Beat

Hannah Prosser

This book is a memoir and reflects the author's recounting of experiences over time. Some time frames may be approximate. Some names may have been changed for privacy. Any possible mistakes within are not deliberate.

Written and edited by Hannah Prosser

Contact: hannahprosser@beatnotnormal.com

Cover and illustrations © V Shane

ISBN: 978-1-7373033-2-9 (paperback)

First Edition

About the Author

And Creation of Beat

The horrors from the many traumatic years spent trapped with Ahaz and the Holdeman Mennonites affected me to the point I felt as though was unable to escape from the past, nor truly thrive. I couldn't even begin to process what had been done to me, much less *talk* about it to anyone. From intense flashbacks and nightmares of the abuse to an incredible number of triggers and near- crippling social anxiety, I found navigating 'the real world' to be very difficult. 'Not normal' continued to ring throughout my mind, from which I could not escape.

Relationships and friendships of any kind were very complicated, and working was difficult as well. I wound up starting a business, Hooligan's Forge, which made working a bit easier since I didn't have to be around as many people.

In fall of 2020, after fourteen long, worldly years of painful silence from holding in the full truth of what was done to me, I had a complete breakdown. Unable to bear the heavy burden of the past, I planned to end it all just to finally stop the pain within. Only there was one thing I *knew I had to do first;* I had to tell my story *in full* before I went out.

It was kind of like one final f-you to Ahaz; that he may have, indeed, succeeded at breaking me, even to the point of what lead to years of silence; only now *everyone would now know*. To him, Ahaz's reputation was very important, yet I held the power to tell the truth of the monster he is.

It seemed incredibly cruel that such a horrible person could have gotten away with everything, and still even be a practicing doctor, while I was left to suffer through the daily torment from the PTSD. I felt certain that the only person any of it even mattered to, was me. I alone had been left to pick up the shattered pieces, only I couldn't do it anymore.

So, I started writing. It was difficult to stick around long enough to complete it and there were moments I did not think I'd be able to accomplish it. I didn't even know what I was going to do with this manuscript after it was completed, the only focus I had was to get it all out, then somehow make sure a large amount of people would have access to it swiftly and be done, end my suffering.

I wasn't sure if it was even worth it; would anyone even read it? Would anyone care enough? Did it even matter? Would anyone hear me now? Would anyone believe me? Or would I still just be dubbed as bad, a liar, or 'not normal'? Would people think that being abused had, indeed been my fault for not blindly following my abusers every wish and whim?

I didn't know the answers to my questions, but still, on I wrote for months, all while severely depressed and fighting to stay alive long enough to finish it. I barely slept, for when I did, the night terrors haunted me. Yet I struggled on, because at that point telling my story was of the upmost importance.

I began telling people around me, slowly, agonizingly, one tiny piece after another. In fact, the first person I *ever* told my story to, was to a stranger. Somehow, it was easier than telling someone close to me.

Somewhere along the way during this process, impossibly, I finally processed and healed from the pain within. This changed everything and through many positive conversations with multiple people, I began to realize that my story, my book, just might be able to *help* people who were also suffering or had suffered through terrible things.

There is even the chance it could help bring about recognition to and hopefully change, at the minimum, the fact Holdeman Mennonite minors are brainwashed into believing its ok and even holy to kiss many adults on the lips. Just think of how much the pedophiles within those churches enjoy that.

Those kids are under socialized, under educated and are not taught how to survive out in 'the world'. The Holdeman Mennonites also make it difficult to leave by instilling fear within everyone, even young kids. My next book will cover that aspect deeper, and much more.

Can I help others like me, cult or abuse survivors? I simply do not know for sure. But I'm going to stand strong and try. I don't want anyone to wind up the way that myself and far too many others have. All I ask is that you listen, you hear, you understand and accept. And if you have a story to tell, *tell it. It is never too late to break the silence.*

Prologue

Pure Panic

I feel like I am suffocating. Drowning in the darkness that surrounds me, squeezing out the life and joy from my body. It's too difficult to keep breathing. I try to stumble blindly through the dark, seeking the light. A glimmer shines in the far distance; freedom. But I cannot reach it. Attempting to propel my body through the foggy night is proving fruitless. I cannot go forward, nor can I go back.

Trapped in this life, I stumble, the air rushing from my chest. Heart thumping wildly, yet blood slowly slugging through my veins, thick and poisoned from the monster surrounding me. I cannot see him, but he lurks, just out of sight. Panic fills me, reaching all the hidden crevices of my soul. It chokes out the good, the joyful, the light.

****

Chapter One

Ages 4-8 years, 1993-1997

In Tompkinsville, KY

My very earliest memories are of the fighting. Screaming, loud fights that generally started in the living room or kitchen and ended up in my folk's bedroom. I'd watch Ahaz grab my mom by her face and screaming, horrible, demeaning things at her with his face mere inches away from her own. Then he'd force her to go into their bedroom with him and he'd lock the door, all while the screaming argument continued.

I'd be standing in the hallway sometimes during those fights, crying and yelling through the locked door for them to stop screaming at each other. I'd try to twist the doorknob as hard as I could, desperately trying to open the door so I could get in-between them to make them stop; but it was, of course locked. And I was just a little girl, powerless to do anything.

Those terrible arguments were usually started by mom fighting against the utterly ridiculous rules that Ahaz imposed upon us all. Us girls were forced to wear only dresses or skirts, and none of us were allowed to watch tv or even have friends. He also forced mom to homeschool all us kids, which she made no qualms of admitting she absolutely hated doing; for both hers and our rights to freedom to attend public school, and so much more; yet it was never enough to change Ahaz's mind. And she refused to leave no matter how bad things got. I never could understand why she didn't just take us all and run.

I was the third kid out of five during this time. Thomas was the oldest, then Sarah, me, Travis and little Dennis fell in at being the youngest. My sister and I were a mere eighteen months apart to the exact day, but we were never actually close despite being so near in age. We did share a bedroom and occasionally played together, but for the most part she saw herself as far more sophisticated than little ole me and held herself distant.

Sarah was always treated with kid gloves and protected. Mom acted as though she was the most tiny, delicate and fragile of flowers. Sarah was her most precious, favorite first darling daughter, while I, on the other hand was always a secondary thought. I was aware of that fact; and I had no idea why I wasn't valued every bit as highly as my sister.

Ahaz worked as an E.R. doctor, but he also had his own private practice located beside the small-town hospital where he saw patients. Sometimes, we'd have to go spend the day at the office. I noticed that this happened after especially big fights when mom would threaten to leave him. Ahaz forced us to be there so he could keep an eye on her; to make sure that she couldn't leave when he wasn't looking.

Even though Ahaz was a MD, he did not allow us to have immunizations of any kind, nor did we have any form of doctor checkups. But to anyone who asked, he proudly claimed to take care of all our medical needs and personally nurse us back to health when we were sick. Over and over many people, patients especially, loudly praise his efforts and the excellent care of his kids.

However, the harsh reality was that he wouldn't so much as look in the direction of his sick wife or kids. And generally, when one of us caught something, we all got it, right along with mom. She'd be dreadfully ill, trying to keep up with everything all of us sick kids needed while even she was vomiting right along with us.

He wouldn't lift so much as a finger to help; we were nothing more than property to him. We were worthless museum pieces, trophies of his manhood; only needed to be kept around in order to showcase his perceived value as a man.

The most painful thing for my siblings and I was not being allowed to play freely with other kids. Ahaz told us repeatedly that public school kids were horrible, undisciplined, disrespectful and overall, far too wild for us to associate with. He wasn't going to allow his kids to 'learn how to be disrespectful', or to be contaminated by the outside world.

Even other homeschoolers were not good enough for us. Nor our male, little cousins that lived in the same town. They were a part of that forbidden public school world; and possibly even worse, their parents, one of whom was Ahaz's only sister, were public school teachers. We did get to go to their house occasionally, but only if Ahaz went, too. We were never permitted to go without him since he had to supervise us in that debauched, tv watching household.

My aunt treated my mom disdainfully, as though she was nothing more than trash. She made it incredibly obvious and even I picked up on her snide comments and rude tone of voice directed at my sweet momma. I saw the hurt mom tried to hide from it and it angered me that my aunt would dare to be so openly rude to her, all while pretending she wasn't.

Mom used to take us to the local library just so we could be in the same room with and *see* other kids. Even though we were not supposed to speak to them; I sure did try to! If I could sneak around one of those tall shelves filled with books and whisper "Hi!" to some strange little girl quick, I did. It was a high that would stick with me for days, a victory, and an accomplishment.

I especially enjoyed going to the free summer library programs because Ahaz wouldn't go to those; it was our tiny bit of freedom. I'd imagine that I was just a regular kid, blending in with all those around me for even just a few minutes, simply doing fun craft activities.

That was all put to a crumbling halt one day after mom took us see a magician show in the upstairs portion of the library. It was fascinating, and I laughed and giggled in pure excitement, engrossing myself in the show while surrounded by kids I couldn't even speak to. The magician pulled a white rabbit out from a tall black hat, and I was instantly convinced magic was truly real. I revealed in the delight of it all, soaking it all up with wide eyed innocence.

Later we went home, all still chattering excitedly amongst ourselves about what we had seen and heard. Ahaz overheard us, and he exploded into an absolute rage. He was yelling at mom, wanting to know why she would dare to take us to such an awful thing. Mom loudly argued right back that it was a kid's magic show; she was fighting for our rights again to simply be kids. But he wouldn't listen to a single word she had to say; he just yelled even louder, drowning out her own voice per usual. He was shouting things like magic was evil knowledge because it wasn't even real, and he refused to allow his kids to become contaminated from such sinful, false imaginations.

The fight was... absolutely horrible. Terrifying. But I was confident my mom would reign supreme since she was clearly correct, and Ahaz was crazy. He dragged her back to the bedroom and eventually she came back out... but as a more broken woman with the bruises to prove it.

I did try to fight for us, too, after she'd given up. I tried to be strong like she had been and told Ahaz that he was wrong; the magic show wasn't evil or wrong. In fact, it had been quite nice.

That only served to get me whipped savagely, until he eventually whipped me so hard, I told the *lies* he demanded from me. I told him I was sorry, that I was wrong, and he was right. But even while saying those words, the rage of injustice burned within me. It infuriated me that he dared to whip me until I lied, even though he claimed to value honesty above all else. The burning, red, raised, lightly bleeding welts he left streaked across my tiny body only continued to increase my anger and resentment.

We weren't allowed to go to the library programs after that, and I hated Ahaz for it; but I also hated my mom for allowing him to lord over us like we were nothing. Worthless, barely human beings, without intelligent thoughts or feelings.

My supposedly debauched, rebellious ways didn't stop there. A boy about my age lived across the street from us, with his grandparents. We weren't allowed to play with him of course, but he and I managed to sneak in a few conversations when no one was looking. I'd sit on the grass on my side of the road, and he on his side; separated only by the open air and blacktop.

I'd ask him questions about public school and what it could possibly be like to have so many kids around him that he was allowed to be friends with. He mostly said things down the lines of school sucked and didn't ever go into the details I was so desperate to know. Even though *he* may have hated it, I was certain that I would absolutely love school. I had no idea what it felt like to walk into a school, or have a teacher other than my mom, nor could I truly comprehend the joy of having friends to chat with. I was just a little, lonely girl.

Sometimes mom would let that boy come over to play outside with us, when Ahaz would go out of town to work in an E.R. My favorite game of all was cops and robbers; I always wanted to be the cop so I could rid the world of wrongdoing and all the bad people.

There were times Ahaz would find out the boy had been over in his absence, and he took it out on mom and us kids. Public schoolers are forbidden, he'd yell and whip Thomas and me. He'd bruise mom up from behind the closed door to their bedroom, leaving her arms and face frequently bruised and I'm sure more places I couldn't see as well.

That horrid man was determined to ensure each one of us knew we weren't our own individual people with thoughts of our own; we were *his*, from mom all the way down to little Dennis. We were nothing without him to make choices for us; or so he portrayed. He was the head of household, and we were nothing more than merely his property. He even frequently made it clear even our toys and clothing were *his*, not our own.

We were expected to follow his every wish, whim, and command without a single hesitation or question; even our thoughts belonged to him as well, or so he claimed. He demanded that we were to be fully compliant, plus *happy and thankful* to be so restricted. It was for our own good, he'd say.

Ahaz's parents lived about a mile away, and we saw them often. However, we were only occasionally permitted to see them without Ahaz coming along to make sure we weren't watching their TV; or even possibly even worse, playing with the Nintendo system.

Their basement held several forbidden treasures, including supposedly sinful barbie dolls. According to Ahaz, barbies were sinful because they could be stripped of their clothes and had defined bodies underneath.

Both my Grams and aunt got in yelling matches with him specifically over those barbie dolls. They'd say Sarah and I were just little girls, and there was no reason we shouldn't be allowed to play with something so innocent as barbie dolls.

Their fighting scared me, but I was secretly, silently rooting those women on, hoping that perhaps some of what they were hollering would get through his thick skull. But it was to no avail, and the barbie dolls were doomed to remain off limits for the unacceptable evil their shapely bodies held.

My Grams didn't seem to like me too much, and I asked my mom about it. She said she thought it was because Grams couldn't stand facing a mini verson of herself, since we were too similar and stubborn. I wasn't so sure if that was the actual reason or not, but it was all I had to go with so I accepted it as much as I could. Sarah was Grams' favorite, and Thomas was Gramps favorite.

Paw was a retired public-school principal, ironically enough. But he liked to pick up the odd printing job at the printing shop he owned, which was located right up the street from his house.

I liked going to the printing shop. It always smelled of dust, plus of the ink and oil from the machines. I couldn't seem to touch hardly anything without becoming smeared in something, even if it was just dust. I remember Gramp's church also smelling of must and dust, but it wasn't quite as strongly.

He also had his own Baptist church, which smelled old, musty and dusty. Our crew made up about half of the regular attendance members, the rest of whom were elderly. Occasionally another young cousin would come, or Gramps would talk someone who had kids into come which was even more rare, but of course those kids weren't good enough for us for us to be friends with.

On one of those Sunday's when a couple of cousins came to church, all us kids were outside talking after the service. One of them was teasing me, and said I looked like I had a black nose cause when I'd get mad my nostrils would flair too widely for me to be all the way white. The kids laughed and I covered my nose with my hand, embarrassed that my nose must be too wide.

Being the curious girl that I was, I later asked if I was part black in the presence of both mom and Ahaz. Well Ahaz must have saw red over this, because his eyes flashed darkly and he severely whipped me for even having suggested our bloodline 'wasn't pure', as he said. I then dared to question what was wrong with being black and was whipped further for asking such a 'not normal' question; why I couldn't just talk and act normal, he demanded to know.

I absolutely hated watching as Ahaz 'trained' my younger brothers to sit still through church. They were just little boys, and he made them sit on a hard wooden chair in the basement for hours on end to practice. Every time they moved, whimpered, wiggled or spoke he whipped the heck out of them, streaking their small bodies with raised, red welts. Their tiny cries cut through me, and I wanted to take that dadgum switch and turn it right back around on Ahaz for hurting them. I wanted desperately to protect them from it; they were practically babies.

Of course, I had personally also endured this type of 'training', but it being done to them just hit different. I cried for them as they cried, and one day I even gathered my courage and screamed at Ahaz to stop hurting Thomas and Dennis, they were just little boys. But it was to no avail, and only served to turn his anger over being 'disrespected' on me. Because normal little girls never try to interfere with what the head of household is doing... and I wasn't acting normal. Not normal... not normal.

Surprisingly, I found myself wanting to please that man. I thought if he was happy with me, he would stop being so crazy. Maybe he'd even stop hitting me so hard. For some reason, I thought that if I wrote a Christian song, this would make him very happy. Make him see reason; since he'd be happy about it, instead of so incredibly angry and mean. So, I told him that I'd made up a song and asked if he wanted to hear it? His face lit up proudly as he told me to wait while he went to get one of his journals; he wanted to write it down word for word.

He came back and we sat on my white metal daybed together. I started slowly spouting off some random made-up on the spot words, in some form of a bad tune as he wrote. As I sang and he scribbled, the big grin began to slip from his face. Once I had reached the end, he asked angrily where I had heard that song before.

This confused me; I'd never heard a song exactly like it and I told him so, while reminding him that I had made it up. But this wasn't the response he wanted, and he instantly flew into a rage at me for 'lying' because he 'knew' that was a real song and I was trying to pass it off as my own. I repeated yet again that I had never heard it before.

Ahaz didn't say anything more; he just got up and half-ran across the hall to his room for the switch and returned with it in hand. He grabbed me by the arm, pulling me from the bed and up onto my feet, asking again where that song came from.

Once more, I told him the truth. But the truth was never the right answer for Ahaz; the truth was only what *he* believed it to be.

"Normal people do not lie; normal people do not pass off someone else's work as their own", he said, and began whaling on me, hitting my back and legs, wherever he could reach with the stick. I was jumping around in my struggle to get away from this sudden turn of unjustified events, but he held firm to my upper arm, pulling me back. He struck me repeatedly, all while demanding that I tell him the truth like a normal person; as soon as I told, he would stop, he said.

But I didn't *want* to lie, and I held out, per usual, as long as I could bear while he whipped me on and on. Eventually though, I couldn't take it anymore and blurted out the lie he was forcing from my lips; that I had heard the song before. This didn't stop him though. Instead, he continued to whip me as he insisted on hearing the 'important' details; where had I heard it and what was it called.

I cried out that I had heard it on the radio with mom, and I made up some sort of quick name for it. Did that stop him? No. Instead, he said he now had to discipline me for having held out so long instead of telling him 'The truth' straight away when asked the first time.

He did manage to teach me a very important lesson that day and on many other days as well, believe it or not; that the truth doesn't matter. If he believed something to be true, then no matter how wrong he was, there was no escape from eventually being forced into lying and agreeing simply to save my own bruised skin.

Lying, even though Gramps preached in church that lying was a sin. And even though Ahaz himself lectured long and frequently about the value of telling the truth; he couldn't have cared less about knowing the truth about anything. It was extremely confusing; how could I *not* lie, when I was forced into lying repeatedly? Was I going to hell for having lies whipped from my lips; could God judge me for that? Was I bad? Was I really 'not normal'? I *tried* to be a good girl and not lie, but Ahaz *made* me lie? It was all incredibly strange.

One day, Ahaz decided that he wasn't getting the respect he thought that he deserved. In order to gain more power and control, he forbade my mom from answering any type of permission questions, since only the head of household was intelligent enough to answer.

Now these deep questions he had in mind that only he was able to answer, were the mind bending, complex type. Such as "Can I go play in the backyard?" Obviously, my mom couldn't possibly be capable of answering such a thing, right? That is legitimately what he believed, firmly and loudly. Ahaz made it clear to us all that mom was far beneath than him, as a female, as his wife, and was not able to make decisions for herself.

I fought against this rule in the only way I knew how; by asking mom everything first. I'd go to her in the hopes she would kindly respond just so I didn't have to deal with Ahaz, and in the beginning she automatically would until Ahaz beat her further into submission as punishment. He broke her down to the point she seemed to actually believe that she could no longer answer. I was very frustrated when her responses turned into depressed answers. She'd duck her head and say she didn't know; to go ask Ahaz instead. Sometimes I just decided it wasn't even worth it, other times I'd bite the bullet and go find him.

In combination to this, Ahaz got on the kick of forcing us to wait for his acknowledgement prior to speaking. It was like waiting your turn to speak, only it was his version on steroids, which involved something he called 'stand and present' prior to speaking.

In order to be granted acknowledgement to even ask anything, I had to stand by his side in complete silence to present myself. And once in position, I couldn't shift my weight, speak, sigh, nor even get tired of waiting and walk away even if he waited 30 minutes to acknowledge me. He could be reading a paper or writing in one of his journals; it didn't matter what it was; he'd pretend he was terribly busy and that he couldn't see me. But he knew, and I knew, that I was standing there. Waiting. For no reason other than he was using the time to prove his power over me.

Eventually, he'd slowly and deliberately turn to look at me as he smiled with satisfied satisfaction and say, "Yes, what can I do for you?"

If I broke one of the rules of being completely still or giving up and walking away after I was in 'position', he'd drop what he was doing and jump up to immediately grab me by my arm roughly, drag me to his bedroom and proceed to whip the heck out of me. So, I carefully considered each time if the long wait was even worth it; how bad I wanted to go outside before I even attempted. Up to a 30-minute wait is forever in little kid time.

Chapter Two

Perhaps not surprisingly, baby dolls were permitted for Sarah and me to play with. Ahaz was big on us girls learning how to be proper moms ourselves; since he made it clear our *only* purpose in life was to marry, and obediently and unquestioningly serve our Christian husbands and have a whole passel of kids. He pointed out often that this was to be our only goals.

I did enjoy having my dollies, and frequently played out scenarios of how I imaged public school and having friends was like. But I wasn't actually supposed to make the dolls talk back n forth to each other even in play; because Ahaz said they were babies; and since babies cannot speak, it was un-natural to have them do so even in pretend. He told me 'Normal girls don't do that'.

Several of our neighbors were elderly women, and there were times I'd sneak out to go see them while seeking to escape from my own stark, lonely reality. They gave me sweet peppermints and one even showed me how to knit. Another gave me a soft dolly that was very old and dusty smelling. I thought it was the most special thing I had ever got, just because I was so starved for attention. Even though it smelled poorly, I decided even stinky dollies need love, too, so, I snuck it back to play with it.

Those sweet, stolen moments of brief freedom remained with me, and instilled an intensely special place in my heart for the elderly.

I also had an adoration and obsession for horses, and I dreamed of getting one and keeping it in the backyard... surely no one would notice, right? Horses reminded me of fresh air and freedom; they were my spirit animal and I imagined racing through fields and mountains, clinging to a beautiful, muscled stallion as we blended into one. Hair blowing back, bare tanned legs in shorts and my face speckled with freckles from the sun... Riding free.

In the meantime, I was gifted beautiful, plastic Breyer horses from my aunt, Grams, and mom. These were my most prized possessions, and I played with them for hours on end, taking them on the very best of imaginary adventures, and playing out fun friendship scenarios repeatedly.

One day, I asked Ahaz to come play horses with me because I wanted him to know just how much I *needed* a horse, and I also wanted to show what a good, normal girl I was being. I had no thought that he could possibly ruin my fun, other than him being irritating to be around. But per usual... he did manage to ruin it.

Right away, he realized I was having my horses 'talk' back and forth to each other, out loud in my own voice. This displeased him greatly and he informed me that normal people do not do that, because it is unnatural for horses to speak English. He said I could, however, allow them to whinny, neigh and snort to each other, but that was all. He was in a good mood and didn't take the switch to me that day for some reason. Instead, he chalked it up to a teaching moment and 'let it slide'.

I knew he was being incredibly ridiculous, just like the baby doll rule about having them talk. As soon as he was gone, I went right back to having them talk back in forth. It didn't take long until he caught me doing this again the next day; and he whipped me until I was sweating, sobbing, stinging, and was covered in bleeding raised stripped welts across my back, hips, legs and arms. When I tried to put my hand up to stop him, he got my hand instead and it painfully welted up as well.

Ahaz forced me to apologize for my unnatural, not normal play and for outright disobeying him before he'd finally stop. He also forced me to promise not to disobey him again. I felt guilty for lying, and it even angered me to be forced to apologize for something that even at my tender age and grossly under socialized that I was, I fully understood was ridiculous. Insane, even. I was *not* sorry.

After that, I continued to play the way I wished to regardless, only just far more quietly. When the floor of the closet would be cleaned out enough, I even played with them within there to help muffle my quiet words.

I tried to listen out for the sounds of him coming down the hallway so I could switch from having my horses have conversations, to loudly neighing and such so he could clearly hear my supposed obedience. He'd stop in my bedroom doorway and smile contentedly at my horse sounds. Except for those times when I'd become too engrossed in my play to notice him coming, and he'd catch me being 'not normal' and would whip me terribly all over again.

I was just a little girl... pretending to save the world from injustice, one tiny ole plastic horse at a time, immersed within an imaginary world of friendship and fun. Not normal... not normal.

Mom got me a soft plush, white and grey horse at one Christmas. I named him Clippy, because he had a box inside him that made a clip-clop sound when I moved him this way and that.

Dear Clippy wound up getting a hole in his shoulder from a scissor mishap, and my great grandma sewed it up, with a purple patch, of all things! Then since she thought it looked lopsided with purple on just the one side, she added a second purple patch on the opposite side to complete the wild look.

Poor patched up Clippy! But I loved him regardless, slept with him, and dragged him all around the house. He was also an excellent listener to all my troubles and a comfort when my body stung from fresh oozing welts and bruises on top of healing ones.

My two great- grandmas I absolutely adored, and in their eyes, I could do no wrong even if I was feeling mischievous. They both saw me for the girl I truly was born to be; charming, smart, kind and gentle. Never once was I called 'not normal' by either of them.

One, my Gran, would read to me for hours on end while rocking me in her lap; she'd quite literally read until she was too hoarse to speak, just to please her darling little granddaughter. When I grew too large for her lap, I'd sit on a small foot stool beside her old wooden rocking chair and listen intently, to the same books read out loud over and over.

Gran also had beautiful peacocks and fowl inside of a large a kennel in her backyard, and an absolutely massive garden of flowers. Another garden included delicious strawberries, which I absolutely loved to help her pick; and eat!

She also had a dog and cat; but the cat she made no claim to which I found to be confusing and hilarious. Even though she fed it daily for many years, she always insisted it was a stray. I tried to tell her that cat was clearly hers whether she admitted to it or not, but that just seemed to aggravate her.

The other great- grandma was just as sweet, but one strange thing she always required was to be called by her first name, Betty, instead of by a grandma type title.

Betty gave me lots of moon pies which I secretly hated, but she was always so excited to give them to me that I didn't have the heart to tell her. Instead, I ate up every single crumb each time, so as not to disappoint her.

She wound up with Alzheimer's and cancer, but I barely realized how sick she truly was until toward the end, because she never forgot me. She couldn't recognize anyone except for me; her precious girl, her little Hannah. She didn't even recognize her own son, my Gramps, yet she knew my name all the way up until she could no longer speak.

The cancer got to her first and her death nearly shattered me; even Clippy could not be of enough comfort. Betty had been one of my only allowed friends; and the thought of never seeing her kind face again nor to feel her gentle touch was very traumatic to me.

After that, I refused to eat for days on end and sobbed myself into such a stupor mom talked about being worried I'd wind up in the hospital. She attempted to force food down my throat by holding my nose, so I had to open my mouth. She'd fork food into my mouth and then hold my jaw shut while I tried to fight her off, refusing to swallow. When she'd finally let go, I'd spit it right back out.

I wasn't trying to kill myself; I was just literally physically ill from the horrible emotions of knowing I'd never be able to see my precious Betty ever again. Eventually though, I was slowly able to eat a few bites here and there until I was back to eating regularly after a few weeks or so.

Mom said that if I prayed and asked God to talk to Betty, that she'd hear me, too. So, I did, and had many one-sided conversations with her after she was gone. I prayed for her to answer me back; to just hear her voice one more time. I even prayed for God to please let her come back to me because I still needed her. But of course, that didn't work.

I was always finding myself in trouble it seemed like, for the type of things I wished for. I just wanted to be a kid and explore, to dream out loud and be a horse trainer, veterinarian and even an astronaut. I wanted to shoot up through the beautiful sky in a spaceship and be able to explore the mysterious wonders above. To be a strong woman and to never, *ever* be a mere weak female. I knew that I was one day going to be somebody and make a difference to many. I wanted to help save people from whatever their troubles may be.

A rough and tumble tomboy; that's what mom would call me. But I wasn't supposed to be one, according to Ahaz. I was supposed to be normal, delicate, non-thinking, and non-dreaming; a no one.

I liked to play amongst the few pine trees that ran in a straight line down the side of the house. I'd pretend that I was a big wild cat climbing up high amongst the branches to find a cozy spot to watch my surroundings, or even a bear going after honey in a beehive.

Ahaz would get very angry when I climbed the trees or turned summersaults in the grass because that was 'not normal' behavior for a girl. I love to dance and spin in circles so fast my skirt would flare out; but that wasn't normal either, apparently. I wanted to wear pants so I could do those things modestly without showing my underwear but was told that normal girls don't ask to wear pants, and I was punished for daring to be so disrespectful as to ask.

I didn't understand how a dress could be modest when it only seemed to mean that I wasn't allowed to play freely. It made no sense that a dress could be considered modest when the wind would blow my skirt up around my waist, and even the wind was also supposedly, somehow, my fault too. Yet, how can a mere girl control her skirts in the wind? I wanted to be a boy, in that case, and said as much, which yet again I was painfully welted up for. As only a mere female, it was not normal to even think of being an almighty male.

I was not normal... not normal. It continued to ring in my ears as Ahaz never lost a chance to remind me of it. I was just a girl... a girl called not normal.

Despite of television being forbidden; mom actually kept a TV tucked underneath the staircase in the basement. No one was supposed to touch it except for in an emergency, such as during tornado warnings, for which the news was permitted to be watched at those times.

Sometimes though, when Ahaz would be far away at an out-of-town E.R., mom would pull it out on the rolling table it sat on and plug it in. She liked to watch cops and robbers, and I sure did, too. I even saw the kids show Barney which I loved; it taught me that real friendship existed. And it also made me even more sad and angry because friends were a big no-no. Yet it seemed as though everyone else had them. I loved watching those singing, dancing little kids prancing around happily on the TV screen.

One night, the very instant Ahaz pulled out the driveway on his way to another E.R., mom rushed downstairs to plug the TV in. Us kids all crowded around her, excited to see what fun, forbidden thing we'd be able to watch that night.

Suddenly, the door at the top of the stairs opened and Ahaz came storming down the steps; he'd forgotten something and came back for it. He wasted no time in yelling at mom, asking how dare she disobey and disrespect him. He shouted that she was a terrible influence on us kids and called her an awful wife.

Mom yelled right back at him that we weren't doing anything wrong; we were just going to watch one little ole innocent show. But per usual, he won eventually and overpowered her voice with his own, and demanded she put the TV away immediately. Then he slammed his way back out of the house.

It was obvious to me, that Mom felt beat down and broken. She quietly put the TV away amongst our many tearful protests and sent us all to bed without giving an answer as to why we had to listen to that man. She never had an answer.

Holidays were another thing that was done differently than others around us. Mom made sure for Christmas we had a small tree and a few gifts, but Ahaz hated the gift giving.

When Halloween would roll around, we weren't allowed to participate in the evil festivities of dressing up cute, nor going trick or treating for candy. He said it was the devil's night and he'd turn off every single light in the house and force us all down the stairs into the basement. We had to stay down there for hours, just sitting in the dark, and in complete silence because he forbade us from speaking, playing or doing anything that made any sort of noise.

I could hear the sounds of the laughing, giggling, happy kids walking up and down the street, knocking on doors for treats. I didn't care about any night of the devil; I just wanted to be out there with those kids, wearing a costume and blending in. Traveling the streets on foot, surrounded by a crowd of others my age, laughing and collecting sweet, yummy candy. Making friends, even. But to no avail; it was completely forbidden.

There were a couple of Easters we were taken to Easter egg hunts with a group of home schoolers. But of course, those homeschoolers weren't good enough for us. We were allowed to be in the same place at the same time, merely in the presence of those other kids. I could look at them at least... and sneak a few words in... that's almost kind of the same thing as friendship, right?

Nope. Not even close. This was *not* socializing, friendship, nor even a remote form of freedom by any means. I still tried to challenge the strict rules and to play freely with the little ones around me but was stopped many times. You see, many homeschoolers still had TV and were therefore completely unsuitable.

On very, very rare occasions, we were grudgingly permitted to play at the houses of a couple of other homeschoolers, but Ahaz lectured before and after on how they *still* were not appropriate enough for us.

The natural curiosity I was born with was made out to be more along the lines of a curse. Ahaz did not wish for myself nor my siblings to have any form of knowledge beyond what he himself chose to grant us. He was incredibly big on perfection, and as he'd say; "normal people obey their authorities without question."

By the definitions of 'normal' he laid out over the years, I didn't even *want* to be normal. Being normal seemed like it was a terrible thing! I only wished to be free, and true to what was well and good.

The things that Ahaz forbade varied from ridiculous, to completely insane. I was whipped for trying to shorten sibling's names into nicknames, and for using the word kids instead of saying children. 'Kid' is an exceptionally common term and 100% acceptable, but you'd have thought it was a curse word from the way terribly way he'd whip me for uttering it. According to him, since the word kid also defined baby goats, it was rude and only said by undisciplined people who were not normal... like me.

One very strange evening, my siblings and I were playing outside in the front yard, hitting a ball around with a softball bat. A car drove by that I didn't recognize, nor could I see who was inside. The driver within waved, and in delight I cheerfully waved right back while excitedly jumping up and down and shouting out, "she waved at me!"

Ahaz spun right around on me quick and in a hurry and demanded to know if I had been able to tell who was even inside of the vehicle. I responded back with no; I could only see that she had waved.

He decided to first calmly educate me on the inappropriateness of my response to the situation, stating that normal people do not say 'she' when they do not know whether someone is a man or woman; they say he or him.

Well, this made zero sense to me, and I said as much. There was a 50/50 chance I was correct either way so what did it matter? I could say 'she' if I wanted to.

His face started turning red while I held my ground. "No," Ahaz insisted. "You cannot ever take the risk of calling a man 'she' by mistake; it would be a great insult to the man." He was obviously growing angry.

Being a female myself, this was a huge insult and made me absolutely indignant. I was positive that he was incorrect, because men are *not* better than women. I also knew that even little me was far more powerful than Ahaz claimed. So, I flat out stated I would *never* do as he said, and the very next person that drove by if I didn't know for sure if it was a man or a woman, I'd still call them 'she'.

He lost it instantly and grabbed me by an arm to drag me into the house to fetch his switch and proceeded to whip the absolute heck out of me until I was hurting badly enough to finally be willing to lie to him in the ways he demanded. I agreed to do as normal people do, apologized even though I was not the tiniest bit sorry, and was forced to thank him for 'disciplining' me. I even went so far as to promise to refer to gender unknown people as 'he/him'.

Inwardly, I fumed at being forced to lie yet again, and he only succeeded to instill within me that he was clearly below me in intelligence level. In fact, that moment along with similar ones helped shape me into firmly believing all people are equal no matter their race, sexuality, or gender without exception. Excluding those who are genuinely cruel, of course. They hold an entirely different category of their very own.

I felt as though I was living in a glass fishbowl. Everyone in the tiny town of Tompkinsville recognize us as 'that weird, skirt wearing, homeschooled family', and staired at us while scowling rudely when we went out anywhere.

Things like that, combined with people being so taboo and off limits, wound up being the building blocks for severe social anxiety for me. It was an intensely aware, uncomfortable feeling from how all those forbidden people would stare.

In addition to this, my Gramps would drive by the house multiple times a day, especially when Ahaz was out of town. If he didn't see the van in our driveway, he'd then proceed to drive around the small town until he found us, generally at the local grocery or occasionally at one out of the few, big-chain fast food restaurants. He would then report our activities back to Ahaz.

I didn't know if this was something Ahaz had his dad do, or if Gramps did it himself out of retired boredom, but it was quite strange and most especially drove my mom crazy from feeling spied on.

Thomas and I would sometimes sneak to the nearby gas station to use a few prized coins to get a Coke can from the outside soda machine. Now Sarah would never take the risk to get said Coke, but she sure was willing to participate in drinking it.

After we'd acquired it and quickly ran back, she'd be waiting for us in the pine trees by our house, and we'd pop it open and share it. Sarah always got the first drink since she was too prissy to drink after us, then Thomas and I would take turns to finish it off. That secret pop was the best tasting one I'd ever had; it must have had something to do with my sibling's backwash.

Ahaz was especially cruel to my older brother. Now, Thomas was quite mean himself, but he was a smart boy, socially withheld, left mentally unchallenged, lonely and whipped even longer and more often than I was at the time. Personally, my whippings were only perhaps one to two times per day; his was far more. Especially when Ahaz was home and would try to whip him into absolute, broken submission. Thomas was even more stubborn than I was, and he could hold out far longer.

Thomas was turned into a monster by that man, and I was quite terrified of my brother. He'd chase me around while I cried and screamed, running as fast as I could because I knew what would happen when he caught me.

Eventually Thomas would catch and tackle me, throwing his much stronger body on top of mine and crush me down onto the floor, taking my breath away. Then he'd put his smelly hand over my mouth and nose to cut off my ability to draw any more air into my lungs. It was terrifying and painful; I always tried to fight him off but never had a chance to succeed. He wouldn't let go until little white spots danced before my eyes within the deepening darkness, and I was too weak to fight back.

Then he'd just let go while laughing about how much fun he'd had watching me struggle, and continued to laugh as I gasped for air, still laying curled up on the floor. I'd attempt to crawl away but was too weak from the lack of oxygen to be able to do so. And scared... so very scared. I'd try to scream for mom, but it would only come out in a fearful, gasping whisper. This was something that happened far too frequently, and mom was never able to stop it.

Too often, I watched as Thomas beat my mom in the living room, punching and kicking at her while screaming out his rage. She'd have a switch and be striking out with it, hard and fast, somewhere between trying to get away from him and trying to dominate the situation. Hitting the angry boy did nothing to calm his rage of the abusive injustices being done to him; it only seemed to rightfully add to it.

A deeply shaming thing happened was that Thomas molested me, perhaps starting when I was around eight years old or so. He did it many, many times and I felt both bad and guilty when he touched me. He said things like no one would ever believe me and gave me shiny quarters to help keep me quiet. I was very uncomfortable with him touching me, but I did like quarters... I figured that he was right; no one would have believed me anyway, so I said nothing about it.

This usually happened concealed within the walls of the log cabin playhouse in the basement, or in one out of the two bathrooms down there. At one point, he started something new instead of just touching me, and cut little holes in a pair of my panties. He demanded that I put them on and stand over him while he lay on the floor underneath me, touching himself and looking up between my legs.

Eventually, the small holes were not enough for him, and he cut bigger ones, which wound up turning into completely crotchless ones over time. He also insisted I sway over top of him as I stood with his head between my legs. I felt incredibly uncomfortable and hated it, but what else was I to do? If I didn't, Thomas would have suffocated me. At least this way, I could get a few quarters for a soda, instead of having his stinky hand over my face cutting off my air for refusing.

I thought that my brother was just terribly cruel. But the reality was that he was just an abused little boy himself.

Chapter Three

Ahaz decided he wanted to build an office in the basement so he could see patients without ever leaving his unruly, out of control wife and kids, as he called us. He talked about being so excited we'd all be together now every single day, which would give him more time to 'correct' us throughout the day.

Mom was definitely not thrilled and fought against it, or at least tried to. We all needed *more* freedom, not *less*. In fact, it felt like we would now be even more trapped under his unrealistic rules and 'discipline'.

I straight up told him I *didn't* want him around more, and obviously that ended terribly for me in the form of many bleeding welts. My opinion did nothing to stop him from emptying his office by the hospital. Nor from building walls to form three separate rooms: a waiting area, an office and an exam room. A long hallway connected the rooms and ended with one of the already existing bathrooms. The waiting room even had an outside door to it, so patients didn't have to walk through the entire house.

Ahaz would have me file his patient's paperwork into the proper folders in the file cabinets in alphabetical order. He said it would help me with my reading, but I am sure that this broke some laws, of both child labor and HIPPA. I saw very personal information on those papers that I am certain patients would have been mortified to know a little girl knew about them.

My mom was now essentially his nurse/ receptionist and she absolutely hated it. Her plate was already incredibly full before this; yet she could never do enough in her eyes no matter how hard she worked, homeschooled us kids, and tried to take care of the house. He frequently called her lazy and worse during their yelling matches. She was never able to do even a single thing correctly in his eyes, even though she was constantly busy with everything there was to keep up with. Having five kids in itself was no joke when it came to the number of things to be done, all of which he refused to offer any assistance with.

Ahaz had always been a health fanatic, but he went on a health kick even worse than he'd been on previously. He was focused on being the longest living man in the world and achieving that apparently was going to be accomplished by eating plates full of tomatoes and drinking mysterious smoothies. Some of his concoctions smelled pretty decent, some not too bad, while others smelled more like a dead animal.

His obsession wouldn't have bother me in the slightest other than he decided some of us kids had to drink them, too. Sarah, of course, was protected from it by mom, and the youngest boys were too small to have it forced upon them. But Thomas and I... he made us drink them. Entire glasses worth. I have no idea what was in them; whatever it was, was very foul and I wouldn't even give it to a snake.

Before I knew it, the things I was forced to drink became even worse. He had this clear glass bottle of brown vinegar he kept under the kitchen sink. There were large chunks of something at the bottom of the bottle, while smaller pieces floated throughout. Ahaz decided he wanted me to drink full cups of this nastiness... for the sake of my health, he said.

I was forced to drink it straight, while seated at the kitchen table. He'd hold the switch, ready to swing, after having already whipped me terribly for refusing to ingest that disgusting liquid to begin with. It was the most horrible thing I had ever tasted or smelled in my short life. I choked and threw up right away, which got me whipped more until I agreed to drink that awfulness just to stop the pain. He'd stand beside me while I sobbed and remind me that to disobey was of the upmost disrespect since he was trying to 'help me'.

After I somehow, someway, managed to get all of it down which did require many more strikes of the switch in-between choked sips, he'd change from angry and stern to happy, and point out how much easier it would have been on me if I'd have just done it right away in the beginning. Then he wanted to ensure I didn't undo his work and go throw it up; so, he forced me to sit there for at least a half hour. The taste in my mouth and the painful roll of my stomach was terrible, but I had to fight through it or else I knew he'd make me drink yet another glass.

And no... I was not ill prior to drinking the vinegar, there was no reason to be forced to drink it for a health reason, other than that he was sadistic. I was the picture of perfect, little girl health, minus the marks and bruises my body was constantly streaked with of course.

Ahaz wasn't the only one whipping the heck out of Thomas and I; he forced my mom to get in on it, too. He'd yell at her and demand that she had to hit us harder; more painfully. The harder, the better, and when she didn't strike us hard enough for his liking, he'd be furious and hit mom as her own punishment. She also left welts across my body, but not quite as terribly as he did.

36

Group time outs were also handed out by my mom, but this wouldn't be for just a few minutes; it could easily be for hours at a time. She used it primarily to weed out who had done something naughty, so she'd know who to whip the heck out of. My sister Sarah generally did not have to be a part of this because she was the perfect, reliable kid. (Who lied and snuck around daily, but she was just too smart to get caught in the act).

It could last for half an hour, or an entire day while Thomas and I clung to refusing to lie and confess to something that we may not have even done; but of course, we couldn't prove it when it was Sarah's crime; and one of us was definitely going to go down for it in her place.

Eventually, either Sarah would point at one of us to label as the guilty party, and mom would believe her beyond a shadow of a doubt, or Thomas or I would confess just to avoid having to spend the day in the chair. It was better to get being welted up over with, even if the confessor was not the wrong do-er. Or... we'd just sit there for hours, protecting our own innocence; or guilt, depending.

Due to the boredom in those many hours that I frequently spent in a chair, I named all my fingers and would dance them around my lap and along the arms of the chair to entertain myself. I pretended they were real people and used them to take my mind away from that place, imagining all sorts of great adventures. But of course, I did have to be careful that Ahaz didn't come upstairs and catch me doing that, since such pretending would result in getting the heck whipped out of me.

We did take a few trips to see my mom's parents on very rare occasions. They lived just a few hours away in Lexington,

Kentucky; in the horse capital of the world. Nana and Granddaddy were kind, and I relished those few times I got to go see them.

Walking into their house felt like walking into freedom, even though Ahaz would still be there to lord over us. They had a huge fireplace in the living room, and beautiful, delicate crystal pieces and trinkets placed all throughout the entire house. On the walls of the kitchen and dining room were a hundred or so colorful mini pitchers, all hanging on various accordion style racks.

There was a special, adult sitting room with the floor covered in a soft, pure white carpet. That is also where the family haunted candle sticks were kept, and I loved hearing the stories about them being mysteriously tossed across the room without anyone touching them. We weren't supposed to go into that room unless Nana specifically invited us in for just a few special minutes.

They had a big inground swimming pool in their small, fenced in backyard, and that's where I learned how to swim on one of those trips. Well, where I at least learned how to dog paddle, anyway. The pool started off at 3ft deep and went all the way down to 9ft. There was a diving board on the deep end, but nana and mom said I wouldn't be allowed to jump off it until I learned how to swim better than just doing the doggie paddle.

Granddaddy was a kind, busy, hardworking man. Nana was every bit as equally strong and every bit as hard working. I knew I wanted to be exactly like her; powerful and unstoppable. I didn't feel like they liked me too incredibly much, but they didn't hate me, either. I was family, and I knew they'd have done anything for me.

Ahaz hated both of my precious grands, and he didn't like my mom talking to them, much less us going to see them sometimes. He knew they could clearly see what a black souled monster he was, and he didn't want them to talk mom into leaving; she was his property, just the same as us kids were. And the grands were a threat to his furious control over us.

He went on rants about how 'normal people' do not insult a high and mighty doctor such as himself. According to Ahaz, he had a flawless reputation and was such an amazing man. And my grands made no qualms over that being complete bull.

I overheard a couple of quiet conversations between the grands and my mom. They basically offered her the world if she would leave him. A house, new clothes for us all, literally they'd cover 100% of everything because they were quite wealthy and could afford it. Even though there was six of us all together, between mom plus us five little ones, the cost simply didn't matter to them. This was a long-standing offer with no end date, but she wouldn't take them up on it.

My very favorite thing was when mom would take us to the park. It was generally a quiet one with very few or no kids there. I loved the monkey bars, but the swings were the best of all. I could swing endlessly into oblivion while tipping my head as far back as I could to gaze into the vast blue sky above. I loved the clouds and found companions in the shapes of beautiful animals amongst the fluffy white. As they moved slowly across the sky, I imagined they were running wild, free and untamable, the way my own spirit was.

One day, Sarah came up with a sudden religious saved experience in order to gain even more positive attention and to keep her role secured as the golden kid who could do no wrong. In light of this, I followed suit right away and had my own story to tell. Honestly, I hoped that if I was a Christian, Ahaz would stop being so cruel to me and not lay a finger on me; perhaps I'd be treated how Sarah was treated.

But I was wrong. Terribly, horribly wrong. Ahaz believed Sarah right away and was so proud of her. But with me... he decided I needed to go through some tests first, in order to *prove* I was a Christian.

Ahaz took me into the kitchen, sat me down at the table and told me that normal little Christian girls obey without question, no matter what is asked of them from their superior, head of household. He grabbed a red tomato and cut it up in front of me, while telling me that if I was truly a Christian, I would eat every single bite and love it.

I *hated* tomatoes, mostly because they were one of his very favorite things; and he made my skin crawl. But I also desperately wanted to prove I was saved and get that golden kid status, same as Sarah had. I managed to eat it, one slice at a time, hating it all the while.

There was a very odd moment in which he placed his hand under my jaw while I chewed and held lightly it there for several moments, feeling me chew and swallow. He had a very satisfied look on his face all the while, which made me feel uncomfortable. I didn't want him to touch me and couldn't understand why he'd do that in such a weird manner. But I did nothing to push his hand away since I was trying to please him.

I thought my 'trial' was over once I had finished the last bite of that tomato, but I was wrong. He praised me for it, but then said he had one more test for me in order to further prove

I was a Christian, and he led me by the hand to his bedroom. I let him because I was trying so hard to be such a good girl.

Once there, he grabbed the switch and told me that if I was truly saved, I wouldn't fight as he whipped me; nor scream, cry, flinch, run or put a hand in the way. Because normal Christians are happy to be disciplined, and even though I wasn't in trouble, this one final test would prove it to be true. If I failed, he promised to punish me more severely than had ever been done to me before. I knew I couldn't fail this one last test.

With a smile, he told me to put my hands onto his bed, and I did. He began hitting me with that stick incredibly hard, putting an immense amount of force behind it. I gritted my teeth and refused to move even the tiniest bit. Tears stung my eyes and I struggled to not let them fall. I *had* to prove I was a Christian; I could do this; I pep talked myself through the awful strikes from that horrid man. Somehow, someway I made it through having the daylights walloped out of me without breaking his rules.

Afterwards, he insisted that I give him a full body hug, and I complied even while the disgust boiled in my belly and my tiny body burned in pain. He made me thank him for putting me through the tests and made me say that I loved him. I lied and said what he wished, and he said he was so happy I was truly saved since this meant I would be acting normal from then on.

Not long after, once I was tucked into bed for the night and my welts were still seeping a bit of blood through onto my nightgown, I decided that if being a Christian meant I had to do everything that man said and it got me whipped so dreadfully, I didn't want anything to do with it. It would be better to just be me, a strong little girl. Tough as nails, independent and in control of my own mind. I was a born leader; and Ahaz was nothing more than a grown-up bully.

I overheard many loud conversations and screaming fights between mom and Ahaz, about him wanting a more conservative life for us all. Amish, perhaps. Somewhere the women and kids were kept firmly in their place with the men even more firmly in the position of being the respected head of household. Mom would scream right back at him that he was nuts; there was *no way* he could ever make her do something like that. We needed more freedom, not less.

He took us to an Amish church one time, and he was speaking frequently with several men there over a period of months. Mom made it extremely clear that she would never go without electricity and other comforts, and said she'd leave him before ever letting it go that far. Ahaz tried to get me on his side of it and asked me how I'd like it if we turned Amish, because the kids there would be appropriate for me to play with. He expected me to be thankful that I'd be allowed to play with others my age.

However, instead I told him that I didn't want to be Amish; I wanted to go to public school and have friends there. This made him very angry, and he punished me dreadfully for it. I didn't understand why he'd ask me such a question in the first place, when he only wished for me to lie instead of knowing the truth. He told me normal girls do not tell lies, yet he forced me to lie after having been honest.

Then he discovered The Church of God, in Christ Mennonite (AKA Holdeman Mennonite) located in Muddy Pond, Tennessee during his search; I'm not exactly sure how he came across them. But he first began making trips by himself to check it out.

Gramps was very angry over this, since he believed *his* Baptist church was the only place Ahaz should attend. And Mennonite wasn't exactly Gramps's idea of being a true Christian; he knew they were religious fanatics. The two of them had huge fights over it, and even Grams and my aunt pitched in their own two cents about it in yelling form as well.

I was so tired of all the screaming and fighting. So tired of watching my exhausted, broken mom fight and let herself lose to the insanity. Of watching her never leave, to never free us from the horrible overbearing ruling of Ahaz. I thought for sure she'd *never* allow a transition to Mennonite; she'd run away with us all first, for certain. So that we could have friends and go to school, and be pants wearing, TV watching wild women.

Once Ahaz had been to that church enough times by himself and had spent a good amount of time within the community, he began forcing us all to go along with him. Mom hated it, but he broke her down with the yelling, and hitting her until she was finally too broken to refuse him. Then we'd have to all get into the van and head out, to appear a couple hours later at the church as one big, fake happy family. It was all only forced happiness for show; Ahaz would take his rage out on whomever dared to show a hint of the truth.

Walking into the Mennonite church was different, for sure. The church was large, clean, and didn't smell even a little bit like dust. There were so very many people there, and their reactions to us varied. Some were very friendly, some distant, and others outright stared, especially the kids.

For one of the first times, I wasn't being stared at for being forced to dress *too* conservatively, but rather it was now because I wasn't dressed conservatively *enough*. We stood out like sore thumbs and knowing that made me feel nervous. No one else there was wearing what we were. As it turned out, 'worldly' people didn't walk through those church doors very often.

All the women and girls there were wearing handmade long sleeved, one-piece dresses made entirely from the same fabric, with a belt at their waists. The belt was also made from the same fabric as their dresses. They all had puffy sleeves, and their bodices were puffed out too. They wore panty hose except for the littlest ones who had on plain white socks. The women and most of the teen girls had on a black handkerchief looking head covering on their heads, which came down to tie underneath their chins. The younger girls and toddlers had their hair all in braids; not a single ponytail to be seen. There was not a single piece of jewelry in sight apart from wrist watches.

The men and boys all wore long sleeved, store bought dress shirts and black dress pants. The men all had beards; there wasn't a shaved face to be found there. And 100% of everyone wore black dress shoes.

After church, Ahaz would take us to the elderly deacon's house. I liked his wife a lot, because she was kind and sweet. We'd eat lunch with them, and then the deacon and Ahaz would spend the rest of the afternoon talking about all the ins and outs of the Mennonite lifestyle. He was most interested in and asked a lot of questions about how restricted and obedient the women and kids were. We'd finally head back to Tompkinsville around supper time.

Gramps was even more furious once Ahaz began taking us all, since we made up at least half of his entire church attendance. There were more screaming fights that resulted in Ahaz coming up with a begrudging agreement to go to the Baptist church one Sunday, and to the Mennonite one the next, in rotation to keep it fairer. This still wasn't satisfactory to Gramps though, but it was better than the other option.

I watched as my mom grew more depressed during all this. She was giving up on even attempting to do any sort of successful school lessons and crying so much more. When she wasn't crying, her eyes remained puffy and dull from having been. Gone was my strong momma; the woman in front of me was drowning deep in pure despair. And I couldn't blame her for that; but at the same time, I was aware she had a way out; we all did. But no matter how bad it was, she refused to leave, and us kids were all trapped there like rats. We might not have been in a physical cage, but we sure were not any form of free. All she had to do was take us to her parents...

Chapter Four

1998, Age 9 yrs.

Ahaz began treating us all worse, and the fighting, screaming and yelling seemed to intensify on the daily. I could clearly hear it; sometimes they would be fighting in the dining room, other times locked within their own room. The thin walls did absolutely nothing to drown it out at the volume with which they screamed at each other. Mom was arguing all the fine points of putting us kids in public school, having friends, wearing pants, watching TV and more. She loudly refused to homeschool us for another year.

On the other hand, Ahaz was demanding we move to Tennessee and join the Holdeman Mennonites, pointing out how it would solve 'everything' because then we'd be in the church school. He said we'd all be under more control in that lifestyle, and finally learn how to all be obedient and follow him, as the head of household, in both his, and The Church's teachings.

There was so much crying, so much fear and rage cramped up in that house, building and threatening to destroy us all. It felt as though I was in limbo; scared, not knowing what was to come.

I truly did not believe that Ahaz could make us turn Mennonite, because I just knew mom would stand up for all of us and not allow it in the end. She would win, and we'd go to that ever allusive, always just barely out of reach public school and finally be allowed to have true playmates.

In July of that year, admis the chaos, Mom decided she wanted a picture of all five of us kids together. I wasn't happy about having to go because I didn't like the jumper that she insisted I wear. The buttons running down the front of it kept popping open cause the buttonholes were too loose, and I cried in frustration.

But one way or another I got out the door with it on, and off we went to sit for the photo. This would turn out to be the very last picture taken of all five siblings together, although none of us knew it. In fact, it would be the last picture taken of most of us for many more years.

The trips to Tennessee were becoming very frequent. Mom refused to go anymore, so Ahaz took me, and he said I was allowed to play freely with the kids there. I actually loved going, just because I could be around the kids; it was such an amazing relief to be permitted such a luxury.

After one Sunday church service my new friend Joyce and I were hanging out chatting near the front, by the coat rack. Her dad came walking by and as soon as Joyce spotted him, she took off with a skip to go straight to him; and gave him a great big, squeezing hug.

My little mind was utterly shocked, and I stared at them, watching the interaction. I truly had no idea why anyone would hug their dad, because dads were cruel, unreasonable, uncomfortable and disgusting to be around.

When Joyce happily came back to the coat rack, I asked her incredulously why she had done that. Now it was her turn to look surprised. "Do what?" Joyce asked, trying to understand. "You mean hug my dad?" She questioned, and I nodded.

"I love my dad," Joyce said. "Don't you love your dad?" She asked, her face still scrunched up in confusion.

"No, of course not! He is mean," I told her. "Isn't your dad mean?"

"No," she answered. But we didn't wind up being able to really discuss it longer that day, as Ahaz was ready to leave to go to lunch at the deacons' house and visit the hours away. But I determined that the next time I saw Joyce, I'd find out more, because I truly did not understand since I'd never seen anything quite like it. At nine years old, this was my first introduction to what a real daddy/ daughter relationship was *supposed* to look like.

It wasn't too much longer before my tiny world was flipped completely upside down around August of 1998.

The sun was shining brightly outside through the window, and it was hot. I was playing on my bedroom floor, with my most precious of Breyer horses. I could hear so much noise and yelling coming from outside of my door, and I'd been trying to ignore it for a while. But then the shouting turned into absolutely blood curdling screams, with mom shrieking "No Thomas, stop! No, No, No Stop! Get off him!!!" I could hear the sounds of some sort of a scuffle.

I was so afraid... but I crept out of my room and down the hallway, heading toward the living room where the source of the horrible noise came from. Once I was close enough to see them, I froze in pure, utter terror. Little six-year-old Travis was on the floor with the much bigger, twelve-year-old Thomas on top of him.

Thomas's hand was covering both Travis' mouth and nose entirely. I saw Travis's own hands barely lift from the floor as though to push Thomas away, then drop back down. He turned some sort of purplish- blue color; and his body lay limply on the floor.

I couldn't move; couldn't scream. I couldn't even hardly take in what my eyes were seeing, but some part of me recognized that Travis was dead.

Mom was standing over them both, desperately yanking on Thomas with all her strength and screaming dreadfully, still trying to save her poor baby boy. I wanted to help, but I didn't know what to do. I lived in dreadful fear of Thomas, and I didn't want to die too. I was too little, and too scared to try to help.

She finally succeeded to pull Thomas off somehow, and mom dropped on her knees by the limp Travis laying lifeless on the floor. Thomas screamed a few angry things as he grabbed and dialed the phone, calling for Gramps to come and get him quick. Then he ran through the kitchen and outside. I watched as Mom started CPR on Travis until he started gasping and breathing again on his own. There were loud, broken, sobbing sounds coming from her.

I ran back to my bedroom, shut the door and slide down onto the carpet in front of it, with my back pressed tightly against the door. I was shaking and had no idea what I was supposed to do.

After I'd had a few moments to try to process what I'd witnessed, I went back out into the hallway. Ahaz was in the living room now; I think he'd been in the basement when all that was going on. Mom was still sobbing on the floor, holding Travis in her arms and rocking him back and forth on her lap. Ahaz started yelling at her saying all this was her fault; everything was always her fault.

A car pulled into the driveway; it was my Gramps. Ahaz went running out of the house and I followed. Him and Gramps screamed insults back and forth at each other while Thomas dashed up from along the side of the house and dived into the car. Gramps peeled out of the driveway just as soon as the car door slammed closed and they took off down the road, with Ahaz still yelling after them.

We went back inside, and the yelling picked back up right away between Ahaz and mom. She was crying and looking more hopeless than I had ever seen her before. She looked like she had nothing left, no more strength to fight anymore. Completely defeated. Broken.

Ahaz yelled that was it; we were out of control, and he was moving us to Muddy Pond, TN at that very moment, and after a lot more screaming and mom tearfully agreeing, all of us were forced outside amid much confusion and fear, and into the van. I wasn't allowed to go get Clippy or my prized horses, much less a single stitch of clothing other than what I was wearing at that moment. All us kids were crying, scared and breaking the rules trying to ask questions. Ahaz told us to shut up and said that he would give us information when he decided to.

He went through the local bank to pull out cash. Then my Grams pulled up behind him in the vehicle line, got out of her car and started screaming all sorts of things at him about the current situation, Thomas, and how insane Ahaz was. Ahaz yelled back at her angrily and then speed off with us all.

We drove for quite a while, headed straight to Tennessee and got a hotel room. For the next week, that's where we stayed. Mom was so quiet, cried a lot, and when we tried to quietly ask her what was happening, she told us to not ask questions. She gained more bruises from Ahaz when she tried to speak up against him. He even hit her for crying because she wasn't allowed to show that she was miserable.

That week, Ahaz didn't yell over the TV, I think because was the only thing we had to keep us occupied. Since us kids were so tickled with watching it, we mostly sat still in that small room. Cartoons were a good distraction to focus on and to help me stop thinking and feeling for a little while. The uncertainty and fear were powerfully overwhelming.

A house was found to rent, not too far out from the Mennonite community. It was an old A-frame house in the country, and we moved into it with nothing. Ahaz announced we were now going to be Mennonite as he believed in the family values they portrayed, and he thought it would help get us more under control. He said we were finally going to get to go to a school, at that church, and pointed out how grateful we should be to him for having found the right path for us all. He believed this was the one true way to save our souls, so we'd one day go to heaven.

I kept trying to talk to mom, to ask and beg her to save us, to get us out of there and head to Lexington. I also tried to talk about what had happened that day we'd left, but she wouldn't say much of anything other than to tell me to not talk about any of it ever again. She looked like a dead thing, all while still somehow walking, breathing, and fake smiling for Ahaz.

The Mennonite women gathered up old homemade dresses that others had outgrown and gave them to my mom, sister and me. They also rounded up some old store-bought clothes for the boys. Mom took off her wedding rings, since no jewelry other than a simple watch was allowed there.

Ahaz took a trip back to Kentucky to load up some things, and made mom go with him, while us kids stay with another family. This was so he could keep a leash on mom and to ensure she couldn't up and run away while he was gone. And to force her to return to Muddy Pond with him; for us kids. We were literally separated from mom to keep her 'under control'.

It was decided that even though I had just finished the third grade in homeschooling, I was too far behind in order to move up. I was upset I had to do the third grade again, but honestly mom simply hadn't been able to keep up with everything on her plate and had been unable to teach me much at all that year. It was what it was.

Further education beyond the eighth grade was not considered necessary among the Holdeman Mennonites, and they were religious exempt from their teens attending high school. Ahaz claimed that this was wonderful for us kids. He said that we should be *so happy* we wouldn't be attending any form of high school, since was no benefit for us to have any more schooling than the eighth grade, anyway. Especially for my sister and I, since we were only supposed to grow up to become quiet housewives and moms.

The school had been built into the right side of the church. There were two classrooms, one for the lower graders 1-4, and another for upper graders 5-8. There was only one teacher per classroom, to teach ALL grades and ALL subjects, and there were under twenty students for all grades combined in the entire school.

The exceptions to having more than two teachers in that school, would be the few weeks toward the end of the school year when any incoming kindergarteners would start. One of the small Sunday school rooms would be turned into a classroom just for them, and they got their very own teacher. Also, in the case of needing a one-on-one teacher for a special needs student.

On my very first day of school ever, I felt such anxiety, fear and excitement all at the same time. I didn't know exactly what to expect, nor how to behave. I watched the other kids carefully to try to fit in and to do as they did.

School started off at 8:30 in the morning with devotions and forced group singing, which was done all acapella. No musical instruments were allowed because the Mennonites did not permit them, not even a guitar or a tiny harmonica or flute.

We got three recesses, one in the morning, one after lunch and another in the afternoon. Lunch, which all students brought from home, was eaten either in the classroom at our desks if it was raining or cold, or outside on the playground when the weather was pretty. School let out at 3:30.

Both classrooms had the exact same schedule, and the recesses had to be played in a group. Each day, students would take turns picking the activities. We played tag, softball, 6 squares, dodgeball, and even volleyball. The best breaks of all were those all too few times free play was allowed, and I could hang out underneath the giant willow tree with Joyce and dream up adventures.

My teacher was such a sweet, tiny, petite woman with a willowy build and light brown hair, which just showed a little in the front, beyond her daily wear head covering. It looked very different from the church handkerchief looking one. To me, she was the best person in the world, and I happily soaked up every little thing she taught. I even liked to pretend that she was my mom.

The other kids often looked at me like I was crazy when I said or did something, which made me more anxious and uncertain. Such as the first time I needed to use the bathroom in class, I simply stood up to go without asking because I didn't know any better. And I frequently forgot to raise my hand before jumping to answer the teachers' questions, which made some giggle.

I quickly learned that not everyone wanted to automatically be my friend, although most were polite and friendly. I was very aware I still stood out from having come from being one of the 'worldly'.

Then there came the day when I innocently asked to play Cops and Robbers at recess... I just wound up embarrassed and confused when those around me were shocked, and it was explained to me that Mennonites do not participate in games like that. They believe if everyone was Mennonite, things like the police, government and military would be unnecessary.

I also made the mistake of casually mentioning wanting to get a picture made with my best friend, Joyce. This was also a highly frowned up comment, and I was swiftly told that photographs are forbidden. Treasuring a picture was likened to worshiping a false idol, which didn't make a lot of sense at all. However, they could have calendar's containing pictures of cats or nature, etc., which just seemed completely contradictory.

Standing out always in all the wrong ways, from first being stared at as the weird homeschooler, and then standing out among the Mennonites themselves was making a terrible impression on my slowly growing social anxiety. Mom and Ahaz referred to this to both me and others as 'being fake shy/ acting not normal'.

It was shortly after school had started, that Ahaz did something strange. He told me, and only me, to get into the van, and he refused to say where we were going. After a bit of a drive, we arrived at a small farmhouse, where there was a man with a Shetland pony waiting in the yard. When Ahaz told me that the pony was mine; I simply couldn't believe it and was nearly tripping over my own feet in my excitement to get to her.

I rode her around for a few minutes in the yard while the guys discussed the reason she was even being sold. It was because the man breed ponies, and she was already five years old and couldn't seem to get pregnant. The man didn't want to keep feeding a useless, sterile pony.

Her name was Butter, and she was soon delivered in a small trailer to the A-frame house. There was no fence to put her in, no barn, stable, shed, or even hay to feed her with. I had to tie her lead rope to the trampoline Ahaz had bought until something was figured out.

The purchase of the pony was actually a power move of his, because he knew mom would never leave him if she couldn't take all her babies; and he anticipated correctly that I wouldn't want to go without ever being able to take my long awaited, treasured pony. She wasn't a gift to please me; Butter was simply a new pawn he'd found to pull into his game.

One of our few neighbors agreed to let Butter have a stall in his small barn for the time being. Ahaz found someone to buy small bales of hay from, and bought a saddle, blanket, reins and brush from the community leather shop.

I absolutely loved her instantly, with all my heart and soul. She was my guide through the darkness, my champion over the uncertainty and stress, my escape from the screaming within the house. Butter became my calm throughout the storm when the anxiety was too much. She was freedom; and she was *mine*.

Mom and us kids were almost relieved, in the very beginning of being in the Muddy Pond community, because we finally were allowed to go to school, and have friends. But I also knew we'd all much rather be free from it all and run wild and worldly. I still couldn't help but to believe that this would happen at some point, once mom was strong enough to truly fight back, and win our freedom from that horrid man for good.

One day that fall, mom picked us kids up from school when it let out. I had already been dreaming all day of getting back to my pony as soon as we got to the house, but before we were even out of the church parking lot, she announced we were leaving for good and going to live in Kentucky with her parents.

I panicked immediately, and loudly cried out for my pony. I asked if we could at least take her, too, because I simply had to have her with me; I couldn't bear being without Butters. I *knew* I was being dreadfully ungrateful, especially since I had already begged mom to leave Ahaz for years. I only wished for Butter to be able to come with me, too.

Mom was very upset with the way I was acting, but on we drove on a break to freedom. She had filled up the gas tank prior to ensure we didn't have to stop along the way, and said we weren't even going to make a bathroom stop. A few hours later, we arrived at Nana and Granddaddy's in Lexington. I was tired from crying, stressed and anxious, but a part of me was still happy and relieved to see the grands.

I told them about my pony, and how important she was to me. I asked again if I could bring Butter there, but that was a solid no, and I was told to just stop being so selfish. I continued crying anyway, although there wasn't a lot left in me by that point.

In the upcoming days, Nana took us shopping. We all were bought entire, brand new wardrobes, complete with shorts and pants, among other things. Even though I had wanted to wear pants all along, the stress of all the new things made me cry again over even that. Mom said we were staying for good, and the grands were going to get us our own place to live and even Thomas was going to come live with us there. She promised that Ahaz would never touch us again, and we would be free forever from his insanity.

Every single one of us got haircuts. I had never been to a hair salon before and when the woman asked me what style I wanted, I didn't know what to say or ask for. Mom told her what to do instead. Then Mom, Sarah and I were off to get our ears pierced. I wasn't prepared for it to hurt, because Mom said it wouldn't. But when it came for my turn, but it did hurt some. Both my ears turned bright red and I cried. Neither moms nor my sisters turned red, nor did they complain of it hurting.

We were at the grands house for about two weeks. I was adjusting and learning a whole new world that did not include Ahaz, and it was a beautiful world indeed! I accepted, after a few more tears, that I would never see my pony or Joyce again. And I was ready to tackle and embrace the upcoming school adventure, even though it was still overwhelming.

Granddaddy, Nana and mom continually reminded and reassured us of all the good things in life and said that everything was going to be just fine. We listened to music, danced, swam in the pool and watched cartoons. All five of us were so happy, laughing and just barely beginning to enjoy life and the promise it brought along with it; of all the wonderful things to come.

Next up was getting us enrolled in public school, and we were taken to meet the teachers one Friday after classes had ended for the day. This private tour was specially arranged so that our under socialized selves would be able to see the school and meet the teachers before our first day there, to help ease us into it. We were to begin school that following Monday.

I'd never known how large a real school truly was inside, and all the turns in the halls to get to the classroom made me afraid I would never remember the way, get lost and be made fun of for it. I was also very surprised to learn just how many kids would be in each class, not to mention in the entire school. I had never been around so many kids in my life, and it was pretty terrifying to think of. I was too afraid to talk to my teacher, and mom told her I was faking shy.

That Sunday, mom loaded us up in the van to drive back to Muddy Pond all over again. I was right back to crying, this time because everything I had newly been given had been ripped away. No more pants. No more earrings. No more cute character shirts, no starting public school, no future high school possibility, no grandparents, no place of our own free from that man, no tv and no radio. No freedom.

Back to the horrible, abusive Ahaz and the Mennonites we drove. I tried to tell mom I was so incredibly sorry for throwing a fit for leaving my pony and making it hard on her; I promised to try really hard to be a perfect little girl, if only we could stay in Lexington. I thought that it was my fault for having complained, that I must be the reason it had all been ruined and we were forced to return to the unknowns and abuse. Mom told me and the others to shut up and to stop asking any questions. We were all very upset, and helpless to stop her from returning us all to Ahaz.

When we got to the A-frame house, Ahaz was happily waiting outside and held his arms open like he expected a hug as though I would be so pleased to be back there with him. I ran past him into the house, and straight upstairs to my bedroom to cry. He yelled angrily after me, but he was too focused on mom to put-up chase and whip me, like he typically would have at any other time.

I threw myself down onto my bed and soaked the pillow with my tears, still believing it was my fault we had been forced to return to all the crazy; it truly must have been because I begged for my pony, I thought. No one came to check on or bother me, and eventually I cried myself to sleep.

The upcoming days, weeks and months I threw myself into school, getting lost in learning, in my friendship with Joyce, and in the comfort my sweet teacher offered. Mom wasn't getting out of bed much, and sometimes my hair wasn't braided when I got to school. My teacher would braid it for me on those days, at least until I learned how to myself. Her hands were incredibly soft and gentle.

Back at home, there wasn't an awful lot of food choices in the kitchen, and a lot of times mom would just yell through her bedroom door for us kids to find our own supper, or to make our own school lunches in the mornings. One day I took a pack of just macaroni powdered cheese to school to eat; it was very dry on its own, to say the least.

Ahaz went back to working in E.R.s, although a few of his former patients did make the drive and come to the house occasionally to talk to him in the small dining room.

He wasn't welting me up daily anymore. This was a very brief respite from it, primarily to do with the false promises made to my mom about how he had changed, and in part to him being away working in the E.R.s. Also, because I spent all my waking time outside when I wasn't in school, so even when he was at the house, I avoided him as much as possible.

I stayed outside with my pony every spare moment of daylight I had, and then some. We would ride, adventure, and have long, deep conversations about anything and everything that popped through my head, which was a lot. Butter never did answer, but I knew she understood my despair. I had very little, to no supervision at all which was a peaceful relief from before.

At night, I would lay on the trampoline and look up at the stars, finding within them the constellations and various other patterns. There were a lot of frogs out in the country, and they made sure everyone knew it. The sound of their little frog songs was soothing to listen to.

Chapter Five

1998- thru 1999

Age 9-10yrs

I wasn't being given much information on what was happening with Thomas, but there were a few things I picked up on through overheard conversations. After we'd left our hometown in Kentucky, Grams & Gramps had apparently gotten emergency custody of Thomas due to him having been abused, and then abandoned when we moved out of state without notice.

It seemed like an open and shut case, however Ahaz appealed it in an attempt to get custody back. Him and mom kept leaving town to do this and other things to do with the case, while placing us kids with another Mennonite family during their absences. I was not actually, directly told much of anything.

Then Sarah and I were taken for physicals somewhere. Mom had told Sarah just a tiny bit about why we had to do this, and sis whispered it to me just to show off. She told me that our grandparents wanted custody of Sarah, too, and since they knew Ahaz never laid a finger on her, they were trying to use me to prove it; so, they could get only Sarah. Knowing that my grandparents didn't want *me* made me cry; I really just wanted to be wanted, too.

Ahaz had anticipated something like that would happen, and it was the true reason he was no longer whipping me. So that all the evidence would have enough time to heal and fade if I was to be court ordered to be examined.

The younger two boys were not ordered to do physicals. I think this was because they were still little and were not being abused to the same extent of Thomas and I; but what Thomas had endured so far was worse than me.

Ahaz just kept saying that Thomas 'would be joining the family soon'. I dared to comment the truth; that I hoped for Thomas's sake he wasn't forced to, and I was scared of him, anyway. I said that I wished I could go live somewhere else, too, because I didn't want to have to be around Ahaz since he was a horrible, mean person.

I got the daylights switched out of me for that, and it was quickly back to the regular, bloody, fiery red welts I had never wished to have again. So much for the break! He whipped me for such a long time, until I eventually apologized and lied by 'admitting' to lying. Because of course, Thomas *should* come home to his loving family; especially since Ahaz was such a self-proclaimed amazing, upstanding person, family man and doctor.

He gave me a long, boring lecture on how normal people are not so disrespectful, and do not tell lies, especially in happy families. Yet he forced me to lie after whipping me?

Contrary to the popular belief at the time, I hated lying. And I most definitely was not sorry in the slightest for speaking facts. When he forced me into lying on the daily, I'd cross my fingers behind my back to turn what I was saying into the opposite of that. I had heard this meant I wasn't actually lying, as though being forced to say I love you to him, was silently changed to I hate you simply by crossing my fingers. He figured this out and began forcing me to keep my hands in sight when he made me lie, so I'd cross my toes instead.

Mom continued to pack us kids up a couple more times after school and take off to her parents again. It was never for as long as the first time though. A day or two of empty promises of freedom; then right back to Ahaz and to the Mennonites. It became a blur. As the end of school neared each day, I would become more anxious while I watched the hands of the clock tick tock its way to 3:30.

When I walked outside that school room door, I never knew what awaited; a drive to the horrid A-frame house to see my precious companion pony and the awful Ahaz, or to false freedom. On those few trips when we ran away, I didn't cry quite as hard for Butter as I had during that first escape. But when I did, I cried only out of sadness from missing my furry friend. In no way on earth did I want to be in that house with Ahaz, even if it meant leaving my precious pony.

Each time, I begged for mom to let us stay gone for good, with her parents. Free. But she always dragged us back in the end.

There was a beautiful blue house with striking white moldings we passed every day on the way to church or school, located just barely outside of the Muddy Pond community, technically in Monterey. Mom always turned to look at it as we went by, but I looked to the opposite side of the road without fail. Directly across the street was a very tall fence, and within it was some of the most fascinating of animals; elk, deer, buffalo, and even at one point there were a couple of ostriches. I thought it was a safe place for them to stay or something, but it turned out to be a wildlife hunting ground.

In winter of 1998, that exact house became available for rent to own. Mom contacted the owners right away, and hardly anytime at all later we moved into it. It was only three bedrooms, so sis and I shared a room, and both Travis and Dennis took the other. Mom exclaimed over how much she loved it many times and was so happy over it. Butter was moved onto the deacons' farm until a pen could be put up behind the house that summer.

The house was most definitely not a Mennonite approved style. The lavish molding on it and the frowned upon window shutters were much talked about. Ahaz told the Mennonites that it was only temporary housing, and as soon as a house or property within the Muddy Pond community came available, he'd take it to have something more appropriate.

There was debate over what was to be done with Ahaz having so much schooling. It was determined that since he had gotten his degrees before 'knowing better', he would be allowed to continue to use it as a Mennonite and work as a doctor.

Mom, Ahaz and Sarah officially joined the Mennonite church all on the same night. Mom was so pale, quiet and looked sad, like she was fighting tears even though she was forcing a fake smile. Ahaz was beaming from ear to ear, and sis was somewhere in-between on the day they were baptized.

The Holy Kiss, aka The Kiss of Peace, was how members would formerly greet each other, no matter how young or old. Females kissed other females directly on the lips, and males kissed males on the lips. No air kisses or cheek kisses; it was literally lips, to lips. If a 9yr old boy was a baptized member he would be required to greet other males of any age, no matter if they were kissing a 15, 25, 60, 90-year-old man, and vice versa with females. Even if it was with a complete stranger from another congregation.

They use The Holy Kiss to greet new members, when seeing them with each other, at church, when visiting inside the community, or even when meeting a new person. For example, when meeting a complete stranger from another Mennonite congregation, they'd automatically kiss the stranger.

It was gross and incredibly strange to see it done over and over, and to even watch my own mom kissing women and girls, and the same for my sister and Ahaz. It was made out to be an honored thing, and none of the Mennonites appeared to visibly find it wrong, bad or out of the ordinary. It was literally a requirement for them to do, not a suggestion, and this was deeply ingrained within their religion.

Another part of them joining meant that my mom and Sarah now had to wear a solid black head covering from the moment they got up, until the moment before they laid down to go to sleep. They could not pray without it, and since praying was expected many times throughout the day at any given moment, it must never be removed except for bathing and sleeping.

For church, a second, larger head covering was required over top of the smaller daily wear one, and it was secured with a straight pin at the top and then tied under the chin, with the loose ends past the tied knot tucked up into the covering for a neater look.

And yes, it would have been immediately, extremely obvious if they had not worn the daily wear one underneath. Anything less than having both on during church was unacceptable. This was only expected of the baptized females; the men were holy enough all on their own without having to cover their heads.

I was still wearing braids. Ahaz had told the ministers that although I was a baptized member of my Gramps church, he knew that I wasn't saved because I was not obedient and moldable enough. Obviously if I was a Christian, I would love him and follow his every command without question.

Oh, and let's not forget those other reasons he conveniently left out, such as for not willingly thanking my abuser after severe whippings and being forced to drink terrible things. Yep, let's just go ahead and judge everyone's Christianity on how they submit to and react to abuse; that sounds like a fantastic, fail proof plan indeed to judging whether or not someone was saved.

I did believe in God. In all my little kid innocence, I trustingly prayed to God to please stop Ahaz from being so cruel. I promised all sorts of things in exchange for this 'deal', but it never worked. I even tried putting scraps of fabric over my hair just in case that was the real way to get answers to prayers, but still nothing happened. I tried asking in so many different ways, but to no avail.

Around this time, Ahaz told us that Thomas was being sent to a boy's work camp in Florida, and once the camp had improved his attitude, he would then come back to live with us. He was gloating and obviously incredibly proud of himself. What actually happened was this...

Ahaz somehow managed to get secret custody of Thomas back, and I do not know exactly how he did it. But a judge signed off on it, which was completely unknown to my grandparents who'd had custody of him all this time.

Professional thugs were hired to pick up my brother while the grands were not at home, and Thomas was there alone.

One of these thugs was later described to me as looking like Arnold Schwarzenegger. These guys trespassed into the grands house and woke my brother from his bed. They told Thomas he was coming with them and forced him to dress and leave with them. Then they held the poor boy hostage as they drove him all the way to Florida to this camp.

My grandparents did not know what had happened until it was too late. They spent the next six months desperately searching for Thomas. Once they found him, they managed to, again, get emergency custody. The moment they had the papers in hand, they immediately went after Thomas and got him out.

Back in the Mennonite community, all I knew of this situation was that Ahaz was running around like a crazed fool, furious and screaming because his authority had been under minded. I was happy Thomas had got out. At least one of us could live free.

But poor Thomas... having been in a work camp was no joke. It was serious, painful labor, with the purpose being to work the boys there until they broke, in order to turn them into the role model kids their parents desired. When my grands picked him up, he was horribly sunburned, on top of more sunburns. He was blistered and his hands oozed from it, and he had cuts and bruises in multiple stages of healing. Thomas was so traumatized from the things done at that camp, that he didn't speak more than a word or two at a time for the next six months, and was never, ever the same again.

Although Ahaz continued to attempt to fight through the courts like a dog with a bone, he never regained custody. He did not do it out of any form of parental love for Thomas, but for his own personal interest; because Thomas was, in Ahaz's eyes, his property. He was the head of the household, and absolutely no one could take away his power; until his very own parents and the judge did exactly that. He refused to fully relinquish control within his own mind.

He liked to endlessly point out that he'd make sure the rest of us did not wind up being as disobedient as Thomas. This is really what seemed to begin his spiral to seeking even deeper control over me. Only 100% submission would do. What proceeded next turned out to only be the beginning... Thomas had been his test subject. I was going to be his final project.

Christmas that year was a surprise, because Mennonites do not believe in putting up holiday trees. At least before, we were, at minimum allowed a tree, but no longer. And although Christmas gifts were not completely forbidden, they were also not highly regarded.

At school, we were allowed to draw names and exchange a small gift. In homes, very little was exchanged. Perhaps a pair of handy work gloves or something else useful like a candle, or a handmade gift. Ahaz forbid any gifts at this point entirely, but even though my mom said she always had to pay the price for it, she still tried to make sure we had little something, even if she had to quietly sneak it to each one of us kids.

The Mennonites were big on making cards and sending letters. In fact, many of the women and especially the teen girls got ink stamps for dressing up homemade cards. And some even sent out mass monthly life updates to other Mennonites in other Holdeman Mennonite communities around the USA, Mexico and in Canada. They'd write or type the letter once, then make enough copies for their list of people to send it to. There was quite a lot of pen- paling amongst the congregations.

The one and only type of musical instrument permitted was a pitch pipe, in order to get everyone started off on the same note during singing at church or school. And dancing was forbidden, completely and utterly. To me, that was very frustrating. I enjoyed the sweet, gentle, soothing tones of music. And although there hadn't been much dancing before, there had still been a small amount I'd gotten away with. For it to not be allowed at all seemed just crazy.

Butter grew more round in her middle as the months passed. I wasn't able to see her very often anymore since she was now a few miles away. But one day, the deacon called to say there were an extra set of 4 legs in his field! As it turned out, the pony that couldn't get pregnant had already been with foal at the time of sell.

I now had two ponies, and my new darling foal I named Spice. She was a beautiful shade of light brown. Spice was so tiny, innocent, and signified to me everything would be ok; there was still hope of a new life and freedom within it.

Over the summer, the heavy underbrush amongst the trees was partially cleared out on the hill behind the house, and a fence put up. A shed was built within it as well.

I said that I wanted goats, and Ahaz decided that would be just fine since it would help clean up some of the plants and small trees remaining. So, he went out and bought 3; a nanny named Bonnie, and her twin kids, Snowflake and Molly. Butter and Spice were brought over from the deacons' farm, and I was so excited to have so many animals right in the back yard.

I milked Bonnie, which I greatly enjoyed doing. Ahaz argued with mom about wanting her to make goat cheese from it and he demanded it and belittled her until she gave in and tried just to shut him up. She gathered all the needed supplies and carefully followed the steps to making it, but it turned out pretty gross. I believe that was the one and only time she attempted it; truly she was never one to want to have to make things from scratch. Simply didn't have that natural knack for it (which there was nothing wrong with).

Butter hated Ahaz, and he decided to enlist the assistance of a fellow Mennonite named Maxwell who used to break horses, to show him how to 'change Butter's attitude'. You see, Butter wouldn't stop trying to bite Ahaz and even kicked him in the head; obviously due to her being a very intelligent pony, she knew evil when she saw it! Well, this was a deep insult to Ahaz, and he wouldn't stand for it. He expected even the pony to respect and honor him as the head of household, and as her owner.

Maxwell agreed to help, and he taught Ahaz how to lung Butter, while showing her who was boss without question. This was accomplished by using a long whip. Once Ahaz got started on that route, it continued, and he escalated it terribly. He didn't simply use the whip as a guide or tool for assistance; he quite literally beat the heck out of her. On and on until she was frothing at the mouth and drenched in sweat. He wouldn't stop the abuse until he was too tired himself to continue. He was so incredibly cruel.

I did try to stop him from hurting my pony. I screamed at him, as he brought that whip down across her body repeatedly. But being told he was wrong by a mere, useless girl only ignited his fury, and I was whipped for it mercilessly. Normal people do not question his authority, he'd say. Normal people would understand he was simply forcing the pony to respect him by simply lunging it.

I only knew I did *not* want to be 'normal' if that's what normal people would see. I saw abuse; I *knew* it was abuse. I tried to tell mom, and she witnessed him beating Butter as well from the kitchen window. But instead of her trying to tell him to stop, she turned away and tuned out what I was saying.

Mom was trying to learn how to cook and sew, even though she absolutely hated it. There was a large sewing group every month in the church basement, and she began going to them at Ahaz's forced insistence. Some women brought their own sewing current projects in various stages of completion, and others showed up simply to get in on the fun of helping others. It was a great way for bonding and getting work done, or even for learning new things.

All the other women there had been sewing since they were kids, unlike my mom. She was decades behind, but the others tried their best to teach her how it was done, and how to make patterns, etc. In the meantime, the ladies were sewing dresses for myself, my sister and mom to keep us in clothes.

As far as the cooking was going... it was rough going. She simply wasn't the chef Ahaz insisted that she be. He decided the issue must lie in her cooking materials; she surely only needed a more expensive set of pots and pans.

A man came over one night and spent over an hour doing a demo of how his fancy pots worked. Ahaz ordered quite a few of them; they were heavy and the amount he spent was utterly insane. For the record... it did not improve mom's cooking. And there was nothing wrong with that at all, not everyone is a born chef! However, he would frequently become very angry over it, because he expected his lowly, modern- raised wife to be able to cook and bake like the Mennonite woman, whom had been trained for it all their lives.

He truly made her feel like she was a terrible, useless person. But honestly, how could anyone expect delicious food to come from someone forced into doing it, who has no real desire to cook? You simply cannot. Good food is made with love and happiness, on top of a good dose of skill, be it learned or natural.

One thing that I didn't like, was that books were very restricted there. Even something as simple as 'Little House on the Prairie' was a controversial set. The reasoning behind it was because the kids written into the story were too ornery, which did not set a good example. We couldn't have books with tv characters or cartoons, such as Mickey Mouse, and goodness forbid if there were the simple words like 'gee' or 'gosh' in a book!

Forget books about the military, police, etc. And you could just forget even the Christian novels that had a peck on the lips kiss, or forbidden dating. Reading was allowed, just as long as it wasn't the wrong books.

I wanted to learn everything about absolutely everything, and not be held back. It was swiftly becoming a deeply ingrained need to read anything I could get my hands on, not just what was graciously handed to me as 'approved' reading. I needed more and had to learn about the real world since it was clear not a soul was going to be willing to teach it to me. Even so young, I knew that I needed to prepare for my future through modern education in order be ready for when that moment of freedom arrived.

I was highly aware that I could only succeed through pressing forward toward my goals, becoming a powerful woman, and to not allow myself to be buried under the life within which I was forced to live. There was a wide open, big world outside the tiny walls and community where I was, and I was going to go out into it one day. I still believed this would happen far sooner, than later, in the form of mom finally taking us all away for good. Or someone else would surely recognize the evil which oozed from Ahaz, and get all of us, mom included, out of there and away from him forever.

In truth, reality was far different from that. Ahaz considered himself essentially an honored king, whom should be bowed down to. But what he portrayed to others was that he was a kind, loving family man. One who doctored his family and wished only the best for us. He would insistently talk many circles around people about all his self-proclaimed good deeds, how could they have stood a chance to ever doubt it? He was such a holy, devoted person who did no wrong, according to him.

The Mennonites had church 3 times per week. Every Sunday morning, Sunday evening, and Wednesday evening. Church attendance was considered far stricter than in the modern world, and they always seemed to notice if even one adult, teen or kid was absent.

Fun fact: the woman and teens not only had to wear long sleeves to church, but also panty hose. No bare legs in church; unless they were a young girl then a few inches of skin might be shown between the top of their socks and hem of their dress.

Thankfully, they did believe in electricity, heat and air conditioning, unlike the Amish. And of course, vehicles were fine as well. But strangely enough, certain vehicle types were off limits, such as SUVs, because the very name stands for Sports Utility Vehicle, and it was not allowed purely for this reason. Despite the fact the Mennonites permitted the playing of casual softball and volleyball, they upheld that they do not believe in sports, and somehow, they tied in supporting sports, to having an SUV.

They were also forbidden from having certain colors in both clothing and on vehicle's, such a bright red, lime green, and hot pink because bright shades are considered gaudy and worldly.

When a new, or used vehicle was purchased, the radio was immediately to be removed from the dashboard, and it had to be confirmed that it had been done in order to maintain the strict guidelines. Generally, a little wood box was made to fit, and then placed inside the open hole, to use as a cubby, of sorts. For pen and paper or whatever someone may choose to place there.

One of the young men there purchased a brightly colored, brand-new truck all decked out with all sorts of goodies, and he was literally forced to return it for something more Mennonite approved. However, a brand-new vehicles value goes down sharply immediately after signing the papers and driving it off the lot, so he lost a reasonable sum of money on it. But he did return it in order to purchase something more sedate, in order to prevent being *excommunicated over it.*

The cleaning standard was impeccable, and I'd liken it to homes of those with a cleaning OCD. Everyone in the community had to be prepared for visitors to drop by at any given moment, especially since Mennonites commonly made a habit of visiting one another.

Chapter Six

There was somewhat of a hierarchy amongst the Holdeman Mennonites. The older and purer the bloodline stretched back, the more respected they were within not just our small community, but throughout the entire sect. It was nearly as though it was the Mennonite version of being wealthy or being the spawn from the original Dracula. (Yes, I am aware fictional vampires have absolutely nothing to do with this, but I found it amusing).

Being that we were brand new blood, we were at the bottom of the totem pole and stood out like sore thumbs amongst the others. Which was ironic, since the restricted lifestyle we had been forced into living prior by Ahaz, was already incredibly similar to the Mennonites. But alas, we were nevertheless considered as coming from being 'worldly', before having switched over to the ~~cult~~; oops, I should have said switched over to the right path, my bad.

Wearing the same clothes as those around me did not actually make me blend in within the community. I felt like I was closely watched and was told repeatedly that I was immature for my age. But they didn't understand where I came from; other than being around some elderly, I had never before been around so many people, much less kids regularly in my short life. I lacked the social skills and experience needed to have blended in better. Somehow my siblings did not suffer this same difficulty though. Ahaz of course continued to point out it was all because I was 'not normal'.

Strangely, even though I was aware that Ahaz wasn't right in the head, I still didn't know enough to actually recognize in full that I was literally being abused. I didn't know then that it was illegal to leave oozing welts across my body, or that the thing's he'd say were mental and emotional abuse.

I wanted to get out of there; but I didn't want things to go back to the way they were previously of course. I hoped to soon experience the real, true world; one that did not include the unreasonable, cruel Ahaz in it. I waited to be freed from him by my mom, and by grandparents.

Ahaz did not join that Mennonite congregation and force us into the community in order to save our souls; or because it was a true 'conviction'. He did it to gain even more control over us all, all under the guise of religion. It was a power move that would enable him to hide his monster within more easily, right underneath everyone's noses.

It also gave him a higher level of protection for himself under the laws that allow for the Mennonites to practice their religion freely without consequence; even if it was something as completely screwed up as The Holy Kiss. Disgusting ole man, that's exactly what he was.

My friend Joyce's family was absolutely amazing, and they did not give 2 figs that I hadn't been born a Mennonite. In fact, they were a hair on the more lenient side as far as the standard went. I found so much happiness in going to her house and playing with her. We pretended all sorts of wonderful things for hours, played games, and simply enjoyed being little girls. I found immense freedom while there, an escape from reality.

There was no one at her house to grab and whip the heck out of me for daring to so much as blink 'not normally' at their house. It was so peaceful, and to see the innerworkings of a true family was wonderful. They were a down to earth, fantastic family who also loved to tell jokes, play small pranks and most of all, make each other laugh!

My eyes began frequently bothering me for some reason for a while, and automatically caused me to blink more often, hence the blinking comment. I wasn't even doing it on purpose; my eyes just felt weird; dry, maybe? People noticed and commented. At church, at school, and at the blue house. I felt so incredibly self-conscious especially when I was asked why I was blinking like that? But the more I tried to stop it, the worse it seemed to become.

Well apparently, that was me just acting weird and doing it to draw attention. Ahaz whipped the heck out of me for it several times, then forced me to apologize and 'admit' that I was just doing it to irritate him. Then he made me 'thank him for correcting me', and to say I loved him. The lies kept piling up, one after another, forced from my lips with a mere painful stick and it made me feel helpless and angry. He demanded that I stop acting not normal; I had to promise that, too.

On the bright side, I guess my eyes were, indeed, far more moisturized after he welted up my backside and thighs. Perhaps if anyone had taken the bother to get me a small bottle of eye drops... oh well. It thankfully went away after perhaps a few months or so.

One strange fact I learned was that it was considered worldly to have a dress that was too long, as well as too short. It seemed completely strange that I couldn't have a dress down to my ankles, nor even just below my knees. Dresses literally *had* to fall to a certain sweet spot midway between knees and ankles. It made absolutely zero sense, and naturally

I felt the need to point that fact out, which did not end well for me.

Naturally I also debated the limited fabric color selections, since bright shades where not permitted, and I found that rule to be quite senseless. I asked if I'd go to hell for wearing hot pink, lime green or bright red clothes? And if not, then why wasn't it allowed?

No one could give me a solid answer to back it up that held any real logic to it. They couldn't answer whether or not someone would go to hell for it, and therefore had no way to answer the second question; it simply wasn't permitted and that was the whole of it.

Ahaz whipped me for even having the thoughts; and for daring to ask around about it. I wasn't allowed to think as an individual, much less ask questions. It was 'not normal' behavior for a little girl. Not normal... not normal. That was me.

In church, the almighty males sat on the left side of the church, while the women and kids on the right. There was a nursery with a one-way glass mirror in the back on the women's side for those with feeding/ crying infants. When a small boy would be old enough to sit quietly through an entire service, then he'd be moved to the left.

For both sides, the youth ages 15 plus walked in moments before service began, in a straight line together just prior to service to sit in the second and third rows from the front on their gender designated sides. This was done for a couple of reasons; to single out those who were unmarried and of marriable material, and so everyone could keep an eye on them from behind.

The males wore only store-bought clothes although they still could not wear anything with visible words, pictures or even logos on them. Take for instance; Polo brand has a small polo horse and rider the front of each shirt; they could not wear those for that reason, even though it was tiny. Attire rules were very strict and taken seriously.

On the other hand, females wore handmade dresses from the time of infancy and up. And just as soon as the tiny wisps of baby hair could be swept up into tiny braids, they sure were- even if those small twists only resulted in an inch of actual braids! Until they were baptized into the church, girls could have *no other* hairstyle. They had a choice between one or two braids, from early morning until bedtime, period. Ponytails were completely unacceptable and wearing it down and lose was the absolute worst of all.

I dared to question why that was even an issue, to wear hair down. But it was simply the rules. There was nothing in the Bible saying a girl's hair must be twisted into a braid or else go to hell, so again... *why?*

Short sleeves were allowed for both genders and ages for daily wear, but never, ever sleeveless. For church, absolutely everyone had to wear long sleeves. Yet, the females were not allowed to wear long sleeved dresses outside of church, even in winter. The men could wear long sleeve shirts anytime, which didn't seem very fair at all.

Speaking of cold... there was a single accepted allowance for females to wear loose fitting sweatpants under their dresses. If, and only if there was a good bit of snow on the ground, it was permitted if one was going outside in the snow. All the rest of winter in the frigged air, all I was allowed to have was bare, frozen legs. So incredibly cold!

Being forced to spend winter in just a thin dress and coat didn't make sense to me. There was simply no reason whatsoever to endure being so cold simply over a religion, for the sake of supposed modesty. I am sure many built up a resistance to the cold, but I couldn't seem to.

In summer, not even the males were not allowed to wear shorts. But again, there is another single exception of swimming. Males could wear long shorts and a t-shirt, and females the exact same. Mixed swimming with the opposite gender was forbidden for all ages, as well as for swimming with anyone who was worldly.

The local lake was considered a lair of sin, and we couldn't go there. But there were other spots, such as Mennonite owned ponds, and a good swimming spot along the river where swimming was tolerated as long as no one else was there. I very much enjoyed swimming, not just for the fun of it, but also because I felt like if anyone worldly did happen to see me, they'd assume I was one of their own.

The no jewelry rule included no wedding rings, necklaces or earrings. Makeup was a serious offence, not even a tiny smidge could be used. Strawberry flavored chap stick was as close to lipstick as I could get.

Not even battery-operated, little learning toys for kids were permitted. Obviously, those toys were worldly and most also contained a forbidden little sweet musical jingle. However, other battery powered things such as flashlights were permissible since it was a useful tool.

Both alcohol consumption and cigarettes were forbidden for all. They were made out to be evil.

Breaking any rule or dress code could get a person put on something called 'Church Concern', which is up to a 6-month long probation period to either shape up or be excommunicated if you refuse to repent; or do not have a believable enough repentance story. Instead of only seeking forgiveness from God, you also had to *convince* the Mennonites you had truly repented, and whether or not it was believed was determined by a majority vote of members; even though some of those members were mere kids/ teens.

Within the community, there was a local General Store, Bakery, Leather Shop, and a Sorghum Mill. I absolutely adored going to those places!

The Leather Shop smelled absolutely amazing, and I loved running my hands over all the smooth saddles and other goodies that could be found there. I imagined that one day I'd love to make all sorts of beautiful leather things, too. I was crafty and creative, and l knew that I could do it.

At the General Store, I at first thought they made *all* the many candies on the shelves. They did make a large variety of homemade treats but here is the truth; they also bought sugary gummy worms, candy corn and even powdered Jell-O *and put them in their own simple, innocent, basic packaging and resell them for profit.* Hmmm... so that's how they tasted exactly like worldly bought sweets- they actually were!

Mom would laugh about how the worldly tourists who'd swarm there during the summer most likely thought they were purchasing *all* homemade candies in those little bags. Now on the other hand, many things were truly handmade such as the maple pecan candies, coconut balls, bread, etc.

My favorite things to get from there were the Cow Tail candies, and Root Beer in glass bottles. Sometimes Joyce's dad would take us to that little store just for those things, and we'd sit on the wooden furniture outside on the porch, sipping our drinks and pretending we had forbidden beer in those bottles.

I loved going up to the top floor at that little store, although the floor creaked and cracked so loudly I sometimes feared it just might break underneath my cautious footsteps. My favorite things to look at up there were all the pretty handmade wooden goodies, everything from cute little dolly highchairs to beautiful trinket boxes. There were also hand stitches quilts and much more.

And as for as the Sorghum Mill, they harnessed up giant Belgium Ponies to walk in a slow circle in order to turn the machinery that squishes the juice from the sugar cane. Tourists could watch the ponies go round and round, and then see inside the mill building itself where large amounts of sugar cane were flowing, appearing to come from those Belgium's to those who did not know better.

My mom used to laugh over this, because of the way it was portrayed, she said that tourists would easily be under the impression they were buying jars of Belgium- power squeezed sorghum; but that simply was not true. They had a large set up of machines which did it so much faster and handled nearly all, or literally all of it, and it was then funneled into the mill where tourist could see it. Those giant ponies were primarily used as an attraction to those people.

There were quite a few holidays that were different or not allowed to be celebrated. Halloween of course was a major no-no with zero exceptions. Easter was celebrated in the form of a church service, the Easter Bunny or gathering of plastic eggs with candy in them was far outside of the relm of what was permitted. The 4th of July was not celebrated at all, absolutely no fireworks, cookouts or appreciation celebration for freedom. Veterans Day was also completely overlooked.

Mennonites do not have veterans, and they are exempt from being called up in a time of war. That might sound alright, but they take advantage of their freedom daily to practice their religion without persecution; *without* honoring those who died to give them that freedom! The least they could have done was celebrated it. Something, anything would have been better than nothing.

Labor Day was also ignored. Naturally, I was whipped dreadfully for protesting how ridiculous it was to not be allowed to participate in all holidays, because 'normal people do not question the head of household'. Not normal... not normal.

Ahaz continued attempting to dominate my sweet pony. Only now he decided he was going to force her to let him ride her, since he was her owner; she owed him that much. Butter completely disagreed and did NOT go along with that plan at all; she recognized the evil within him.

He would lung her first, while beating the absolute heck out of her, chasing her round and round in a circle, bringing that horrid whip down with every ounce of force he could muster while I helplessly watched and cried over the horrendous amount of force he used. Telling him not to, or begging, stopped nothing except to turn his rage toward me.

And so, on it went... until Butter was, I am sure, in an immense amount of pain, and her entire coat soaked and dripping in sweat. Ahaz would be drenched in sweat too at that point. Then he would swing his leg over (there was no 'hopping' on her, she was literally just a little Shetland pony!) and after such a dreadful beating, she'd stumble under his grown adult weight. A few different things would happen next; either she'd still have the strength left in her to rear and get his ass the heck off, or she'd seemed to more collapse; just went straight to the ground and when he toppled off to the side she'd leap back up.

When he'd get on her, it tore at my heart with how she stumbled, and I'd be screaming for him to get off, that he weighed too much for her. It made him incredibly furious at my horrified 'disrespectful' screams and pleas, on top of the insult of Butter absolutely refusing to allow him to ride no matter how he beat her. There were times after she tossed him that Ahaz would then make a beeline for me with a riding crop, to lash it across my back, bottom and thighs in his fury. He'd be shouting out that Shetlands are able to carry up to 500 pounds; that he wasn't hurting her, and I was disrespecting him as the honored capable one to make proper decisions, and 'normal people do not do that'.

She was my precious pony, and mine alone to ride. I treasured each and every moment of time spent alone with Butter. Of course, Spice, the foal, was quite nice as well, but I did not bond to her as tightly even though she was cute as could be.

Ahaz decided that my mom wasn't whipping me and my brothers hard enough. He declared that he was now going to be the only one capable of dishing out discipline, as the head of household it was his responsibility. And his gaze was beginning to focus primarily on me, more and more as time went on. Although he welted my little brothers some, he didn't spend nearly as much time dedicated to it as he did on me. Nor did he hit them quite as hard; they were 'normal'.

No matter how many times I begged my mom to stop him, she always preferred to pretend the things her eyes saw was false, and not as terrible as what they truly were in any given situation. The truth of harsh reality was too painful a burden for her to face head on.

My mom felt helpless to do anything other than follow Ahaz in everything; the screaming fights were becoming less frequent and further spread out. Not because of an increase in happiness, but due to her having been broken so dreadfully, she could hardly function anymore. She was in a suicidal blur of fake smiles to attempt to hide it, and she was sleeping a lot more during the day.

This seemed unbelievable to me since my mom had personally been raised up to be a strong woman, and been given every single comfort, convenience, and privilege that her wealthy parents could offer. She had chosen to marry Ahaz only because he was going to be a doctor, since she dreamed of having six kids; 3 boys and 3 girls and wanted a husband that could afford them all comfortably.

The first signs he was going to be controlling had started happening a couple of weeks prior to marriage, but she still went through with the wedding. And stayed. Even though she had been taught to be a powerful woman and never take any of a man's crap. Its mind blowing to me. But there she was, as a very unhappy, powerless Mennonite woman, completely broken from the awful way Ahaz treated her.

Ahaz was quite simply obsessed with having absolute control. He began demanding that mom and us kids walk slightly behind him and to the side, since he was the head of household and should be revered as such. No, this was not actually a rule in the Mennonites; he said that he got this idea from the strict deacon.

He was especially intent on enforcing that I personally did it, since I was not his equal and therefore not superior enough to be anywhere but behind him and to the side.

I was always too busy running ahead to stay away from him. The mere thought of dropping behind and being a lowly, mere, insignificant female grated on me, because I knew I was worth more than that. I protested this ridiculous command and was severely whipped, and later beat, many, many times for it.

There was a day when we arrived at church one morning, and I had, of course, sat in the far back right of the van per usual in order to at least distance myself as far as possible from him in the driver seat, while trapped in the van with him.

Once parked, Ahaz reminded everyone what he expected of his little ducklings (no he didn't use that term but what he wanted reminded me of that). He got out and walked to the right side of the van and waited with a disgusting, slimy, expectant smirk. Mom opened her door, and my brothers in the middle seats followed suit, then me. My stomach twisted at the grin on his face, and I felt sick with distaste. I got out and my sister followed behind me.

He deliberately and slowly turned toward the front entrance of the church and began to walk slow and proud, expecting first mom right behind and to the side, then all us kids. Panic and disgust set it; I was *not* a lowly follower, and I would never follow such a nasty person. I broke free from the pack and ran to the nearby side church door and straight to the woman's bathroom. I stayed in there as long as I could get away with so he couldn't come after me before the service began.

The horrible whipping which I received for this... bleeding, racing stripped welts as soon as we got back to the house. He swung that switch on, and on, and on, until the church dress I was still wearing had small holes throughout the fabric. He forced me to lie in order to make it stop; to apologize for not acting normal, and to tell him I loved him and to promise I would obey. I did eventually give in and lie; but I meant *none* of it. There was nothing wrong with me, but something was dreadfully wrong with *him*.

Ahaz whipped me often for this same offence, just in different instances. I refused to bow down to his righteousness; I was too smart to be a minion. I was my own, strong little person. Around this time was when the shift slowly began to slide from being severe, terrible whippings, to what I would definitely refer to as beatings. The length of time got longer, the fury behind it more forceful, and it would eventually spiral widely out of control on down the line.

He became determined to beat away everything he deemed to be 'wrong'. I was beat for thirsting for more knowledge than I was permitted to have and continuously pushing the bounds of what a little Mennonite girl should know by carefully reading many, many books, including scanning and reading through encyclopedias while bored.

Also, for insisting I was going to be a police officer when I grew up, which was literally forbidden. For crossing my arms when I was chilled, because 'normal people only cross their arms when they are angry' and I was not allowed to appear angry. I was not allowed to feel or react to things he deemed unacceptable to react to, like the cold. I was expected to act like a tiny, little perfectly oiled, smooth running machine at all moments with zero exceptions, or else I was 'not normal'. Not normal... not normal.

Chapter Seven

2000, age 11

I loved during the summer when I could go pick the gorgeous wild Blackberries that grew quite near to the house. Only perhaps half or less of those berries actually made it into the bucket, to go inside to my mom who would make a cobbler from them. They were the best Blackberries I had ever eaten, and I simply couldn't seem to get enough of them.

There was a worldly girl around my age who lived nearby, and I snuck over to her house several times to play with her. Her parents were quite nice and seemed very cheerful. The girl had some awesome tiny dolls called Polly Pockets. They had rubber clothes and I was instantly obsessed with them.

When Ahaz found out that I was going over there, he nearly lost his mind in a furious rage because I had dared to play with such an awful, worldly, public school kid. He not only beat the heck out of me for it, but also told her folks they were not allowed to have me in their house, yard, or even to play with their daughter at all.

I was devastated, and still tried to sneak over a few more times. Only now, I was greeted with the parents acting awkward and turning me away at the door. Of course, I got caught in their yard and was tattled on by my brother Travis a couple of those times, too, which just led to more beatings.

Why did I continuously go against what Ahaz demanded instead of being such a good little obedient kid? Because I was willing to fight for my rights; and he was a controlling, narcissistic, downright evil person. I was naturally compassionate, kind, gentle, strong, and intelligent with a thirst for learning. Even though I had truly never actually lived freely among worldly people without extreme restrictions, I had picked up on enough from mom and a few others to know some of the freedom's others enjoy.

Books also gave me a fantastic look into it as well, and I discovered The Constitution of the United States. Mennonites focused on their right to religious freedom; I focused on the fact that since I had the right to religious freedom, too, that meant I had the *right* to be able to attend both high school and college and learn *everything*.

I decided that since Ahaz didn't own me, as he claimed to, I could and *would* be able to attend proper schooling no matter what he said. I had rights, too. The Constitution did *not* have an age limit stating only adults were capable of religious freedom.

I told Ahaz and other's things like that frequently and said that no one would be able to stop me from my allowed rights. Ahaz would beat me, trying to force me to believe he did, indeed, own me. I was a mere, female kid, nothing more. Not normal in my thoughts, he said.

Seeing real relationships, such as between Joyce and her dad, just showed me even more that I should never, ever accept such awfulness. I should never give up, stand down, stop being myself or give up on what was right. Standing up for everything I knew was not actually wrong, only made me into the powerful little lady I was born and meant to be, and I was determined to never, ever let him change who I was, no matter the cost.

Although yes, I was repeatedly shoved back into the tiny box within which he wished for me to remain. And yes, I was a liar; in the form of every single time he'd beat me extensively to force me to. I eventually gave up during the lengthy beatings he doled out, but not in a helpless sort of way. I lied to make it stop, because in the end, it was senseless to permit myself to suffer longer than a couple of hours just because Ahaz was a complete idiot.

Of course, before giving in, I first had to tell him just what I truly thought and repeat the truth over and over whenever he'd stop, to see if I was ready to give in and tell the lies that he wanted me to. I screamed and cried from not only the pain, but also from the fury, the injustice, the insanity of the situation. I wanted to claw his damn eyes out; but ironically, I never did out of pure fear. Even the strong are afraid.

He may have beat me and given me bloody stripes until I did as he said, but I held tight to the facts that it still didn't make him right. *I was still right. Just because he was a grown adult, and I was forced to remain in residence with him did not mean he could steal my very heart, soul and personality from me. Just because I was forced into lying, did not make the lies the truth.*

My siblings had all fallen easily into routine quickly past those original 6 months or so, and were quite happy, settled and unbothered. They were never targeted like I was but neither did they fight for their rights.

Travis and I play fought a lot and sometimes it got quite rough. I was bigger and tougher than him, and although he occasionally won our tussles, in general I primarily did. We'd wrestle as though we were real opponents, then hang out and chill and chat before diving right back in again. The two of us also spent hours relaxing or jumping on the trampoline and riding our bicycles together.

Several times Travis wanted to try to ride Butter, and I did my best to coach and help him ride her. But my Butters was finicky with anyone other than myself, and although she never treated him as she did Ahaz, she still didn't like him much or make it too easy on him. There actually were times she would bite or kick at him; I can only assume it was because she just didn't like males since Travis himself was quite the gentle, quiet little boy in spite of our frequent rowdiness.

Sarah and I couldn't stand each other. She continued to believe she was better than me and lying to get me into trouble. The fact she held so much power to do such things over and over hurt deeply. She'd frequently do some little naughty something and then proudly point her finger at me, to blame me, then laughed hilariously when I'd be beat for it. The power appeared to excite her.

All around me, I was surrounded by ridiculousness I could not escape. Even though I fought for truth and my right to freedom of choices, I was left voiceless. Powerless. My words, thoughts, hopes and dreams were 'all wrong' and unacceptable. I was treated dreadfully by most of my family, like I was nothing more than dirt on a boot that needed to be scrubbed clean.

When the weather was right at night, I liked to lay on the trampoline by myself or sometimes with a sibling or two and gaze up toward the sky at the beautiful stars. I'd watch for the falling ones, and quickly squeeze my eyes shut tight, face turned up and wish to be free; for something dreadful to happen to Ahaz, or for mom to take us all to a real, true home.

There was one Sunday after church while headed back to the house, Ahaz began talking in the van about how we were so lucky to have such a wonderful home, to all be together in, and he wanted us all to say how thankful we were for it and how thankful we were for *him*.

'Home.' That word struck me hard like a blow. It wasn't my home and would never be and I dared to say as much. I also blurted out that nowhere could be a home where he was, because a home is supposed to be a happy, safe, loving place, and I would *never* refer to that house as a home for as long as he was there, nor *ever* be thankful for him.

Should I have lied instead and acted like a passive little submissive to speak what he wanted from the get-go, simply to avoid disaster? *No.* I *had* to show my honesty. Obviously, I had been taught all my life to speak only truth by that two-faced apple, so I continually felt it was 100% fine to do so and I could defend it as such since it was true. He never saw it like that; the only truth that mattered was what *he wanted the truth to be.*

Ahaz was incredibly infuriated, and upon arriving at the house, he beat me on and on. I told him I simply couldn't and wouldn't lie... I declared that I would *never* call that place a home or be thankful for him, since he was a horrible person.

I believe that was the first day he beat me for around three hours in length because I simply would not give in. He took breaks periodically during it, forcing me to lay over the side of the bed as he rested for a few minutes here and there. I only gave in to staying still in that position because I was hurting so much.

After a couple of hours, he was actually ready to quit since he was exhausted, and he tried to switch over to forcing me to write sentences instead of 'confessing' my 'lies'. What he demanded I write was something down the lines of 'I love my home and am I am thankful for my f***** (Ahaz), I will not lie, and I will show respect to my f***** (Ahaz)'.

Well, it took about an extra whole hour of beating me until I was too worn out, exhausted, shaking and hurting to do much other than give in to the sentence writing. He was also exhausted, sweaty, and breathing hard.

He forced me to sit at the kitchen table and start writing. My hand holding the pencil was shaking from weakness, my eyes were painfully swollen from all the tears that had passed from them, head pounding, throat hoarse and sore from screaming, and the stinging pain in my body was rampant. The wood seat and hard back of the chair made it unbelievably even more difficult to sit.

I had to stay put to write until it was time for evening church, then was forced to clean myself up to go. After church, I had to go right back to the house and continue the lines for a few more hours until I could finally go to bed. I felt like a cloud of misery was hanging around me, and I hated writing every single, lying word. It made me feel like I had betrayed myself.

The following days were spent going to school, heading back to the house and then being beat all over again. He demanded over and over that I call that place 'home'. Heck no. "Home Sweet Home" did not and would not ever apply as long as I was trapped with him. More bloody stripes were layered across my back, behind and thighs. I shook from pain but refused to give in, tried to toughen myself up to stop it. Everything felt blurred and hazy.

Mom did nothing to stop it, she just looked the other way and ignored the screams of me being beat; ignored seeing my hands shaking as I struggled to hold the pencil to write for hours after the terrible beating. My siblings openly laughed and mocked at how funny my screams had sounded, while I was sitting trapped at the table. They laughed at my red face, swollen eyes, and shaking body. Sarah laughed the loudest of all.

However, Ahaz noticed and enjoyed how I could not control the shaking. He would stop as he was periodically walking by, lean over me so, so close, breathing his nasty stinking breath on my neck and face, and act as though he needed to get that near to see the writing. It made me feel ill, like I was going to throw up, and made me freeze all while both my body and mind screamed at me to run.

I remember him grabbing my trembling, cramped hand clutching the pencil, and wrap his fingers over mine. So sick at his touch... bile rose to the back of my throat. He ordered me to keep going through my frozen state, and 'demonstrated' by using his hand over mine to continue writing.

He stayed that way far too long. This was not a parent helping a kid. This... was an animal stalking its prey. I didn't yet know why I felt so incredibly sick around him except for him being odd, unrealistic, cruel and overall terrible. It wouldn't be too much longer until I found out what my innocent, accurate, instinctive intuition had been telling me all along... but not quite yet.

When he finally let go of my hand, he'd straighten up with such a big, happy, disgusting smirk and saunter off like he owned the world. The odd incidents would bring on more tears all over again, this time of powerlessness, feelings of being trapped, hopelessness, helpless, fear, rage, and pure hate.

By the time I was finally allowed to go to bed on writing nights like that, it was generally quite late, long past the time my siblings had laid down. My hand and fingers hurt so much I'd cradle my right in my left, head thudding dully from the terrible headaches, body hurting.

Did this break me? Oh, heck to the no, this was only the very beginning. I was still determined to never, ever allow that horrid Ahaz to force me into following along. I would always stand for the truth, for the right to have an opinion, for the right to be curious and smart, to not simply be a lowly female as he wanted. I was not lowly; I was good for far more than birthing babies (which I still didn't know exactly how that even happened).

The older I got, the more I questioned and became even more curious about all sorts of things. From basic knowledge, to learning about so many more things than the information I was permitted to learn about. I read everything I could get my hands on, but it was never enough. I needed *more*, always *more* knowledge. The topic matter wasn't nearly as important as the learning about something, anything, everything was.

By this time, I had learned to sew quite well. In fact, I could cut out and sew a dress to completion within about three hours. I also started embroidery and began my first quilt that year, embroidering horses and foals onto quilt blocks. I made pillows, curtains, dresses for dolls, and whatever else I could think of to sew or embroider. It was a nice past time to keep my fingers busy in down time, when I wasn't outside with Butter or the other animals, being beat or being forced to write lines.

Fun fact: the Holdeman Mennonites are located all over the USA, Canada and in Mexico and several other places. In the

USA, to the best of my understanding, there was a minimum of one congregation in every single state; some even had more than one within it. These are all connected, all 'The Church of God in Christ, Mennonite'. Many traveled frequently to other congregations, and they marry primarily amongst the communities from other states to keep the blood fresh.

The Mennonites at the particular congregation I was at, were primarily carpenters, at least within that community. People paid top dollar for their woodworking services, which were simply outstanding to say the least. There were of course some that also farmed crops and animals.

My best friend's dad actually had his own trash route he ran for all those too far out in the country for city trash pickup. Which was definitely an unusual job choice but allowed. The primary jobs varied from one congregation to another, depending on location and what worked there. Some places had many fish farmers, or shrimp, or focused on milking or crop farming.

One thing that seemed to stay the same no matter the location, was that married woman were not, as a standard, permitted to generally work except for under desperate circumstances. Girls were raised to become housewives and moms, to tend gardens.

Now, for the unmarried teen females, they would sometimes get a job within their community bakery, or general store to pass the time. At the age of 18, if a wedding was not already set up right away, they were eligible to become a schoolteacher. If so, they attended about a two-week long course on how to teach and what was expected of them.

Then the girls name would be put into some sort of teacher name pool, and she'd be called with a position from another congregation to go teach there. This was done to help them have a new experience prior to marriage. It also helped put them on further, quiet display so more marriable teen boys and men would be able to see and choose them. Teachers weren't supposed to marry mid school term, and upon marrying they'd be phased out as a teacher, career over.

An even stranger thing was these young girls were generally considered as 'old maids' at the age of 20. Those old maids would usually just continue teaching.

When kids graduated the big fancy 8th grade, it was treated much like a (high school? college?) ceremony. There would be a graduation party after, with buffet style food from all the dishes the women brought, and gifts, too.

For the boys, they would be given useful things, such as tools of their trade, pocketknife, a wallet and so on.

The girls would receive gifts primarily for their hope chest. A hope chest is a beautiful, sturdy wooden chest within which useful items are placed, for the girls to save for their own household upon marriage. Such as pretty salt & pepper shakers, delicate China dishes, handmade curtains, hand quilted blankets, beautiful woven doilies and more.

After graduating, the young boys would then standardly go to work with the men. They needed to work this soon in order to make enough money to save enough to build or buy a house prior to marriage; a wife which they would marry within about the next five to seven years, give or take, since males seemed to be granted slightly more time if needed before choosing their wife. There were some occasions in which new couples would rent a home if the boy did not quite have enough for a house yet.

The girls stayed home after graduating, in order to learn how to be a proper housewife. Such as to hone their cooking & baking skills, cleaning, and how to maintain their own house and garden or farm. They would practice their sewing and quilting, singing, and being quiet, demure and submissive. Commonly collecting and making more items for their hope chest and awaiting marriage.

We were not allowed to see or talk to our 'worldly' outside family except for perhaps once every year or two, and for Ahaz's own parents only. Ahaz forbade mom to speak with her parents at all, since he had never liked mom or us kids associating with her parents anyway. He wanted us all completely cut off from the entire world, and the Mennonites encouraged limited and careful interaction with worldly people, anyway.

Several times I caught my mom talking on the phone to nana. I could tell from the tone of her voice coming from behind her locked bedroom door; her voice had always sounded different when they spoke. Hushed, and a completely different tone to it.

Sometimes I would go into an excited panic and knock on the door frantically, trying to convince her to please, please let me talk to nana; I promised I would not tell Ahaz. She'd deny it usually, but on the rarest of occasions she'd permit me to talk on the phone with dear nana.

Whenever he'd catch her Ahaz would scream and scream at mom. Put her down, make her feel like absolute and utter trash for being such a horrible person for daring to go against the honored head of household's wishes, who was an 'honorable doctor and Mennonite, and therefore unquestionable'. Ridiculous, overbearing, abusive control freak, that's what he was.

He was, by then building up his patients in that state because he didn't want to leave us unsupervised long enough to work in the E.R.s. So, patients were right back to calling the house phone and whomever was the closest to that ringing phone was supposed to answer it.

I absolutely hated the phone ringing, because I never knew who was on the other end. Was it a Mennonite? Perhaps my best friend Joyce? Or a patient who falsely believed Ahaz was such a good godly man and who would point out to me how happy and thankful I must be to have him there? Would it be someone who had no expectation of a kid answering a doctor's phone line, and speak harshly to me for it?

He was seeing patients at the kitchen table, where anyone could overhear their very private conversations. Most the time I was outside anyway when they were there, but on very cold or stormy days I'd be in my room, embroidering my quilt blocks and dreaming of freedom. Even though I tried not to cause I hated his voice, I could still hear them. Wonder how those patients would have felt, knowing a little girl could hear? The same went for my mom and siblings; we knew far too much even though we didn't want to.

Sometimes he did still go to an occasional E.R. and there was a period of time over a few months when he started taking me with him to the small Cumberland River Hospital in Celine, Tennessee. There was a small doctor apartment on the lower floor of the hospital, and it had some furniture, a TV and a treadmill within it. Despite hating being around him, I actually loved going, because I wanted to be around worldly people and I also hoped to see something exciting.

I'd bring and wear a little blue apron over my handmade dress and pretend that I was a nurse. He would take me to each E.R. patient and ask if they minded if I was in the room, and no one ever said no; I have no idea why they agreed, honestly. Everyone treated me as though I was the cutest little thing, and I enjoyed the attention.

People came in with both small problems, and some big ones. Mild asthma attacks, broken bones, cuts that needed to be sewed up and worse.

Sometimes people came in with a mild issue and it wound up going terribly wrong after they arrived. I saw a boy who came in a bit sick but conscious and talking, but then went downhill incredibly fast and he wound up completely limp and unconscious and had to be transferred to a larger hospital.

Another man came in with chest pain, and his grown, worried daughter was with him. I watched as he had what appeared to be a heart attack right there in front of me while his daughter screamed. A team of people, Ahaz included, crowded around him with a crash cart as the daughter screamed out that her daddy was dying. I watched her heart break as we both were pulled from the room. She was left in the hallway, and I was pulled away by an x-ray tec who grab me and whisk me away to the x-ray room.

The tec gave me some snacks, juice and answered all my little questions about how x-rays were read and more. Yet all I could think about was wishing I could still be watching what was happening; I could still hear the daughter crying out in the hallway, through the closed door.

Then he stopped taking me. For one he wasn't going often anymore, and another I was learning too much there, I think. And it was making my thirst for knowledge even stronger, amongst such a worldly, active place. I *had* to learn, no matter what it was.

Chapter Eight

2001, age 12

Everything had always been, still was, and always would be mom's fault in the eyes of Ahaz. He blamed each and every tiny thing on her; from losing Thomas to me being too curious and questioning things. Me standing up for myself, the truth, and what was right was also her fault, for not having 'taught me better'. She couldn't cook good enough for his taste, she wasn't submissive enough, should never question his authority in front of us kids, etc.

Mom no longer fought the process as much anymore. She had given up on standing up for herself or for her kids.

I had always adored and looked up to my mom; she was always the only consistent comfort amid the darkest of storms, and the sane amongst so many things that made little logical sense. And yes, I was emotionally bonded to her despite the fact she refused to get us out of there, and therefore was a part of the abuse cycle herself, by forcing all us kids to stay in that awful place.

Her allowing her beloved kids (first Thomas, then me) to be abused made no sense. The other kids did not seem traumatized nor affected by any of it; they just rolled with the punches, and I could not wrap my head around why that was. Why were they just going along with and accepting every tiny thing they were told? Why did they not feel the desperate need to seek answers?

I begged her to at minimum to protect me; like how she protected Sarah so he couldn't touch me, either. I'd cry and plead, but it was to no avail. I was only the girl called not normal. I was nothing. I wasn't worth fighting for. Freedom from Ahaz was seemingly so easy and close, yet it was a complete impossibility. I had no choices, not option to get out because for some reason it was dictated that my voice, my opinions didn't matter. I was born to both mom and Ahaz; so, there I must stay until eighteen years of age.

In the meantime, the animal horde continued to expand with one little ole addition after another. It started with just one calico cat named Cassie, which multiplied into many litters of kitten quickly. Mom always let me keep one or two kittens from each litter, but of course I always begged to keep them all. I consistently snuck them inside, even though they were supposed to be outside cats.

I found and befriended stray cats as well, taking weeks at a time to slowly lure them closer to me with ham and turkey meat. Eventually I'd be able to touch them lightly, then more firmly until they realized just how amazing pets and snuggles were. By that time, they had absolutely no chance at resisting my affection and joined the gaggle of existing cats.

At one point I put a stump under one of my bedroom windows and would leave it open so the cats could freely hop in and out by jumping on it. Mom also liked a couple of the cats, but to me every single one meant a great deal. They were sweet and special.

Another animal I snuck into the house a few times was my pony Butter. She never once went potty inside, guess I just got lucky because she most definitely was not house broken.

I wanted rabbits, so Ahaz found a local man that had some, and he took me to go pick a couple out. I adored those bunnies, and mom even bought a special harness so I could take them out for exercise. Yes, I literally walked those bunnies. They didn't seem to mind it, since for them it meant fresh grass to munch on, and we didn't go far at all. Plus, it was more of a slow mosey with lots of grass- munching nibble breaks.

Then there came Renaldo! He was a registered Golden Retriever puppy who was incredibly sweet, adoring and loyal. His favorite treat was hot dogs, and as he grew, he rarely allowed me to leave the yard without him when I went adventuring in the woods or on a ride with Butter. He was such a handsome, loyal dog.

My mom wanted a cockatiel bird, and thus Paddy came to join us as well. We taught him to say, 'pretty bird' and several whistles, etc. He would only say good morning once a day, and only when my mom first walked out of her room each morning. She absolutely loved that, because it made her feel just a little bit better.

One of the twin goats liked to stick her head through the fence and then baaing loudly until someone came to help her get out. But that goat was never actually stuck! If no one would go to her rescue soon enough for her liking, she'd eventually stop baaing, calmly turn her head just right and pull herself out without any trouble. Mom in particular caught her doing this many times while watching from the kitchen window.

There was one strange morning when I woke up and went out to feed & water my bunnies; Travis was usually the one to tend to the ponies and goats' water and hay. But the ponies and goats were acting strangely, and it caught my attention. They were all completely silent, and the two ponies and two goats I could see were facing toward the back corner, yet turning their heads to look at me, then back, almost as though they were trying to tell me something.

A strange, uncomfortable feeling came over me, and I slowly and apprehensively walked up the hill to see what was going on. Then I saw what they were looking at.

That goat had stuck its head between the wires for the last time. Its body lay within the fence, where it was supposed to be... only its head lay on the ground, outside of the fence. It was attached by only about an inch wide, thin strip of hide still connecting the head to the body. Whatever had happened, had resulted in a nearly completely clean decapitation of the animal.

I ran into the kitchen hollering and trying to explain what I'd seen. Immediately I was laughed at and called a liar, because what I was describing simply wasn't possible, and I was told to stop acting not normal. Ahaz and Travis eventually went outside to see for themselves after mom looked out the kitchen window and realized that the other animals were, indeed acting strangely.

Mom figured that the worldly neighbor dogs, or some other animal, had tried to attack the goat when its head was through the fence. Whatever it was had terrified it so much it yanked back hard and fast enough to decapitate it head on its own. That was the only reasonable explanation.

Ahaz and Travis buried it in the woods near the fence but didn't dig it deep enough. The next morning, I found the same goat... again. This time it was partially eaten and smellier. They had to re- bury it, this time deeper and they put rocks on top too.

A short time after that, the remaining twin was put outside the fence on a tether to eat fresh grass. By this point, there was no remaining grass or plants within the pen itself, just dirt. It was something Ahaz had come up with doing, and he had been doing this for a little while even though goats should not be tied out since they startle easily.

This time, that goat was found on the tether line dead with a broken neck. So, then it was down to just one, the momma goat.

Ahaz put a garden out in the front, side part of the yard. This was not only a regular new job for me, but also a new punishment. Such as getting all the rocks out of there, which honestly seemed to be unimaginably endless, and every new rain would turn up even more rocks. He'd have me out there for many hours at a time in the hot sun, without water or being allowed to stop to use the bathroom when I was put out there as a 'discipline'.

In his mind I think, it was an excellent way to force me to learn how to follow his nonsense man-made rules in addition to those of the Mennonites. So, to him it made perfect sense to dehydrate and withhold bathroom 'privileges'.

Hoeing the entire garden was of course yet another big task. My hands blistered dreadfully, yet I wasn't allowed to stop. Blisters take a good long while to heal, and while continuously working it simply made them worse and worse. I would be forced to be out there an entire day, or full afternoon/ evening until it was too dark to see anymore. The rocks and hoeing seemed near endless.

Travis also had to work the garden, but even then, the amount of time within which he was required to was vastly different from mine. Dennis was younger and mostly played or threw rocks right back into the garden.

Early on, I resented how Sarah wasn't forced to work in the garden. Ahaz did attempt to make her to several times, but she pretended she wasn't capable of using a hoe or planting anything. In fact, she just deliberately chopped actual live plants down and acted like she was helpless to comprehend how to do anything else.

So, mom would say she needed Sarah in the house to help her anyway, since her precious daughter was 'too delicate' for outside work. Ahaz permitted mom to have her favorite, although from time to time they did argue over it. That was the one and only argument type my mom truly won.

Sarah would smirk, giggle or even outright laugh over me being forced to work so much during growing season. She thought it was very funny that since she was 'better' than me, she didn't have to. I was just a grimy little girl, and her, the princess. She always treated me like an outsider, as though I truly was not normal.

Sis and I were still sharing a room and had bunk beds. We were not fond of this at all, but it was what it was. She mostly ignored me, and although I attempted to converse with and befriend her, she simply never wanted anything to do with me, unless it was to laugh and mock me.

Others praised her for how exceptionally mature and old she was for her age; people always had. Oh, how little they knew! But no one ever believed the truth, because she would never confess to how manipulative she was. Thanks so much for adding to my torment, sis.

Ahaz was a hoarder, and greatly disorganized. He was one of those types that would get very angry if anyone touched his stacks of papers' he left all over the place. The piles ranged from a couple of inches tall to a few feet tall. He even kept a lot of newspaper clippings, and I had no idea why he kept them or what they were about.

In an attempt to maintain the Mennonite expectations of cleanliness, Mom just kept shifting his piles into boxes and mostly putting them their bedroom walk in closet, until she couldn't even walk into it anymore since it was so full. Then they were stacked up in more boxes in the bedroom itself, and in filing cabinets. He didn't like that at all and would go into screaming fits when his precious papers were touched, much less moved. Yet the house was supposed to stay immaculately, miraculously clean?

One positive thing was that he had stopped forcing me to drink brown vinegar, but he still threatened me with the idea of it from time to time. I feared it dreadfully, but it never happened again past age 11ish.

Joyce & her dad invited me to go along on the trash route with them on weekends and in summer. I was so excited, and honestly just thrilled to have any sort of time away from Ahaz for a while, and to feel free with two of my favorite people. With them, I could be closer to acting like myself than I had ever had the freedom to be at any other point in my life.

The work was pretty gross, and we'd came back stinking, but the experience of it was pure bliss. We'd talk about all sorts of things, laugh, just relax and enjoy each other's company. I started to refer to her dad as my dad, since I was that envious of Joyce's relationship with him, and I was comfortable around him. I even willingly gave him hugs when the opportunity arose, which was a very strange, comforting feeling to hug an honest to goodness, kind dad. Neither him nor Joyce seemed to mind.

Since I did not want Joyce's mom to be jealous, I started calling her my second mom as well. Now I did adore my own mom a lot, but there was nothing wrong with having a spare, right? I imagined if she was truly my own mom, that she'd never allow me to be harmed like my own did. In truth, I was just a lost little girl desperately wishing I had my own kind loving family.

Then Ahaz and his god complex came into play. Me calling anyone else by mom or dad infuriated him, and he beat the daylights out of me for it repeatedly until I bled. I was forbidden from calling them that, since 'normal people would never disrespect their (Ahaz) or mom in that way'. He did it for as long as it took, even if that meant for hours, until I was too wrapped up in the pain. I eventually gave up, to protect my own hide and told the lies he wished; that I was sorry, would never do it again, and that I loved him. He forced me to thank him for 'caring enough to correct and discipline me properly so that I would turn into, and act like, a normal person'.

That year, things began to change. Previously, he had occasionally used a belt instead of a switch, but never the belt buckle end. However, during moments of his extreme anger, especially when I stood up for myself, freedom of thought and personal religion, he started using the metal end when he felt the switch wasn't working well enough to get the full, blood curdling, screaming effect he wanted. He most especially did this when he was busy and didn't have time to draw it out and wanted me to be a shaking, crying crumpled mess on the floor more quickly so he could go see his next patient or whatever he was doing.

I unexpectedly grew close to the elder minister all the sudden. He was kind, funny, and going to his house to help

111

him do a few small chores was an absolute joy and a fabulous escape. His wife was so nice as well, and she made the very best homemade strawberry jam I had tasted. Sometimes I got to make cookies with her, and even baked up small pizzas to eat for supper on another evening.

In a very short time, I started calling them by 'grandpa' and 'grandma'. My new grandpa felt honored and adored me just as much as I did him. Their family, on the other hand, I think felt a bit uncomfortable about it. His son was the younger minister at the congregation, and he had a wife and two daughters. I occasionally played with them sometimes.

When Ahaz found out, I was beat and told that I already had grandparents and that it was not normal and disrespectful to call anyone else that, especially while his own parents still lived. Pointing out that I was *not* allowed to see said grandparents on either side because of Ahaz himself, only served to make matters so much worse for me.

But despite his efforts, I never once stopped calling the elder minister and his wife that. They didn't mind; so, what should it matter to anyone who *wasn't them*. This resulted in a great many beatings in the following years, but it was well worth it to have someone, anyone, to call family. I tolerated the pain repeatedly but regretting nothing.

We'd sometimes go fishing at a fellow Mennonites pond located behind the church. The water was such a deep brown, muddy color that no matter how I tried I really couldn't see below the surface at all.

My mom always refused to go on those little fishing trips, so I had to tolerate Ahaz's presence in order to fish, which I hated, but it was what it was. Besides, a lot of times he'd just hang out with the guy that owned it and he wouldn't be too dreadfully near to me. I just wanted him to stay as far away as possible so I could enjoy casting, reeling, and repeating it all over again in the hopes of catching something, all while daydreaming and blissfully pretending that I was a worldly girl on a fun fishing outing.

That same man also had a wooden fence lined with grapes and had a couple of very pretty cherry trees. I hadn't liked the taste of cherries ever before, but these fresh ones were amazing, and I quickly realized that I needed to eat as many of them as possible. The man let me, and my brothers pick quite a few.

Personally, I wanted to just eat the entire buckets of cherries myself, but Ahaz insisted enough made it into the bucket for mom to make a cobbler with. I figured a cobbler would taste alright enough with those yummy cherries, but I wound up hating it. Fresh only was the only way to go in my mind, but at least I'd been able to sneakily eat quite a few of them while picking.

The deacon had a good-sized blue berry grove, and after my cherry experience, I was eager to give fresh blue berries a try too since I thought perhaps, they would be far better than the gross store-bought ones. But alas, after picking and eating them I quickly found out that wasn't the case at least for my taste buds; they weren't my idea of tasty. Of course, I was told that, 'normal people love fresh blueberries.' Not normal... not normal.

9/11

"Where were you when 9/11 happened?"

It may seem wild; but I didn't know about the horrific event that happened on that day, on the day it happened. Keep in mind the Mennonites had no access to TV, or radio, and the newspaper had already been printed off for that day (yes, we were allowed to have the paper).

September 12, of 2001 was the date. On that day, mom had dropped us kids off at school, and I was playing on the merry-go-round in the few minutes I had before the bell rang. One of the mom's dropping off her littles got out of her van; she had a newspaper in hand and began showing it to the other moms. There was a bit of a buzz; tongue clicking and the like. I knew something was going on.

In school that morning, the teacher had a paper as well, possibly the same one that had been brought by that mom, I wasn't sure. She explained to us what happened briefly and told us we would pray for all those involved. So, she led prayer about it and then the day proceeded as usual.

That upcoming Sunday, the minister mentioned it in his sermon, talking about all the souls that were lost. This moment and upcoming similar ones were taken to point out that 'If everyone was Mennonite, such acts of war would never happen'.

And since they were exempt from being called up into the military in the case of a draft, they knew they'd still be able to comfortably rest easy no matter what wound up happening. They'd just stay home and pray while going on with their lives. How helpful. They live in the country of the free, yet none of them have ever fought to have or keep that freedom.

I was eager to understand more about what happened, which was pretty easy since mom frequently bought newspapers whenever she went into town. I was determined to not be like the ones who just flippantly felt that all those people went to hell, or that it was a shame the victims had not lived long enough to come to 'know the truth' of the Mennonite lifestyle.

I wanted to understand and empathize fully, in a real-world type of way. I wanted to know what was happening within the country I lived in, and I wished that there was something, anything I could do to help all the survivors and families left behind.

But I was still just a girl, trapped within a near twilight zone. So, I thought about all those people as thoughtfully and caringly as possible, hoping someone, somewhere could feel they were not completely alone; I read their stories, I saw them, and I cared.

Trigger Warning!

The following two chapters

are not recommended for

sensitive readers.

Please proceed with caution,

or skip to Chapter Eleven!

Chapter Nine

2002, Age 13

Year of the Devil

This was an extremely hard year, filled with an obscure amount of pain and unnecessary suffering. Things went from not good at all, to something so much worse. I had always felt that Ahaz was far more evil than what I had yet seen, but as it turned out; I hadn't even seen anything yet. I had no way of knowing just how bad things were going to get... I was just a girl.... a girl called not normal.

Neither Ahaz's patients, nor the Holdeman Mennonites could seem to see the devil within him. Or at least they didn't acknowledge or react to it outwardly, if they did. I couldn't understand how it wasn't completely obvious to everyone; how they couldn't at least *feel* it.

He was commonly praised for what an amazing family man he was, and how lucky we all must be to have him. If I was near while he was being praised, the person would generally turn to smile at me and wait for a sign of my agreeing acknowledgment. Ahaz would be bobbing his head and smiling, but with a warning glint to his eyes no one else seemed to notice.

So, I'd grit my teeth, stretch my face into a grin and give a barely noticeable nod in agreement just to avoid being beat later. Yet inside, I was screaming, hopeless, lost and desperate for everyone to remove their blinders and see the *truth* for themselves. If only they could see... but alas, they were blind to it all.

Ahaz decided that he needed to have switches in multiple thicknesses, on hand at all times, to change out which one he was using in the middle of my long beatings to ensure I wasn't getting too numb from one type used. I think he mentioned something about the deacon having come up with this idea but of course I cannot confirm that in any way.

He broke them across my body frequently, so he also kept plenty stocked up to quickly grab another. The sharp sting of a small switch was most definitely different from the wallop a thick one. The smaller ones most commonly cut into and took off more little bits of skin, while the thicker ones would mostly leave long bruises.

He'd say he was allowed to hit me with something as thick as his thumb, and this is another way in which he attempted to make it seem like what I was enduring must be acceptable even in the eyes of other people. That he was only whipping me, not beating. It took years to fully understand that what he was doing was beating me. It was not a mere few strikes to 'discipline' a kid; he *beat* me. Terribly. And even though it was awful, and I knew I did *not* deserve it; he also beat into me that it was his God- given right as a parent to do it.

Ahaz added a leather strap from the local leather shop to his switch collection, and there was a large wooden paddle with holes in it that the deacon had so kindly made. At first, he would make a choice and use only one or two things per beating session, such as use a switch for a bit and then the strap. But then he realized it was worse if he continuously changed them out, using them in whatever order but changing frequently between the paddle, strap and switch.

I told him he was wrong just to spite him, but he was actually incredibly correct; and he knew it. He kept extending the amount of time dedicated to beating me, both in frequency and length in terms of hours. On and on and on. He'd take breaks, of course, and he'd either force me to lay over the bed, feet still on the floor with bottom on the edge of the bed waiting for him to hit; or he'd simply force me to stand while he took a break to catch his breath.

After he was finally too tired to continue, he'd force me into apologizing for whatever supposed offense, and force a disgusting hug, and force me to lie and say that I loved him. He made me say 'thank you for disciplining me'. I always felt so dirty and disgusting to be forced into saying those things. I *hated* that he could beat me to the point of complying and saying such lies. And then the disgusting hug on top of it... was pure torture.

Personal fact: I grew hair down below and under my arms, etc. I was scared because no one had ever told me that hair below was ever supposed to happen; I did know about leg and armpit hair because I still shared a room with my sister. But the other I had never seen, and I thought something was terribly wrong with me.

I was absolutely horrified and decided I must be a complete freak of nature. There was no such thing as a female anatomy class or sex ed available to me. It was far too embarrassing and personal to ask anyone if it was an ok thing or not. I'd definitely couldn't ask my mom, and since my sister only lived to mock me, there was no way I could ask her either. She'd have just cackled & hooted with laughter, and probably not responded since she felt she was far too sophisticated to answer questions from someone so lowly.

I turned 13 in December of 2001, just before Christmas. A few days later I got my first monthly, which was very scary. When it happened, I thought I was dying for sure and certain. Told my mom about the blood and she gave me a pad and showed me how to use it. She said I was a woman now, and I decided I did not like being a woman at all, but hey, life must go on, and so it did for a bit longer, anyway.

Ahaz found out somehow that I had started my period. I still do not know how exactly. I can only assume mom mentioned it to him for some reason; but I have never quite dared to ask her that question. Its either that, or he overheard our conversation about it, I simply do not know.

****

Just a few weeks later, on a Saturday, I woke up feeling a terrible sense of dread and I didn't know why. Something bad was going to happen that day, but I had no way of knowing what. I felt a bit sick from overwhelming anxiety and stress. I passed Ahaz in the kitchen at one point and felt even worse. He made my skin crawl from even being in his presence.

That afternoon mom announced that she was going to town, and all us kids clamored to go with her. Ahaz was hanging out in the living room, and she hesitated and glanced sideways at him as though they had a secret agreement of some sort before announcing that only Sarah, Travis and Dennis could go.

My sister looked smug and sly, standing there by mom, while the boys ran by me to get their shoes. Meanwhile, the panic within me increased tenfold. I *knew* that I couldn't be forced to remain there with that horrid man.

As the boys raced back by me, I begged for mom to please let me go, too. But she refused and told me they'd be back in a while.

And with that, Sarah snickered with quiet laughter, while Travis and Dennis outright laughed mockingly, before they scrambled to dash out the door, followed by my more sedate sister and mom.

My eyes caught Ahaz's for a very brief moment, and I could not grasp, exactly what I saw within them. It was some sort of boastful amusement and pure, unstoppable evil; although I had an awful feeling that it went much, much deeper than that.

Instantly, I felt as though I was going to throw up right where I stood. Spinning around on my heels, I rushed through the few steps back to my bedroom and shakily closed the door, popping the handy door lock closed. Backing up, I stared at the door in a panic, listening for any sounds beyond the sturdy wooden barrier. My heart thudded so loudly; I could hear it pounding within my own ears. The small lock on the knob made me feel slightly safer, but not by a lot.

I heard footsteps walking toward my room, and I braced myself as I heard his hand touch the doorknob and met the resistance from the lock. He pounded against it, ordering me to unlock it; but I remained silent within my intense fear. He stopped and just stood there a few moments; I could hear him breathing fairly heavily. Angrily. Some nose sniffing and loud throat clearing later, I heard him turn and the sound of his footsteps walked away. It sounded like he went to his room.

Breathing a shaky sigh of relief, I tried to catch my breath and attempted to calm my racing heart. But mere moments later, I could hear him walking back out. I listened, hoping maybe he'd turn toward the kitchen or go outside; that perhaps it was over.

His loud footsteps kept on coming though, straight to my door. He didn't say anything but stood there silently for a few seconds, breathing loudly and heavily. My heart thudded so hard I thought it might come straight out through my chest, and I found myself holding my breath, frozen in fear. I thought he was most likely going to beat me, yet it didn't feel the same.

He popped the lock on the doorknob. Time seemed nearly frozen as I heard him grab the knob and I watched in horror within as it slowly turned. I quickly tried to push against to keep it shut, but he gave a few good shoves and it sent me sprawling back onto the floor. He walked in...

I felt weak with fear. The glint in his eyes was enough to make me shudder and shiver. I crossed my arms in a defensive move, as though by covering I could protect myself. He had a belt dangling in his right hand.

Moving so fast, he grabbed one of my wrists and yanked my arm away from my body, telling me that normal people don't cross their arms unless they are angry, and I wasn't allowed to show such disrespect to him. Then he strapped the heck out of me with that belt.

I refused to cry at first. Instead, I fought, tried to pull free of him, tried to run but with the hold he had on me I just wound up mostly going in circles while he continued to hit me. I nearly got away at one point when his grip loosened, but he grabbed the skirt of my dress to yank me back.

He beat me until I was shaking, and barely able to remain standing upright on my trembling legs. Still, I did not fully understand what was happening, why it was so different that time, but I knew it wasn't over yet.

Ahaz was breathing heavily from the exertion, and he was sweating. I felt sick. He suddenly tackled me, and I fought back but wound-up crumbling to the floor under his heavy weight. With his face close to mine, he breathed his disgusting smelling breath onto me while I tried to squirm and yell out for him to get off me; it was hard to get my breath.

"I know you're a woman now," he said, drawing the words out slowly and shockingly.

I felt utterly embarrassed and surprised, stopped struggling and froze. How could he know that?

He proceeded to reach a hand down low, in between my legs and grabbed my privates through my dress. I was so shocked that I still couldn't move; I don't think I even breathed. Everything stopped, except for him.

Ahaz smiled, still pinning me down with an arm pressed hard down on my chest. He reached lower and yanked up my skirt, which brought me simi out of the shock and I reacted; screaming and kicking, trying to push him away. Trying to fight.

"You are a woman now and it is my job to teach you how to act like a normal woman", His chilling words rang in my ears. I didn't fully grasp what he was intending but I *knew* it was terribly, horribly wrong, like what Thomas had done to me. I tried to fight back harder; to scream louder. But I wasn't strong enough.

****

It is so difficult to describe what happened next. I didn't actually know the word 'rape' to describe it until much later, but that is what Ahaz did to me. He used something to cover

123

his appendage, which I later learned was a condom, and then forced himself inside my body. It was incredibly painful when he pushed inside of me.

I screamed and screamed, but there was no one to hear me. And even if there had been, no one would have stopped it. Me screaming in pain was not an unusual occurrence by any means. I didn't fully comprehend what he was doing; without having a grasp of the correct words or knowledge. All I knew was that this new form of torture was horrifying, disgusting, terrifying, painful, embarrassing and incredibly wrong.

I tried so hard to get away... trying to gain leverage to push against him to get him off... but there was no escape from it. Ironically, although the thought of scratching his eyes out passed through my mind, I was literally afraid of causing *him* true pain because I knew the suffering for me would be so much worse. Which was a resulting thought from all the years of mental, emotional and physical abuse. No matter how strong I tried to be, I was powerless to stop him.

Finally, he stopped, and it was over. He was huffing and breathing so hard, his nasty, stinky breath surrounding me. He pushed off me to the side, but it took a bit for him to stand up. He took the thing off his appendage and tucked that back in his pants and grabbed the belt.

I was crying, helpless, too shocked and in pain to move yet, except for trying to fumble to push my skirt down to cover myself.

Ahaz told me that I was a real woman now and said that no one would ever believe what happened. He told me that I didn't act the way a normal person should act, and maybe this would teach me how to act right. He said that he expected for me to act like a grown, normal woman now that I was one.

Then he finally left the room, leaving me broken on the floor.

It hurt terribly between my legs and inside my body. I felt disoriented, sick and half out of it. I just laid there and cried for a bit before forcing myself up. I stumbled and felt so weak, and completely helpless. I knew I was going to throw up and started to lift a hand to cover my mouth before I realized I couldn't touch my face; my hand had touched him trying to get him away from me.

I managed to make it to the hall bathroom right by my bedroom. Ahaz was nowhere to be seen. I puked my guts up in the toilet, then leaned on the side of the sink basin as I began to try to wash my hands. There was blood between my legs, and I wasn't on my monthly. I got into the shower and scrubbed and scrubbed, trying to wash it all away, the blood, the pain, the fear, the weakness. I felt so dirty and disgusting.

After I re- dressed, I snuck outside by opening and climbing out through my bedroom window, even though it was dreadfully cold out. I crept around the back of the house trying to stick close to the outer wall and duck below the kitchen window just in case Ahaz was in there, and then on to the woods. I went to my favorite spot, and just cried on the cold ground.

A few of my cats found me. They were meowing and seemed to know something was wrong. I pulled one close and snuggled it, thinking how wrong it felt when it began to purr. There was no happiness here to purr over. But I still took a small amount of comfort in it, knowing she loved me and was trying to make me feel better. I felt alone... yet at least I had my animals.

It was nearing supper time when the van pulled back into the drive. From my favorite spot I could easily see it through the leaf-less trees. I didn't want to go back in, but I was incredibly cold, hurting even more from the hard ground, and I knew I'd be in deep trouble if I didn't turn up soon. I wiped my face dry on my sleeve, even while knowing I wouldn't be able to hide the puffy eyes from crying. Choking everything down, I ever so slowly walked back to the house, feeling pain with each step.

No one seemed to notice that I'd changed my dress. Travis realized my face swollen from tears, and he pointed that out and laughed. Sarah joined in, giggling loudly like it was hilarious, and asking if I had been crying, in between her giggles that turned into uproarious laughter.

Mom told them to leave me alone, and for Sarah to help her with supper.

I felt like they all knew; as they surely could all see how dirty I was now, that they knew what fate I'd been left to. That mom must have known before she even left. So many things were going through my mind that I couldn't process it.

I wasn't hungry. And I most definitely did *not* want to have to sit at the table with that disgusting, cruel Ahaz there, nor all the laughing others and my fake, pretending to be happy mom. So, I went to hide in my room, which was a place that no longer even felt safe; but I had nowhere else to hide.

Too soon I was being called out to eat. I panicked and refused to respond; I wanted absolutely nothing to do with having to go in the kitchen with the disgusting, cruel Ahaz there. But he came for me, and with a relentless smirk, he demanded that I 'join the family like a normal person'; or else he'd be forced to 'discipline' me. I was already in too much pain to take anymore, so I followed.

My stomach felt as though it was rising up my throat, but I went to my assigned seat and sat down. That hard wooden chair made me hurt even more, and I struggled to fight back the tears. I put tiny bits of food on my plate as it was passed around, but I couldn't eat so just wound up pushing it around on the porcelain plate. Being in the same room as him, at the same table, much less forced to breath the same air as that man was unbearable; I hated him so, so much.

Mom kept looking at me strangely, but she didn't say anything other than to ask if I was going to eat. I didn't reply, I didn't think I could. After supper, I had to help Sarah with dishes. It felt more like torture, in the painful condition I was in. Thankfully she washed that night and I got to dry, so it could have been worse. Sarah kept peeking sideways glances at me and giggling about how 'funny' I looked, which only made me feel that much worse.

I couldn't sleep that night, as my entire body, stomach and privates included hurt dreadfully. I laid on the top bunk wide awake, staring at the glowing planets that I'd attached to the ceiling with sticky tack, until they no longer glowed.

The next morning there was church. I told mom I was sick, and since I didn't look so great, she actually fought to stay home with me. I could hear Ahaz grumbling and arguing about it in the living room with mom and was afraid he'd force me to go. But then I heard the front door open and shut, the van start and drive off with him, Sarah and the boys as they headed out to church.

Once they were gone, I thought hard about telling mom. She read a book in her recliner in the living room, while I continued to lay in my bed. I knew she would never believe nor protect me, in fact she'd most likely say I had deserved it; I *was* the girl called not normal, after all. Refusing to follow strict rules without pointing out my right to having choices, always being 'disciplined' for something. I was deemed a troublemaker... I was nothing and no one.

And how could I even tell her, or anyone about the shameful thing that had been done to me, when I didn't even know the proper words to describe it exactly? She would call me a liar, I figured, if I tried to tell her of my painful humiliation. She always denied or downplayed everything that happened, even if it was right in front of her own eyes. There was no way to prove a single thing, no help at all to be had.

At some point, I drifted off into an exhausted sleep. Not normal... not normal.

Chapter Ten

Beat

My chest rose and fell heavily. Panting, I squinted up at the ceiling, barely able to see through the sweat and tears heavily crowding my eyes. The fan above was on, but in that little room it failed to provide even close to enough air to cool my overheated body. Blindly, I stared blankly at the blades as they swished round and round, trying to detach and remove myself from that moment within which I felt such utter shame, humiliation and pain.

The aches from the bruises and sting of the welts burned through my soul, removing any fleeting hope of normalcy. Not that such a thing could ever be expected or allowed in my little corner of the world. I was not in control and would never be permitted to be.

Poking out my tongue, I weakly tried to nudge the damp string of hair away from the edge of my mouth, but to no avail. It was sticky from sweat and essentially stuck to my lips. I dared not attempt to move more, to use my one free hand to brush it to the side because I knew I'd be punished severely for even that. I was a captive, without freedom of movement.

Ahaz lay beside me on the floor, sweaty and worn out. In fact, this brief period of time served as his personal break from beating me; even narcissistic bullies need rest from time to time. His own breathing remained ragged from the overt exercise of beating me.

Nearby lay his choice of weapons for his pleasure; a long, strong, thumb thick wooden switch from a hearty tree outside, carefully chosen for its sturdiness. A heavy, wooden solid paddle, which the deacon had made as a special, custom made piece just for me, and it boasted of several holes which had been drilled out of it. Next to those was a leather strap, which was a bit of a brownish orange color. This, too, Ahaz had gotten with me in mind, from the local leather shop. How thoughtful.

As I laid there limply in pain and exhaustion, the trauma of the day leading up to this moment flashed through my blurry mind.

****

The morning had begun simply enough. I had risen early, washed up, slipped on one of my hand sewn dresses, and worked on readying myself for the day. Brushing my hair, I slightly proofed the front and swept it back into a snug barrette. What remained I twisted, folded and flipped up into yet another barrette, followed by a hair net combined with many pins to hold it all together. The final touch was the head covering slipped over the formed bun and secured with half a dozen bobby pins, and two straight pins at the bottom.

Presentable now, I wandered down the short hall to the kitchen seeking a bit of breakfast. My breath caught in my throat as I realized too late that Ahaz was already at the table. Averting my eyes from his gaze and lifting my chin high, I walked on, determined to simply ignore him- all while the bile threatened to rise in my throat.

"Good morning," he said.

Instantly truly ready to vomit at only the mere sound of his disgusting voice, I spun around and tried to speed back past him, only now he had jumped up in order to successfully block my only path out. There was no other option. Steeling myself, I planted my feet and refused to meet his eyes.

"When someone says, 'good morning', you say it back. That's what normal people do." He smirked.

I refused to respond or acknowledge his slimy presence, hoping he would bore of this, but knowing he wouldn't. I absolutely refused to speak to that disgusting man, couldn't bear to even though I knew how it was going to end. I had to stand up for my right to not bow down to an evil human being; my right to make choices. My right to not look at or speak to my abuser. My right to not show 'respect' to the face of evil. He deserved not even the tiniest hint of such a thing as that.

"Normal people look their superiors in the eyes; look at me! It is disrespectful to not look at me. Look at me and tell me 'Good morning, father' like a normal person," he said.

I shifted from one side to the other, continuing to silently refuse even though I could hear the angry warning in his tone. I would never call this snake father. Just thinking of it made me want to retch even more.

Fully losing his temper, Ahaz pressed his face closer to mine and yelled "I am your father, and you will do what I say immediately. You will not disrespect me; I am your father! Call me father like a normal person; look at me like a normal person! I demand respect and I will have it as your father!"

Gathering up my nerve, I attempted to push past him, but he snagged me roughly by my forearm and nearly dragged me from the kitchen. It hurt, but still I said nothing, just stumbled along behind, pulled back toward my room, my heart heavy with dread. Throwing open the door, he shoved me inside and slammed it back closed, with him on the opposite side for which I was thankful of. But I knew there would be hell to pay for my daring opposition.

I could hear him yell to my mom; "Cancel all my appointments for the day. I have something else more important to do."

"But I can't just do that," my mom's much softer voice drifted back, filled with dismay. "Your first patient is supposed to be here any minute now!"

"It doesn't matter, just do it," I could hear Ahaz commanding as his voice faded out while he walked to the other side of the house. Fear struck my heart, but I steeled myself for the inevitable which was to come from that disgusting man. I knew what was coming; but this time, I determined to be stronger. Faster. I couldn't allow him to win.

Not nearly enough time had passed; mere moment's, really; before the heavy tread of his painfully recognizable footsteps came treading back down the hall. He stepped on a creaky board and the sound made me shiver, and I wrapped my arms around my torso in self-comfort.

The door practically flew open on its own, so swiftly did it open, revealing a red face full of pompous glee. Already his breathing had shifted heavier, clearly anticipating a good time to come. Breaking me in always had seemed to be a highlight pass time of his.

Not even bothering to shut the door behind him, Ahaz tossed out his tools to beat me with onto my nearby mattress, except for the strap. "I will break you of your disrespect before this day is over." He promised with an evil grin. "You will acknowledge me. You will call me your father. You will do every little thing I want of you after today, without complaint. LOOK AT ME!" He ended the last bit in a near scream.

I couldn't bear to look at the monster in front of me; I refused to bow to his will. I stood strong, shoulders pulled back, head up, face averted to the side, eyes staring at the wall to my side. Yet the fear tingled at my spine as a single drop of sweat rolled down my back. My arms remained wrapped about myself in a protective stance. I could feel his eyes upon me, surveying me.

"How dare you cross your arms in my presence!" He rumbled loudly. "Uncross them now. Normal people do not cross their arms, it is a sign of showing disrespect and anger. You will not disrespect me, and normal people are not angry! I am your father, and you will treat me as such! I am the head of this household and second only to God. Uncross your arms!"

Slowly, I obeyed, lowering my arms, knowing from experience what would happen if I did not. Immediately feeling overexposed I instinctively began to raise them again without thinking, desperate to protect myself somehow, to create a wall or a barrier between, even if it was only one of show.

With a hearty, forceful swing of the leather strap against my arms, he put an absolute halt to my movement. The leather cracked across my skin, raking over my arms in a fierce, painfully bruising sting. Dropping my hands to my sides, I waited, the helplessness and rage rising within my throat.

Grinning, Ahaz swung again and again, this time aiming for anything and everything; nothing was safe. I held fast without a sound, taking the beating. If I made noise, I knew it would only serve to excite the disgusting man. My legs, bottom, back, everywhere but my face burned as the abuse continued.

"Call me father," he commanded, not pausing in the swing of the strap. But I still remained silent.

"Look me in the eyes and call me your father!" Ahaz screamed as he increased the force of his swings.

Tears threatened to escape me, but still I withheld. I refused to use that disgusting word. If father was a term of honor, I would never say it to this sorry excuse of a man, nor would I ever meet his eyes. He deserved nothing from me.

Grabbing the back of my neck, he pushed me down hard and fast, onto the edge of the nearby mattress and switched from the strap to the wooden paddle. Swinging forcefully, he used both arms to put the power behind it, over and over until I was nearly blinded from the pain and could not help but to attempt to crawl across the mattress to get away. Snagging ahold of my ankle, Ahaz dragged me back, still swinging and hitting any body part he could reach.

Everywhere hurt, but I would not let the screams break free. I couldn't let him know how awful it was, how much he was hurting me. I had to be strong; I would never let him break me. I would never let him win.

"Call me father" he yelled again. "You will respect and honor me. You will do what I say, when I say it. You will look at me, you will not ever cross your arms, and you WILL call me father and act normal!"

Seemingly deciding that I had become too used to the paddle at this point, Ahaz dropped it and grabbed the switch. Promptly he began swinging it across my already pain-filled body.

Unable to stop it, a scream tore out from deep within me; a deep, wail of pain, humiliation, and hopeless, helpless rage. I couldn't stop the tears that began to pour from between my tightly closed eyelids as the welts continued to rise on my bruised flesh.

Ahaz laughed; it was more of a cackle of pure evil. "I will break you like a horse if that's what it takes to make you act normal!" He hollered. "This is what you are forcing me to do. Just call me father and say how much you love your father, look me in the eyes and all this can be over. All you have to do is act normal."

Full on screaming now, I jumped up and scrambled to reach the bedroom door, but I didn't quite make it. Ahaz snagged the back of my dress firmly in his grasp, yanking and dragging me backward while I reached out my arms to try to protect my body from his furious strikes.

He tired of the switch, and he grabbed the strap again, sending the leather crashing across my lower unprotected legs, and higher. The thin cotton dress I wore did nothing to protect me. In agony I tried to run, but he still had my skirt grasped tightly within his fist. I tried to pull away, I kicked out, I tried to block with my arms and legs, but I was helpless to get away or to stop him as the onslaught continued.

The commotion drew the attention of my siblings, and several came to hang out in the still- open doorway to watch.

"Look at her!" My older sister, Sara was pointing and laughing loudly. "You look so funny!" She exclaimed as her laughter grew louder. I didn't look directly at her, but I could see her out of my peripheral vision just barely, through the fog of tears. She held her hand over her mouth, continuing to laugh... and laugh...

The boys came to join in on the fun, laughing so hard they doubled over, Travis even reaching to grab ahold of the door jamb to stop himself from falling over.

Laughing louder, Sara called out "This looks like fun! You're having so much fun, aren't you?"

Ahaz encouraged their laughter; he encouraged them to watch what happens when one does not act normal. He continued beating me with an added fury, clearly enjoying turning me into an example of unacceptable behavior. He would not be shamed by not being able to conquer a kid, especially not in front of my siblings.

Spurred on by the onlookers, he reached for the paddle once more and swung wildly, striking the lower part of my back so forcibly it knocked me forward and down to my knees.

I did not attempt to rise, just sank lower onto the floor, curled up and cried while the beating continued.

"Look me in the eyes respectfully and call me father," he demanded, now beginning to pant from the exertion.

Snot leaked from my nose, dripping down onto the floor disgustingly. My body was already drenched in sweat from a combined effect of the pain, fear, humiliation and utter hopelessness. But still, I refused to submit to his demands.

"Eeeewwwie," Sara called out. "That is so gross! You are nasty! This is so hilarious!" She laughed. "I can't believe you have snot running down your face!"

Her calloused laughter and words cut through me deeply, and only served to increase my anguish. My helplessness.

On and on it went; I tried to get up to run again, but he forced me back down onto the floor, and onto my stomach. Ahaz sat on my back while continuing to thrash me this time with the leather strap, until I nearly passed out from the pain; from his weight; from barely being able to suck any air in through my lungs. I couldn't even get enough air to scream. I barely felt the warm liquid rushing out from between my legs; I was peeing myself from it; the pain, the fear, being crushed. And I was helpless to stop it.

I could hear dimly hear Sarah laughing uproariously. She laughed like it was the funniest thing she had ever seen in her life, until it made her gasp for air. "You peed yourself! I can't believe you did that! You are so disgusting why can't you just be normal!" I could hear her struggle to say the words in-between her laughter.

Ahaz stopped a few swings after I peed and got off my back. Breathe... I could breathe. But I couldn't hardly move. He told me I was disgusting and to clean up, then he would give me the chance to act normal after- or else the 'discipline' would continue. Him and my siblings left me there, with my sister still laughing as she was walking away.

I could barely lift myself from the floor. Everything hurt; even breathing hurt. But I knew I had to wash up before he came back. So, I crawled to my closet and tugged on the skirt of a clean dress until the shoulders slipped down off of the white plastic hanger. Somehow, I stood up and stumbled to the bathroom and managed to clean up. Then taking a soapy rag back to my room, I scrubbed the urine from the carpet as best I could.

Ahaz came back far too quickly, smiling. "Are you ready to act normal now?" He asked.

I was shaking; my entire body shook even in the aftermath. But still, I absolutely refused. I would stand strong; I could take it. I could not give a monster any form of respect. I had to stay true to myself; to what I knew was right.

The smile slipping from his face at my silent refusal, and he came toward me again...

****

His palm rested on my own. His grasp was snug; mine was like a dead fish. Floppy, limp and unresisting. The touch of his skin on mine gave way to dry heaving, but there was nothing left to vomit up. I was so weak, in pain, hungry, and exhausted that my body held a continuous tremble which I was unable to control.

Ahaz was reading a book while lying beside me on the floor, having his precious down time. I neither cared nor had the sight to see what type of book it was, but knew it was most likely one on discipline. Tears and sweat filled my eyes; eyes that were also so swollen I could scarcely see, much less focus on much around me.

My mom had taken my siblings out somewhere in town. There was no one left there to help me; not that anyone ever did, anyway. I was nothing to them... not normal... not normal.

I desperately wanted to fight, to run, but my limbs would never support my own body. All I could do was think about it foggily, while lying nearly helpless and broken on the hard, hard floor. It wasn't over yet. He squeezed my hand every few minutes, perhaps to remind me that he was still there.

Ahaz forced me lay with him during his breaks, for a seemingly combined number of reasons. Such as for dominance. Forcing me to touch his dreaded skin. Forcing me to be 'a good girl and lie still' upon his order. Beating me so long and so hard until I was nearly incapable of movement to prove who was the boss.

Half dazed, I wished desperately for a mere drink of water. Licking my dry lips; they felt rough and crusty; tasting of tears and snot. I hazily wondered when my mom was coming back. Mom never stopped this, though; she always pretended it wasn't happening. How she drowned out my screams when she was there, was a mystery to me.

Ahaz began to stir, setting the book aside and rolling over to breath into my face. I turned my head to the side, trying to avoid his hot, stinky breath. "Look at me," he commanded. "Call me your father. I do not want to do this all day, but I will if I have to. I'm your father and you will act like a normal person no matter what it takes."

I nearly wished that I could stoop so low as to betray my own self, but I could not. Never for this monster. Closing my eyes and choosing not to lie by calling him a term of respect, I waited.

"Then we will keep doing this" He sneered. Slowly standing, he groaned at the effort, stiffness having settled into his limbs. Picking up the switch, he reached for my upper arm and dragged my body upwards onto my feet. Stumbling, I somehow managed to somewhat stand, and to remain on my feet even when the onslaught began once more. My limbs, muscles and flesh screamed out, but my voice remained silent.

It didn't take long until I was beaten back down onto the floor. I felt weak, and my body burned like it was on fire. I was gasping to try to catch my breath, the fight completely knocked out of me.

Ahaz dropped onto his knees beside me, pushing my own apart to get between and opened the front of his pants. I could hear him pull something out from his pants pocket, could hear the rustle of the package as he opened it. Then he forced himself into me, and painfully raped my already broken body.

I didn't have anything left in me to stop him, so I just squeezed my eyes shut and tried to take my mind far, far away from the horrible agony and humiliation of what he was doing to my body. To an imaginary place where horses ran wild and free, and I right alongside them.

****

I wasn't born broken; I was broken on purpose. I was becoming an empty, weakened shell of the person I'd been born to be. No future ahead, no past behind. Broken, shattered; a weary, helpless freak of a girl. Not normal... not normal.

Chapter Eleven

At school, I kept my head down amid all the other rosy faced kids and felt so deeply ashamed, as though they might could see what had happened. I had to make sure that no one knew. My stomach felt as though it was on a roller-coaster every time the images flashed through and replayed in my mind on repeat, and it was hard to focus on anything else other than reliving what he had done to my body over and over.

On one of the days during school at our after-lunch recess, we were outside in the cold winter air, playing a tag game in the front church parking lot. A boy near my age began to quietly laugh and make fun of how I was running, just loud enough for me and another boy to hear. He said I ran weird because I was so slow and fat. The other boy also began to snicker and joined in to agree and call me fat. "Fatty, Fatty!" he called out and then giggled about it.

I was depressed, anxious, and deeply traumatized by that point. To me, that was a moment of realization that it was true; I was too fat and slow. I needed to be strong and lose weight to run faster. To be faster than Ahaz and strong enough to hurt him if he dared try to do that awful thing to me again.

When school was over and I arrived back at the house, I weighed myself. I was around 110 pounds, the most I had ever been. Since I was already feeling terrible, it was easy to not worry about eating anyway. I started skipping meals entirely, or just eating a very small amount. I was drinking very little as well.

I started to exercise with a determined fury over the upcoming weeks and months. Push-ups, sit-ups and crunches were my favorites. I ran daily, always focused on being faster, and on not running 'weird' anymore. I took my pony out to where the old railroad track was, tied her to a small tree and ran on and on. But the lack of food and fluids was actually making me weaker and more miserable, which was especially evident while working out.

There were times while running or exercising that I would get very weak and had to stop and just lay down until I could force myself back up to keep going. I always had to keep going; had to be stronger. Had to lose weight. Had to have the strength to stop him from hurting me.

Ahaz attacked and raped me regularly, and he'd beat me first to exhaust me.

Most of the time he generally waited until mom was out of the house. She made several trips to town a week to just get out and pretend she was a free woman for just a little bit, and usually took Sarah along with her.

For my mom and siblings listening to my screams when they were there, hearing me scream in pain, humiliation and anger for long periods of time was already a common occurrence. I didn't understand how they managed to endure it; and from the out-right laughter from my siblings afterwards, it was clear that no one cared at all.

No one would help me nor make it stop; I was just the girl they lived with that was called not normal. In their minds, I *needed* to be treated that badly in order to force me to fall in line and to stop me from daydreaming of freedom and the finer things in life.

There was no escape from it; I was never quite strong enough to get him off of my little body, nor brave enough to truly injure him. However, I dreamed of it. I obsessed over the many different ways in how I could kill him. I also prayed incredibly hard for him to die so I didn't have to go through with doing it myself.

Mom was sick a lot that spring. She had been spending extra time in bed or sleeping in the recliner in the living room, and looking even more pale, miserable and depressed than usual.

Then mom walked out of her bedroom one Sunday morning, wearing a long sleeve church attire shift, which was a fancy term for a maternity dress without elastic in the waist. No one was allowed to wear an elastic free dress unless they were pregnant, so wearing one was how it was how pregnancy was wordlessly announced. I stared and wondered if my eyes were working properly or not.

"Mom...are you...???" I started to ask but felt uncertain.

"Am I what?" She asked, pretending to be clueless.

"Are you... having a baby?" I finally got it out.

My mom instantly looked like she was about to cry, scream, throw up or have a complete breakdown, and she refused to respond.

I was worried that maybe I had offended her, but the way she was dressed simply did not make sense unless it was true. We all had to get in the van to go to church. I whispered to ask my sister if mom was pregnant, all while Sarah had that big smarty pants, know it all grin on her face. She just kind of shrugged in a deliberate, sly way as though to say she was old enough to know and I wasn't.

At the church, women crowded around my mom, congratulating her, laughing, and smiling. She was smiling, too, but still kind of looked like she might lose her cookies at any given moment.

Ahaz was receiving congratulations from the men across the way and grinning like he was a nasty, slimy gloating pig. I looked away and felt disgusted I had even glanced over.

Joyce found me and asked when the new baby was due to be born; so, I told her mom had refused to tell me anything. All I knew, was that she'd walked out wearing that shift just moments before leaving for church. Joyce looked at me like I had grown two heads when I said that, and I was certain her own mom wouldn't have kept her in the dark that way. However, I never got to test that theory since Joyce was already the permanent 'baby' of her family.

For some reason, I was left completely in the dark on the new baby situation. Mom took only my sister shopping for baby things with her, and she mostly only slept or read when she wasn't busy throwing up or dragging herself miserably around the kitchen. Ahaz still forced her to cook even though she looked about as good as death warmed over.

Since she wasn't hardly getting out of the recliner now, mom had an even greater need for books. She did still go on some library trips, and I loved it when she let me go with her. I had an intense need for learning, and books were where I found most of my knowledge. She read, slept and looked miserable, like there wasn't much left in her. I wondered if she still knew I existed, and why she wouldn't just get out of the chair and leave with all us kids. Why she wouldn't save me from him.

Ahaz hated it when he knew we'd been to the library, and he tried to forbid it repeatedly. But mom paid no heed and instead we began slipping library books inside of grocery sacks along with real groceries, to smuggle them inside the house without getting caught.

I choose books on history, science, outer space, military, and so, so much more. Including every single book that I could possibly find on horses and horse training, from novels to how- to guides. I read memoirs, I read autobiographies. Mom did try to screen what I got but sometimes she messed up when she was the most distracted and depressed.

On those packed wooden shelves, I came across a novel on witchcraft. The outside cover looked innocent enough, and I managed to slip it unassumingly into the check-out pile. Now, this was not any sort of hard-core magic or spells by any means, more the art of it and a bit of basic information in novel form. But I thought since any form of prayer or physically fighting against Ahaz was utterly useless, I would give witchcraft a try against him.

The few chants within it were simple and unrelated to my situation. But there was something in there about needing a blood sacrifice and a bit of hair for spells. I took matches, a knife and a small pot out to my favorite spot in the woods, pulled out a few strands of hair and tossed it in the pot.

It didn't take much hunting to find a toad, since that area was ripe with both toads and frogs. I had often caught and released them just for fun. Only this time, I found and caught one with the intent to kill it. But once it was in my hands, I had no idea how to proceed. I couldn't bring myself to neither slice, nor stomp on it. So, I thought perhaps I could put it down and smash it fast with a large rock; yet I couldn't do it.

I fought with myself to get up the nerve to do it but just couldn't. Its big ole toad eyes gazed into mine while I frowned in studied concentration over the issue. I needed blood, but I couldn't cut or kill another thing no matter how badly I wanted to find a way to make Ahaz stop. Besides, I knew there was probably no realistic way a spell could actually work and didn't want to harm it for no reason.

So, I let that poor toad go free and pondered on what to do. Eventually I decided to cut myself and use my own blood. So that's what I did, lifting my skirt to find a good spot. The quick, sharp pain in my thigh as I slide the blade gently across my own skin brought a sense of deep relief from the pressure within me, although I didn't understand just quite why. I moved the pot under my thigh to catch a wee bit of dripping blood on top of the strands of hair. Then I put pressure with my palm pressed against the cut to stop the flow of bleeding.

After a bit more thought, I felt that nature needed to be added to the pot. A little dirt and some crumbled-up leaves from the ground ought to do the trick, I figured. Grabbing some fresh spring tree leaves off a low branch, I tossed those in as well.

Then I gathered a few small twigs, some dried leaves and bits of wood laying around the area. I dug into the soft ground to make a hole for the fire then placed the sticks I had gathered within it and arranged it all carefully. Grabbing the matches, I slide one across the outer rough strip of its package, striking a flame and getting my tiny fire going.

Once I was satisfied it was burning well enough, I reached for the pot and started to place it over the burning flames, then realized perhaps it needed one last thing. A few good disdainful spit globs later; it was finally ready. Holding it over the fire with one hand, I snagged up a stick with the other and began to stir the mostly dry contents, mixing it well.

I had no idea what I needed to chant to cast a spell against Ahaz. So, I made it up as I went along, some of it was made up sounding gibberish tossed in for good measure. However, the intent was there; I wanted him to either die somehow, or to at minimum stop him from hurting and humiliating me. To stop him from taking away the power within me, sapping the happiness from within the very depths of my soul from the abuse. To stop him from saying I wasn't normal on and on and on... not normal.

After a while the fire was slowly dying down, so I set the pot down still near enough for it to stay warm and decided to call upon my little-known about, supposed Cherokee heritage. Yes, I have a speck of it in me, according to my mom. And I'd read books about them from the library.

So, I crossed my legs, placed the backs of my wrists on my knees, squeezed my eyes shut and asked for help from my ancestors and continued asking for the same things that I had wanted in my 'spell'. I felt the earth underneath me, tried to find a connection between it and me, deeply breathing in the crisp spring air, envisioning the gorgeous blue sky above. I asked for someone to please believe me, to help, to make it all stop. Or else to let me just die.

For the record... obviously none of that stuff worked. It was just a silly, desperate attempt of a helpless girl who was wrapped up in fear. The pain I was forced to bear between the mental, physical and now the even more horrifyingly awful thing I had to endure was too much. I had to make it stop. I began to contemplate taking my own life and how I would do it.

Yet there was still too much fire within my very soul itself; I saw too much beauty in the many future possibilities to take the step needed to accomplish suicide. The world was a giant playground I knew I'd one day be free to explore. I just needed it to happen *then*, not have to wait years to know freedom from Ahaz.

The struggle to keep fighting was real. I was now incredibly hungry nearly all of the time. I figured out I could make it 24 hours without eating, then would eat a single slice of 100 calorie cheese to make it through to the next 24 hours, and repeat. Pounds were sliding off, and neither mom nor Ahaz liked it.

In fact, Ahaz ordered me to eat, which only made me more determined not to. He didn't like me being so skinny, which made me *happy* because it was one thing he could not control. He could beat my body, he could horribly attack me, he could call me not normal, but he couldn't force me to eat. I was the one in control of my food intake.

Although losing weight did not stop his attacks, I still just kept thinking that if I just lost more fat and worked out enough, I'd be able to stop him. But I couldn't. I also didn't understand that I was making myself weaker instead of stronger.

I was just a girl... called 'not normal'.

Chapter Twelve

On June 18, 2002, it all came to a head. I was desperately depressed. I had been crying off, and on all day, incredibly hungry and weak yet working out obsessively. I'd do pushups till I felt I was going to pass out; stop for a bit and then gear up again to do more among other things.

I had a terrible headache from the tears, the shame, and the utterly hopeless situation I was trapped within. What he did to me spun round and round in my mind and I couldn't escape from it no matter how hard I pushed my body to run, to grow stronger and fight. I didn't have enough strength left. I was not normal... not normal... the words resounded in my head. It felt like the way I'd imagine a carousal ride might have felt like if it never stopped.

That evening, mom forced me to come to supper. I wanted to vomit from the smell of the food, and from being forced to be at the same table as Ahaz. But of course, there wasn't anything in my gut to actually throw up. I watched as mom piled a plate high for me with roast beef, mashed potatoes, peas and macaroni and placed it on the table in front of me and ordered me to eat.

I sat there staring at that plate of food in disgust, feeling as though it would make me fatter and weaker against Ahaz. I had to be strong, period! My brain was working backwards somehow, between the multiple traumas I had endured and the anorexia. I could barely think clearly except to know I was *not* going to so much as lift my fork.

Mom angrily said that I had to eat every single bite and I wasn't allowed to get up until I had. I couldn't do it; couldn't even take one small bite. Tears slipped down my face as I choked back the nausea all while my siblings giggled over my obvious distress; Sarah told me I was 'being hilarious'. I felt helpless, lost and alone.

By the time everyone else had finished eating, mom was absolutely furious. She got up and came around the table to me, snatched up the fork and scooped up some food. "Open your mouth!" she screamed in my face. "You are going to *eat this right now!*".

I solidly refused, keeping my lips clamped tightly closed. She slapped me hard across my face and grabbed my nose to pinch it shut, to force my mouth open and shoved food in my mouth, which was something she had not done for a long time.

I was shocked and humiliated from the slap; she had never slapped me before. Then when she forcefully held my nose shut to force feed me was the final straw; it made me feel helpless. I squirmed and pushed away from her and ran outside through the back door, and fairly flew to the woods to freedom, bare feet and all.

Mom stood at the door and yelled after me to get back in there right that minute, but that did nothing to slow nor stop me. I had to get away; I was in a complete panic.

My favorite spot was too close to the house, and I knew they'd look for me there. So, I kept going, and went higher up the hill to my second favorite place. It was by a cool looking old tree that grew from the earth at a strange, off to the side angle. One of the branches started at the base and went straight up, nearly giving it the appearance of it being two trees if you didn't think about it too hard.

I hunkered down by it to cry out my hopeless fury of lack of freedom of choice, being trapped, humiliated, and hurt. I knew I would face being beat, restrained and force-fed when I went back, and realized the only way to hold it off for a bit was to not go back too soon. I was going to take this night for myself and return to face it in the morning.

There was simply no way I could return to that horrid place that night. To the awful laugher of my siblings who watched me being harmed and laughed hysterically during it. I could still hear their laughter echoing in my mind. To the awful Ahaz, who beat and hurt me so dreadfully in my private parts. To my mom, who was pregnant with a baby who'd most likely turn out to be a horrid little boy, to be raised and praised as an honored male, another a head of household.

I felt intense pain that mom never believed what was right in front of her. Her mind refused to connect and process what her eyes saw, and her ears heard. Even when I had showed her throughout the years, the bleeding marks he left on my body. She'd say I was a rough and tumble kid, and that Ahaz would never have done that to me. She was blind and deaf when it came to my abuse, as well as mute to take a stand against it. There was no peace nor joy in that awful house, no solace from the pain. No one to come to my rescue or to save me from the screams within my own mind.

It felt as though I was choking from the inward pain; suffocating, cracking, breaking. I broke a few thorns off a nearby bush and pressed them into my skin, dragging them along my flesh. I felt so incredibly dirty, and needed to see if my blood still bled red. I felt as though it surely should have

151

turned black; as black as my throbbing heart, suffocated from the intense pain I was forced to endure completely alone. But I still bled red, and I blurrily wondered through the haze how that could possibly be, when I felt like I was surely dying from the pain within. I felt so dirty and hopeless. Not normal... not normal... maybe I really was not normal.

The area I had chosen to settle into offered an excellent vantage point of the surrounding area. I kept quietly repeating repetitively to myself that I was safe, or at least for that moment. I curled up, wrapping my arms about my knees and slowly rocking my body, and continued crying my eyes out over the hopeless situation I was trapped within. Hours passed, and the comforting moon slide out to light up the stary night sky, slipping its beams down through the thick leaf coverage overhead, and I relaxed a bit. Safe. Secure. Alone. Free. No one could hurt me there, except for perhaps a few stray insects.

I heard people move around through the darkness, between the trees and heavy underbrush, calling out my name. I recognized their voices as men from the Holdeman Mennonite congregation, and I felt afraid because I knew they were there for me.

No way in heck did I intend to answer them. I *needed* this night to myself; a night I would be able to keep close as a happy memory of temporary freedom from the agony. I was taking this time to myself no matter what the final punishment would be; I'd face whatever may come on the following day. I felt bad for the men, having their time wasted to look for one who did not wish to be found. I stayed huddled up under that tree and prayed that I wasn't found. I knew no one would ever be able to understand.

A few hours later, there were more people, and even more voices calling my name. I did not recognize them, but they were calling out that they were with the police department; and I could hear it was a lot of them there.

I got really scared and started to panic, because I knew I was going to be in even deeper trouble. I knew they'd tell me how bad I was for 'running off', and I feared what they'd do when I was discovered 'unharmed', at least unharmed in their eyes. No one could see the inward agony... no one could see what was being done to both my mind and to my body.

But I couldn't bring myself to call back out to them; to face their accusing eyes. I couldn't tell them the truth because they'd never believe it anyway. Not even my mom and siblings would say how awful Ahaz was to me; not even when they witnessed it. So, strangers definitely wouldn't, either. All they would see was my 'worried' family with a high and mighty doctor/ Mennonite man in it, and a pretend, 'concerned' mom. They didn't stand a chance to help me.

It would have been everyone's word against my own, and I was just a helpless, broken little girl that used sarcasm and projecting my inner rage out, to protect myself from anyone, much less Ahaz, seeing just how broken he had made me, and how helpless I truly was.

I knew when they found me that I'd just be forced back into that horrid house and left to my misery in the end. The truth didn't matter, Ahaz had made sure of that. Even if they did happen to believe, Ahaz would ensure they were unable to do anything about it and talk circles around anyone who tried. In for a penny, in for a pound. If I had to be in a gut-wrenching situation, I could at least make *this choice* to have this single night to myself.

153

At one point, a search group of officers got quite close to me; in fact, one person was only a few feet away from where I lay. But I was curled up in a ball on the ground and tucked up tight against the tree so that I was not seen. It did pop into my mind to hop up and quietly tell them really quick what was going on.

However, fear was a very real, controlling thing. And I had been thoroughly trained my whole life that not a soul would ever believe what I said, truth or otherwise. I was just a useless kid called 'not normal.' My words held no power. So, I remained silent while they continued to search throughout the night, while feeling guilty their precious time was being wasted to find someone who did not need to be rescued from those woods. Someone whom they couldn't help.

Not too long after first light, I headed down toward the house. Heart pounding and filled with fear yet resigned to my torturous fate. I had taken my night; time to go be beat for it and face my mom's pretend, 'concerned' tears. I didn't see nor hear anyone in the woods at that time and I hope that perhaps everyone had given up and left.

Suddenly, there was a helicopter overhead, the fast-moving propellers whirling and shifting the tree branches and leaves in the woods. I was near my favorite spot fairly near to the house and hunkered down quick as it passed over. It scared me so much that after it passed, I ran back up the hill to where I had been all night. I was crying, unsure what to do. If they brought in a helicopter that meant I was going to be in far deeper trouble when discovered 'uninjured'. So, I hid again and waited for the inevitable.

A bit after 8, I heard the police dog and a group of people following it. They made so much noise, crashing through the quiet woods surrounding me. The dog was following my fresh trail made just a bit earlier, prior to the helicopter. When they got near and I realized being discovered was imminent, I began to run out of not knowing what else to do, leaping and bounding over fallen limbs and briars.

Then they caught actual sight of me and hollered, "There she is!" And chased after. At the top of the hill was a clearing with a neighboring worldly house, and I wound up cornered and surrounded there.

I wasn't sure what to do. All those assessing, accusing eyes boring into me. I thought that I had to be strong and show no fear, so I took a proud stance in order to bear it. On the outside I was smiling to cover up the pain and anxiety. Inside, I was petrified, not knowing what would happen to me.

An ambulance appeared at the top of the driveway swiftly, and a couple EMTs got out of it.

Some men called out a few questions to me, asking if I was ok and why I had run away. Then the dog came near, and unable to resist the fury distraction I reached out to pet it. The sheriff got close while I was distracted and grabbed ahold of me, and literally carted me over to the ambulance as I kicked and squirmed in a panic from being suddenly and unwelcomely touched and lifted up. He wrestled me into the back of the waiting ambulance and then the doors were closed.

The EMTs checked my pulse and such, asking what happened, what made me run; what was wrong. They were very kind and nice. I knew in that moment I had a choice. I could tell them, and they might believe; I felt like they just might. I came so close to saying the words, but they wouldn't quite come out of my mouth. The shame overshadowed me, and I knew that Ahaz would never let the truth the believed.

Instead of telling, I just cried in silence while they coaxed me to tell. Eventually too much time had passed, and they were forced to give up due to my silence. I feel like they knew... but I had to be strong to make it through; I simply couldn't do it. A couple of people believing would never survive the force that Ahaz was.

Then the sheriff took me to the justice center. I was incredibly relieved to not be forced to go back yet, and in keeping with the secrecy, I decided to enjoy every single moment of freedom I could. The sheriff got me something to eat, and I was hungry enough I did eat some; it was also very helpful that he did not attempt to shove anything down my throat.

I met a wonderful female correction officer named Lisa, whom I instantly adored, and I hung onto her every word. Both her and the sheriff gave me a tour of the facility and I was thrilled by the modern world experience, and I happily soaked up every bit of information and every detail of my surroundings. I told them I wanted to be a correction officer or a police officer.

They repeatedly asked me what had truly happened, but I simply couldn't choke out the words to tell them. All the years of never being believed added up. I knew everyone around me would lie and say I was not being beat or attacked, and plus the utter shame was absolutely humiliating.

One thing I did learn there, was a bit of what had happened at the house while I was solo in the woods...

Back at the house the night before, mom had apparently been freaking out. She was very aware that I knew those woods like the back of my hand, and when I didn't return, she feared something had happened to me. Ya know, since her 'dear daughter would never have a reason to not come home'. The Mennonites where unable to find me, and so 911 was called. The police got the following story.

'Hannah got mad at her mom for trying to make her eat supper. Hannah then left the residence and went for a walk. When Hannah did not come back, they called some friends and made a search of the area without any luck.'

Now obviously, this was clear lies. I wasn't just angry; I was lost, abused, and broken. I did not take a walk; I ran the heck out of there just as quick and as fast as I could with zero walk taking involved. And what happened to the fact that she slapped me and pinched my nose closed to force feed me? Hmmm funny how that was conveniently left out. How about that I was anorexic and extremely depressed because Ahaz was severely abusing me, and he was breaking down even my mind?

But I held silent as to the truth. My word over theirs meant nothing; less than nothing. I was 'just' a kid with no voice. A kid called not normal.

Eventually, after a couple hours or so, the sheriff said that he had to take me back. I felt like I was taking a walk to a guillotine as we walked out to the patrol car. When we neared the house, the sheriff said, "Last chance. Are you going to tell me what really happened?". I wanted to desperately, but I couldn't bring the words to come. We arrived at the blue house, and I tried to pretend as though everything was going to be ok.

Lisa had given me her phone number written on a wee scrap of paper, and I clutched it tight within my fist, making sure not to lose it as I made my way inside. Mom was all tearful, acting like how her poor baby girl could have done something like that for no reason. I avoided her and dashed to the room I shared with my sister and tucked the paper into my pillowcase, curled up on the top bunkbed and cried my eyes out.

Much to my surprise, Ahaz didn't beat me that night. But the next day was an entirely different story. Of course, he made sure to not hit me where it would show; he avoided my arms, face and lower legs. He did point out that he was very pleased I 'hadn't lied to anyone' because no one would believe little me, over powerful him. 'Normal people do not run from a happy, loving family,' he said. And if I ever attempted to again, he'd made sure to make my life far harder than I could ever imagine, since right then I had it 'easy'.

Easy... was this really what easy was? There was so much pain both inside and out, I didn't understand how this could be easy.

Ahaz demanded that I eat and gain weight, as I was 'too skinny' and needed to just act normal. But oh no, I was determined to do quite the opposite. It was my body, which equaled my freedom of choice in my own body. Or at least in the few things I could control over it. I didn't want even an ounce of fat to please him; I wanted muscle instead. My anorexia eating disorder was now well established and in full swing and would not end for well over a decade.

Chapter Thirteen

Starvation mode. That's what mom said my body went into as it became harder to lose 'weight' and I continued to struggle with eating just barely enough. She told me that I couldn't lose anymore because my body was now preserving calories, thinking that it was in the midst of a famine and was turning every bite I ate into retaining fat. So, I determined to try harder, work out more, and to survive on as little as possible.

Standing in front of the mirror, I'd turn this way and that, picking out small bits I believed were fat. I thought my butt bulged out too much and my stomach wasn't completely flat. My arms and legs weren't thin enough nor muscled enough; I saw only fat. However, the reality was that I was about 90 pounds. I felt disgusting, fat and ugly. Yet, I could wrap my small hand around my upper arm and be only about an inch away from my fingertips touching each other. I wanted them to be able to touch, believe it or not.

The anorexia actually gave me goals in a way; something to focus on other than the torment I was forced to endure. Something I could control while the rest of the world spun wildly. There was comfort in the obsessive exercising and portion control.

My inward hopelessness manifested outwardly as rage, which was a defense mechanism to protect myself. As my stress and anxiety grew, so did the fury. I felt helpless and I knew I had to prove that I *wasn't* helpless. I *wasn't* broken. I had to stand strong and prove he could not break me.

Everywhere I went, it seemed like people were staring. In the modern shops, and even at school. Our playground was clearly visible to the road, which meant 3x per day there was a total of an hour to be gawked at by those who were 'worldly'. Many times, vehicles would slow to either just get a good eyeful, or so they could take pictures of us Mennonite kids. Now of course photographs were forbidden, but what others do isn't exactly stoppable. I was told to turn away when I saw a camera.

I felt like a caged animal on exhibit in a zoo. The anxiety from this grew the older I got, and to the point I hated going places. I was so ashamed to stand out for a lifestyle I did not wish to represent. I was also jealous of all the worldly people, dressing as they wished, and wearing their hair down or in ponytails. They had the freedom of choice in simple things such as hairstyle, nail polish, lipstick, jewelry and in how they dressed. Education for them was not just an option; high school was mandatory, and I was incredibly jealous of that specifically.

Yet those same people I was envious of and dreamed of fitting in with, whispered and pointed and stared as though I was a freak. Some looked at me pleasantly. Others rudely, some curiously. Some just looked straight up outraged that I even existed as though it was *my fault* that I was dressed in such a way and living such a lifestyle. Some couldn't have cared less one way or another and didn't stare at all. Some giggled. Some worldly people even said they loved how I was dressed, and they wished they could live such a simple life, too.

I wanted to scream at them all, to let them know I *was one of them*. Even though they couldn't see it, even though I wasn't allowed to appear to be one of them. I was just forced to essentially wear a costume on the daily and I wished everyone could *see* that. I wanted them to stop looking, because inside at least, I *wasn't* a Mennonite; I was just a broken little girl, deeply abused and lost, waiting for the day I could be freed.

At the library, within the pages of innocent appearing books, was where I learned curse words. I began to use them at times of intense helplessness as part of proving that I wasn't broken; because although I couldn't stop what was being done to my own body, he still could *not* control my mind, thoughts or words. Ahaz did not like this at all; I was correct in assuming it would infuriate him that he could not control what I said.

I'm sure you have most likely heard of using soap within the mouth of the offending kid for using bad language. Well per usual, Ahaz did no punishment halfway. First, he would make sure to beat me until I was too weak to fight back. He liked to yell for my siblings to come watch both my beating, and what he'd do next. He encouraged them to laugh.

Ahaz would soak a washrag with an obnoxious amount of liquid dish soap until it was quite literally dripping. Then he'd grab my nose to force my mouth open and pulling so that my head was also forced to tilt back, and he'd squeeze the rag rhythmically so the soap would drain straight down my throat until I was choking. I cannot forget the smile on his horrid face during it... Then he'd let go of my nose and push as much of the rag into my mouth as he could. He forced me to remain there with the soap drenched rag within my mouth for five long, long minutes.

He always looked so intensely pleased and smiling during it, all while my siblings in the open doorway just laughed and laughed. Sarah especially would call out mockingly how funny I looked as she cackled, and Travis laughingly would agree with her.

If I dared to pull the rag out during that time, he'd just beat me more until I gave up. I fought a lot; I didn't give in easily. Not until I was so weak with pain and exhaustion that I lacked the strength to continue fighting. It made him so happy when I gave in, but behind my outward submission, absolute fire and hate burned within, which was a close second only to the immense helplessness I felt.

It was incredibly difficult to endure the burning and to be choking on the rag and soap simply on his sadistic whim. After the five minutes were up, he'd remove the rag with a grin and force me to wait an entire thirty minutes before being allowed to rinse my mouth out, have a drink, or vomit. Yes, I was literally forbidden to throw up which was so hard after having soap literally squeezed down my throat. It burned dreadfully.

However, I *was* allowed to choke and gag unrestricted as long as I did not break the other rules. How kind and thoughtful; let's just take a brief moment here to thank and praise the ever-wonderful Ahaz for not taking away my freedom of gagging. My sister loved the awful sounds I made even more and mocked how hilarious I sounded. I felt... so alone.

Not succeeding at holding back from throwing up would mean another reset; back to square one of having the rag re-soaped, drained down my throat and then shoved in my mouth. And yes, there were many times I couldn't succeed at holding back from puking; in fact, very few times was this accomplished without at least one do-over.

Afterwards, I'd be incredibly sick, miserable, puking my guts up and worse. It was absolutely terrible, and I'd be ill for a day or two after.

Not only during, but for hours after every time Sarah would think about me being hurt, she'd giggle and comment about how funny I had looked when it was happening. How hilarious it was when Ahaz crushed me to the floor, sat on my back and continued to beat my bottom and legs; while I couldn't even scream out because he was so much heavier that I was. Could barely even breath. She laughed even harder if I peed myself from it, during the abuse. From the pain and from my tiny body being crushed.

So funny... she'd say. Her giggles and outright laughter made my chest feel tight all over again and made it hard to breath once again. I felt an incredibly deep, deep, dark shame. I was nothing. I was not normal. I was just an angry teen that other people saw as deserving of what I was delt.

Why did I continue to curse occasionally, even knowing the outcome? For one thing, it wasn't ever about the words, it was about freedom. It was about helpless outrage over the situation I was trapped within, and I felt the constant need to 'prove' I was an individual, not a robot; not an object intended only as mere silent decoration.

I was a real person with very real thoughts, feelings and opinions. I was a kid who was beat dreadfully for wanting to learn more than I was allowed. For wanting to understand the entire world around me; no matter what it was; because I simply had an unstoppable drive within me to learn about it all.

I was just a kid, beat for years for all those things and so much more; beat for telling the truth, since the truth was clearly meaningless. The only 'truth' I was permitted was whatever Ahaz just so happened to imagine were facts, even if it made no actual logical sense.

Such as not being allowed to cross my arms when chilled for a wee bit of added extra warmth. In his mind, the true facts were that only angry people crossed their arms; and I wasn't allowed to be angry. I wasn't allowed to ask why things had to be done a particular way; normal girls do not question. Nor ask why religion had anything to do with not being allowed a proper education since it wasn't *my* religion; it was theirs. I wasn't allowed to have my own thoughts; Ahaz believed my every thought should only mirror his own, and only be about the things he demanded. To be his mindless follower... and to stop being 'not normal'.

I talked to the elder minister, aka 'grandpa', and told him about the terrible beatings (I used the word 'whipped') and the soap and exactly how it was done. He seemed a cross between doubtful and concerned, but he called a meeting between the minister, his wife, Ahaz and mom to discuss it.

What the minister later told me from that meeting, was that he had told Ahaz I was too old to continue being punished in such a way; I was a young woman now and not a small girl. He also reported Ahaz convinced him that I was over exaggerating and just mad I was being 'disciplined', and my mom had agreed. Grandpa told me to not over exaggerate, and I felt... hopeless. Depressed and more alone.

It was so confusing and made my head spin from trying to understand; how could something so terrible be ok? And if it truly was ok, was I over-exaggerating like the minister said? Was I just a bad kid? Was I truly not normal? But why did he have to hurt me for being curious and smart? Why did he have to hurt me for wanting to be my own individual? Why did he have to call me not normal when the things I wanted were merely an everyday occurrence within the outside world that was forbidden from me? Why did he have to beat me for wanting to explore it and understand it myself?

At the same time, I *knew* he was simply a mean person and that it was terribly wrong, yet no one else could see. Even my siblings who witnessed my agony thought he was right; that I was not normal. That I was bad for wanting to know the world. That I was bad for fighting back and fighting for my born rights. I had been born in the free world, yet never allowed to experience it. What was the point of living within such an amazing county with so many freedoms, if I couldn't even experience the wonders of it? Everything spun round in my head; it was discombobulating and conflicting.

My voice not being heard and being instantly discredited with no one understanding what was happening was heartbreakingly painful. It was agony. I was so alone and fighting to be strong, fighting to just live long enough to turn eighteen and thus win my freedom from his abuse. Fighting to get my hands on enough books so when that time came; I didn't go out into the world without understanding how to live and interact in it. I was going to have an education of some form no matter what Ahaz did to me to try to stop it.

The word rape: I learned it in that local library. I didn't have an awful lot of information on it, but I knew that was definitely what was being done to me by the description I found and comparing it to descriptions on sex. The next time Ahaz raped me, pinning me down as I weakly tried to fight after having been beaten, I screamed at him that I knew what he was doing; he was *raping me.*

He instantly backhanded me hard, straight across my face. Then covered my mouth with his hand and leaned close, his disgusting breath washing across me as he pinned me down, my body trapped underneath his. He ordered me to *never* say that word again, told me I was wrong and dumb, and said that I misunderstood the term.

He reminded me that I was a woman and as such, I was required to be obedient and serve him as the man. He claimed that I wasn't old enough to know what was best for me; that he was teaching me how to be normal. Then he finished raping me and left me alone, a curled-up sobbing ball of misery and pain.

Ahaz got it into his mind that I was not showing enough respect to him as the head of household. All these years I had been forced to wait quietly in precisely the correct spot in order to say something for up to 30 minutes, but now he upped the time wait to as long as he felt like it being. Just standing there. Waiting on absolutely nothing; could even be for an hour.

He would even come up with bogus reasons for me to 'practice' this, and beat me when I refused, until I gave in and stood shakily on wobbly, beaten legs for whatever length of time he demanded. Even though I absolutely loathed talking to the devil, I was forced into going to him for any tiny little thing. You know, since mom was 'only a mere weak woman', incapable of deciding if I was allowed to, say, get the heck out of that hell hole for a bit and spend an afternoon or night with Joyce.

This 'stand, present and wait' had zero purpose other than how much he enjoyed it so thoroughly and obviously. I hated being in his presence, hated him with every fiber of my mind and body. Only a chance of seeing Joyce could compel me to tolerate it, but more often than not he was refusing it near every time. But sometimes, I got to go see her outside of school and church. And it was worth it just for that, to be able to escape reality and to pretend I was free for a bit, just like Joyce. Well, as free as a Mennonite girl could be, anyway.

Ahaz, mom, and other Mennonites including Maximus, grandpa and more started telling me that I must be bipolar; that must be what was wrong with me. Mom had a long talk with me about what bipolar meant and said I had been born with the wrong chemical combination in my mind.

To everyone except me, they just saw a naturally gentle girl who was 'not normal' from mental illness. They decided that must be why I could go from happily playing with my precious comforting animals to switch to asking real world, curious questions, which was followed by being beat and/ or raped. And then instead of being grateful and pleased that I had been 'corrected'; I instead wanted to kill myself from the horrific abuse I was enduring. The fact I wasn't grateful and genuinely thankful seemed to both perplex and anger Ahaz and others.

They also blamed my anorexia on the bipolar aspect, too. I wasn't normal... normal girls don't refuse to eat. The 'rebellious' thoughts of wanting an education and free world thinking must stem from that too, of course, because no one in their right mind would want to turn from the 'right path' once they had been shown it.... according to mom and Ahaz. Primarily Ahaz, of course. The Holdeman Mennonites that spoke to me about my behavior, depression and eating disorders acted the same as well.

My precious momma from younger years was long gone; I could hardly recognize the shell of a woman in front of me anymore. Where was the strong, powerful woman who had fought back against the injustices?

That fall, my baby brother was born. Naturally Ahaz did not bother going to the hospital with my mom; he made it clear that was the women's job to bear alone, and he had not been at a single birth due to that, even though he had had six chances to. Eight chances in fact, if you count the still born baby boy and an ectopic pregnancy previously. And no, that was not an entirely common Mennonite way; that was simply him being a pois ass.

When I found out that the baby was a boy, I cried as though my heart was breaking. Yet another awful boy had been born of Ahaz's blood; to mold into yet another utter monster who'd be raised to believe he was like a god, simply because of what was between his legs. This was the horrified thoughts running through my mind, and all I could focus on at the time. I could see no other future for that baby boy other than one of destruction.

Ahaz dragged all us kids to the hospital many hours after the birth. I was so upset, that I didn't even want to look at the baby. I did get a brief glance of him though, which just made me cry even harder. The boy, named Alex, looked like the most gorgeous baby I had ever seen, like an angel. It was awful that this poor innocent would be raised as near devil. I could only see the monster he had the potential to become, not the sweet tiny baby that he was.

I was being sucked even deeper into depression. I'd cut my arms, legs, stomach and torse just to make sure my blood still flowed since I felt dead inside. There was all this 'come to

Jesus' talk surrounding me at school and church, but how could I do the whole 'saved' thing if I was a dirty, nasty little girl? I didn't care how everything ended; I just wanted it to end. I wanted to die, and I wrote out suicide notes. I couldn't bear how terrible life was.

The younger minister came over many times to talk with me, but I basically just cried. Each time, I desperately wanted to tell him what was going on, to find a way to make it stop. But I knew no one would believe. No one could make Ahaz stop. I was in an endless loop going round and round.

Like little free-spirited rebels, Joyce and I planned out our escape from the Mennonites. Whenever we had a few moments to steal together, we'd talk about how things would be when we turned 18. We'd have a little cabin all to ourselves and buy a little purple beetle car to share to use for work. Naturally we'd have several snuggly dogs inside, with guard dogs outside to protect us.

We even drew out the cabin layout, complete with a fireplace and a comfy sofa near it to enjoy the fire optimally. We decided that we didn't need anything big, just small and cozy. It sounded like pure paradise, and I clung to those peaceful imaginings for many years to come.

Joyce and I got into trouble for being a 'click' at school. She was my only true friend, but we were ordered to play with the other girls; even though recess at school was already forced organized group play the great majority of the time. We very rarely were permitted free play.

Ahaz beat me for daring to be in a 'click', and the teacher and then the schoolboard had a big confrontational talk to me about it, and from the way they spoke of it they made it sound more like I was in a big bad gang instead of just enjoying being around my best friend. They told me that I should be friends with everybody equally, and that I wasn't allowed to have a singular 'best friend'.

But honestly, it wasn't that I didn't like the other handful of girls that were there; it was that I didn't fit in with them. They weren't nearly adventurous nor inquisitive enough; not at all deeply interested in learning about the real, huge world out there or in standing up for themselves. I most definitely couldn't daydream up a life as a modern working woman with them; much less discuss all the worldly things I was learning in books, like I could with Joyce.

I had zero intention of actual following the orders to separate, even though it came from the teacher, school board etc. I didn't care that it would mean hours more of being beat; it was worth the sacrifice. So, when Joyce and I got to school the next day, I was hurt and shocked when she avoided me, and I felt completely alone.

There was absolutely nothing wrong with having one, singular good friend. In fact, a true friend is so incredibly difficult to find, I felt like even having one should be praised, not put down. Our friendship was never the same after that, and it broke my already lonely heart.

I was considered an outcast, a misfit among the Mennonites. I was looked upon as trouble, as a bad influence because I questioned how things worked and requested valid reasoning behind the answers based on facts. I learned that every action should have an equal and opposite reaction, which meant to me that for every question, there should be a solid reason standing behind it as to *why*. If there had been true answers that made logical sense, it would have rung true based off facts.

I frequently asked grandpa far too many questions. Like why everyone had to wear long sleeves to church, but short sleeves for daily wear. I asked if my arms were extra sinful on Sundays, and on Wednesday nights and therefore had to be extra covered for church? But if not, then why did it matter what the sleeve length was? Why couldn't I wear long sleeved dresses in winter, outside of church? Would I burn in hell if I wore a long-sleeved dress as a daily wear? If not, then why couldn't I wear the length I wished to?

I wanted to know why all church shoes had to be black. Did the Bible say all shoes must be black to enter the church? And if not, then why couldn't I wear brown or white shoes? I also asked about the braids, and would I go to hell if I wore a simple ponytail instead? And if not, then why couldn't I?

What if I wanted to be an astronaut and explore space; would that send me to hell for doing such a thing? And if so, why would it? Why was it so horribly wrong? If it wasn't wrong, then why couldn't I do it?

I asked if since people could be Christian out in the world, then why couldn't I chose too just be a worldly Christian and dress worldly? Since I lived in a country with freedom of religion, why was I forced to dress in handmade dresses and live like a Mennonite and not be allowed to exercise that freedom of choice? Did the law only apply to adults, and if so, why?

Why was the right to freedom of speech allotted only to adults, when nothing about the law specified that I must be over the age of eighteen to be allowed such liberty? Why was it that just because I was a kid, I had zero choices? Why was I punished severely for being honest and for telling the truth? Why must I be 'whipped' terribly for having real thoughts, ideas and opinions of my own? Shouldn't intelligence be looked highly upon?

I wanted to know why were the colors of bright red, lime green, hot pink and more forbidden as worldly? There were those *exact same* shades in nature, and if God had created it all and it was good, why was it still wrong to have clothing or a vehicle in those shades?

I questioned why did the dresses have to have elastic in the waist, when there was no waisted-elastic requirement in the Bible? Would I be extra sinful if I had none in a dress? Would I go straight to hell? No? Then why was it forbidden to wear a dress without it, unless one was pregnant? Elastic left visible marks around my natural waistline and made me sore, so I pointed out that it seemed silly if I didn't have to wear it to get into heaven.

Why did the fabric of my dress have to be all from the same piece? If I trimmed the edges of my sleeves with a different shade of fabric or had a different color collar, would I truly go to hell? If not, then why couldn't I? If none of those things would send me straight to hell, then I wanted to do them all, and so much more.

If watching TV or listening to music with musical instruments in it wouldn't send me to hell either, then what was so terrible about it? Why were they forbidden?

Poor Grandpa... he tried so hard to answer my inquisitive questions in a proper Mennonite fashion. But I needed more; I needed the broken-down, fact-based version of an answer to each and every single question I could come up with. I needed scientific based facts, average based facts, or anything that even remotely resembled it to *prove why it was so wrong, I'd go to hell for it.*

I also tried asking many other Holdeman Mennonites in the community about these things, but no one had quite so much patience for it as my sweet Grandpa. They'd grow exasperated fairly quickly and essentially tell me to fall in line, and to stop questioning things.

I desperately needed to blend in more, to stop the prying, staring eyes of strangers. Needed to slow the overwhelming anxiety from feeling like I had always lived in a fishbowl. I needed more than I was allowed to have, and the freedom to explore it all.

Near to the end of the year, Ahaz decided to build an addition onto the back of the house. He was tired of seeing patients at the kitchen table, and while he was at it, he built my sister a bedroom. Now, at first it may seem he was being nice since Sarah and I couldn't stand each other. But truth be told, this was just another way to get me more alone. This was about *him*. I didn't realize it in full right away, although I did have a very vague understanding of it.

The thrill of having my own room to get away from my laughing, mocking sister at least overrode the full realization of it at first. The addition was finished quickly, and my sister moved into her new room right before Christmas, around my fourteenth birthday.

Sarah was given a brand-new bed and frame to go with her new room. The bunkbeds were moved into the boy's room, and I was given Travis's and Dennis's two old bedsprings since the boys wouldn't need them anymore. Now I had two twin sized mattresses with box springs in my room, but not a bedframe. Everyone else in the house had bedframes; but oh well, right? I was just a little girl called not normal... not normal.

Chapter Fourteen

2003, Age 14

It was around or about the beginning of this year when I was officially baptized into The Church of God, In Christ, Mennonite. Most kids seemed to join between the ages of nine- thirteen or so.

The reasons that I personally did it were simple. Joyce was joining, and I wanted to be allowed to hang out with her again. I thought perhaps if I wore a head covering too, maybe people would stop keeping us apart. I also thought that maybe God would listen to me better and stop Ahaz from beating and raping me if I was baptized. I had no other hope to stop him, so I grasped at any potential possibilities that would make him quit hurting me.

I had to get up and tell the entire congregation I was saved, etc. Then the members all took a vote as to wither or not they believed me; and I was in. A baptism was scheduled for me and for several other kids as well.

Soon following, I was baptized inside of the church with just a few drops of water poured from a tiny pitcher onto the top of my hair. The minister laid his hands on top of my head and prayed, then move down to the next until we were all baptized. Then all the other members of the same sex had to greet us individually as members, with The Holy Kiss, also known as The Kiss of Peace.

I had seen it done a thousand times, but this was my first experience with having to participate in it personally. Of course, I had known ahead of time that that I'd have to do it and had been anxious for days stressing about it.

All the female members formed a line, one by one kissing each of us new members straight on the lips. Some of their lips were wet, which was disgusting. Some were dry, some had stinky breath which was disgusting. Some had on Chapstick; others did not. One after another... I had known this was a part of it, but seriously... yuck. I wanted to throw up, having to kiss one right after another, mouth after mouth. This did not feel holy; It felt like sacrilege to me.

I do not know exactly how many women and girls I kissed that night, but it was all the female members in attendance. Nor do I know how many more woman and even just little girls I had to continue to kiss at church, and while going to other Mennonites houses especially after church on Sundays, and even during rare visits to other congregations in other states or when others traveled to ours. That's a lot of kisses to both people I knew and to complete strangers, as well.

I was a minor, kissing grown adults, teens and even kids. Because as a member it was now something that I *had to do*. If I had refused, I would have been first placed under 'Church Concern' for a period of time and then excommunicated if I had not repented and participated because it is considered somewhat of a holy privilege and young members are not excluded from having to do so.

I did it only because I was seeking protection under the cover of The Church. I did believe in God, but I wondered why God would want people to kiss on the lips because it seemed kind of gross.

As it turned out, joining The Church did not do anything to protect me; God did not strike Ahaz down for raping a

Christian Holdeman Mennonite with a head covering on. And Joyce was still supposed to stay away from me for the most part. I prayed and prayed to make the torment stop. I hoped and believed that surely, God or someone could make it stop. Anyone.

Due to the expansion in my knowledge and increasing interest toward the understanding of worldly things, Ahaz banned any more library visits. However, he did still permit trips to the modern Christian bookstores. Obviously, he was a fool for believing books from there would not influence me 'toward the world' so deeply, because it was in those worldly Christian shops that mom and I discovered the astounding Dee Henderson books.

Her books to me were powerful. Mom bought first one, then another and another. The O'Malley series was especially amazing, as was the Uncommon Heroes series. The characters within held a variety of jobs, such as firemen and military. I both loved and hated having to wait on her next book to come out, and then the next.

The books were suspenseful Christian romance and taught me so much more about the real world outside of my own, then what I ever had learned otherwise. Those books were exactly what I needed to learn about healthy relationships, how strong women could be, and how much there was to look forward to in life.

They gave me a stronger glimmer of hope, shimmering through the darkness surrounding me. I determined that now, more than ever, to either join the military or to become a policewoman, or perhaps even a firewoman. I would be strong, and I would be educated no matter what it took.

In order to get my hands on more of her amazing books cheaper, mom took me to a used bookstore in Cookeville, near to a movie theater. We combed through the shelves of books to find the rest of the published ones I did not yet have. It was so exciting!

After finding several, mom bought them, and we walked outside to get into the van. From across the parking lot, I gazed at the outside of that theater, wondering what it was like to go inside one. In spite of having been born simi-worldly, I had never been through theater doors due to all the restrictions imposed by Ahaz. I knew that one day, I'd be free, and I'd do it. How wicked could it really possibly be, anyway?

Reading all of Dee Henderson's amazing works of pure modern art inspired me to write my own. I had always enjoyed writing so much, and mom liked to secretly tell me that one day she'd be buying a book of mine off the #1 best seller rack.

This was when my writing changed drastically. My own writing style itself was advancing and changing, with the simple short stories I was expected to write at school no longer being enough to satisfy me; I needed *more;* and to show off my true skills by writing real world scenario stories.

With only a few months left before my supposedly 'big' 8th grade graduation, my teacher told me to write a story and gave me about a month or so to do it, because it was to be a bigger story than ever requested previously. I decided to throw my all into this one and make it extraordinary, completely unlike the expected, simplistic Mennonite style.

The title of this story was *Zanzibar,* and it was about a worldly family who lived on a farm, and a little girl who was struck by lightning in a storm while gathering needed items during a difficult birthing of a foal. The girl was paralyzed from it. Although my mom ewed and awed over how well written it was, neither my teacher nor the school board looked highly upon it.

Soon after, I was supposed to write another short story, and this one wound up being considered far, far worse.

It was about a little girl who'd been mistakenly switched at birth with another baby and had been raised with the wrong family. I wrote it since I actually wished, and hoped, that this was the case with me. I desperately hoped I had a true, kind family out there somewhere that I just didn't know about yet, even though mom insisted I wasn't adopted each time I asked.

This story seemed to be a bit of a final straw to the school board, and it quite nearly got me kicked out of school entirely. That and plus I was failing in math; I had always done reasonable in my grades, but that year, my teacher was dreadful. Not mean so much, but she was utterly awful at describing things in a way that I could grasp. You put that on top of me having absolutely horrible depression, anxiety, anorexia, and being severely abused, etc.; well, no wonder I was failing it. I needed a kind math tutor, but there was none to be had.

The school board was called together over these things, and I was taken to the church by Ahaz to meet them all there in one of the Sunday School rooms. They consisted of a group of a few men, since women were not permitted to hold positions of actual power. Maximus was one of these men, and combined, they all had an absolute fit over that story I'd written. Because, as they told me, it was far too worldly and did not hold to their simplistic standards. They said that it was 'unrealistic' (in the Mennonite world, anyway).

The men said I was also doing poorly in math for attention, and claimed I wasn't even attempting to try to do the work. Their idea of proof in this was that I had never had such low grades in it before. I told them that I was truly trying in math; my teacher that year just made it incredibly difficult to follow, and I asked for help, for someone *else* to show me how to do it.

I was called a liar for saying that for three reasons; one, I wasn't making eye contact due to anxiety when I spoke, and Maximus explained to me that people make eye contact when they tell the truth and break it when they are lying. Secondly, they simply refused to accept I needed any form of assistance or tutoring in math since I was so smart. Lastly, their idea of proof that I should be able to easily understand it was because the couple other kids in my grade were passing it, which meant it was *me,* not the teacher.

They said that I was causing a disturbance and being a bad influence on the other kids by having no qualms about announcing how I intended for my future to be; as an independent, modern woman with a Mennonite- forbidden occupation and lifestyle. They didn't want the other kids to be adversely affected by it.

It was also because I simply wouldn't stop talking about wanting to go to public school and college; not simply ending my education at the eighth grade. This was completely unacceptable, unruly behavior by Mennonite standards. (Let's just take a quick moment to appreciate how *unacceptable* continued education is; clearly women are too weak and homely to be powerful and educated).

Maximus threatened to expel me and not allow me to graduate from the eighth grade. I was inwardly excited for just a bit, since I *wanted* to go to public school. But Ahaz made it very clear I would not get to do that; he'd just force me to homeschool until I graduated the eighth grade and then that would have been that. Asshole.

I was crying during the whole thing, because they had taken on a confrontational front and any sort of confrontation made me feel fearful. Their gazes were focused on me, and I could see they truly believed that they had all the facts straight when they clearly didn't.

I tried to tell them that the story wasn't bad; it was just a reflection of real- world happenings and I was certain it would have been appropriate in a worldly school. I told them that I needed math help from someone else, because I just couldn't understand what my teacher was trying to explain. I also pointed out that since I was born in America, I had freedom of choice of both future jobs and extended education. And I had the freedom of speech granted to me by the constitution to speak of my choices.

I'd love to say that I said those things proudly and confidently, but in reality, they wound up being mumbled through sniffles and a throat so tight that I felt as though I was suffocating. My heart was pounding; I felt like a scared little girl because I knew my words did not matter; I knew it would make no difference to Ahaz or the school board members; and I was correct.

In order to stay in school, I was forced to lie and agree that I had *not* been trying in math, just as they said. I was ordered to apologize to the teacher, and say that I was sorry for lying, not paying attention to her and for deliberately doing the work poorly, and for being 'a bad influence'. I also had to write a different, more Holdeman Mennonite acceptable story.

Then, I was whipped hard enough to bruise by one of them with a large wooden paddle with holes; while it was witnessed by the rest, and I was forced to bend over and put my hands on a metal folding chair. This was no easy feat to stay still, and I was shaking from fear, embarrassment and pain. But it didn't last for hours even though it did bruise me, so at least it was still an improvement over Ahaz's treatment.

Of course, Ahaz's personal view was that if the school board had whipped me, he needed to as well. He beat me after, per usual, ranting about what normal people do...

Normal people do what they are told and do not backtalk their superior's. Normal people do not write worldly stories. Normal people do not lie. Normal people accept the rules. Normal people understand that only he knew what was best. Normal people loved their parents. Normal people do not get poor math grades on purpose. Normal people are not unruly. Normal people are thankful for rules. Normal people... normal people...

I was just the little, not normal girl. I was nothing. Telling the truth got me beat, bruised and welted and bloodied up. Lying was forced upon me; forced repeatedly to tell that horrid man thank you. Forced to lie and apologize for wanting freedom of education. Forced to lie about wanting to live free, never again under the rule of a mere man.

At school, I attempted to try harder to figure the math out. The teacher went over all the stuff in lessons again and gave us a quiz. I did it carefully, triple checked over every single problem, and turned it in. I was positive that I was going to get a 100% because I had worked so hard on it and was actually happy that I'd finally figured it out.

Well.... wouldn't you know it, I got a terrible grade. The teacher used her red pen to mark all over that paper and gave it back with a terrible, unhappy scowl. I was deeply confused; if that hadn't been how to do the problems when I was certain I'd followed exactly what she taught; then *how was it done*?

But it still wasn't believed, of course, that I didn't understand it. I was just 'not normal' according to Ahaz. How about poor teaching? Anyone ever heard that one? Just me? Ok cool. How about some kids need a little extra help in certain subjects? Still nope? Yep, then *clearly* it must have been just me, acting 'not normal'.

As far as the story re-write went, they wanted a ridiculous, simpleton story and so I gave exactly that to them, to all my vengeful, rule following ability. I wrote a story titled 'A Day in the Life of a Bulletin Board'.

It was about a kid who went to bed as usual, and woke up as a wall hanging bulletin board, able to think, feel, see and hear but not capable of responding to anything. It described the things going on around that it witnessed throughout the day, including multiple times of being stuck with pins, as papers were pinned to it, which made it think 'ouch' but was helpless to stop the pins.

I expected after I turned that in for the teacher to announce she was angry at that one being too dumb and unrealistic, but she said nothing. In fact, I never got it back, graded or otherwise which was very strange. I hoped it made her angry; simple and near brainless was required of me, and that is exactly what I gave her on a very basic level.

That story was actually a reflection of, and a representation of myself. I was silenced and helpless to stop anything that anyone around me did; no matter how many 'pins' were stuck in me.

There was a boy there who's mom had been slowly dying of cancer for a long while. She wished to see her son become a member before she died, and it was drawing close to her time to go. This boy went in front of the entire congregation to tell his experience story and was voted down by the members. Which basically meant the majority of the congregation did not believe he was truly a Christian; and they told him something down the lines of he needed to go pray more on it.

It crushed the boy, and I felt this cruelty deeply within myself; felt his pain as though it were my own. Who were *they* to judge whether or not someone was a Christian? The Bible clearly stated to *not* judge, and this made me very, very upset as the realization struck me of the power their votes held.

They crushed a mere boy's soul for no reason at all other than perhaps they felt he didn't tell it clearly enough, or shockingly enough, like a bolt of lightning type story. They judged and found him lacking as though they were playing God.

I confronted the elder minister with this and asked why they judge, when they preach to not judge. If only God could judge, then why were mere people acting as though they had the power to judge who was a Christian, and who was not? Grandpa did not have solid answers, and by this point he had about given up on answering most of my difficult questions anyway. He said that was just how it had always been.

We talked a long while about how the Mennonites judge so many others heavily, such as how far too many believe only Holdeman Mennonites will go to heaven. And how most think it is impossible to be a true Christian if you are not a Mennonite, since only they are following the true lifestyle to get to heaven. There were a few who are not so narrow minded, but it didn't seem to be many that *truly* believed that way, even though it was written in as part of their religion to believe such. Grandpa was one of the good ones who truly believed Christians existed outside of the Holdeman Mennonites.

This way of thinking seemed to stem from how everything was so strict. How it was one way, or the highway. And the highway meant becoming one of the excommunicated which would result in being surely bound for hell. It was worse to have been Mennonite and leave, that it was to have been born worldly, since the worldly didn't 'know better', but ex Mennonites did know the one true path to heaven and abandoned it.

I asked grandpa why were those who were excommunicated avoided; why could Mennonites not eat at the same table as one of the excommunicated? Would I be poised by the sin of the excommunicated if I ate food from the same table, as they seemed to act? If not, then why would anyone be so cruel as to tear families apart by having such rules.

Why were families not supposed to speak often to those who left and turned worldly? This seemed unjust, and clearly only added to the fear of people feeling as though they *couldn't* leave. To leave meant to leave everything and everyone behind, and to be bound to burn in hell forever as far as most seemed to believe.

Why couldn't we have musical instruments or dance, when the Bible clearly states people played harps and sang and danced in praise. I wanted music in my life so badly; I wanted to dance, and I did not feel as though that made me a sinner. If God had been pleased by it way back then, why wouldn't he be pleased with it now? Couldn't I at least have a small harmonica to play?

I questioned why the men and boys were allowed to wear store bought clothes when women and girls were forced to only have handmade clothing. Wouldn't a store-bought dress or skirt serve the same purposes? If the men were good enough to have store clothes, why couldn't females, too? Even if it was just a blouse and skirt; what made store bought modest clothes so forbidden? Would I go to hell if I wore them? If that did not define my Christianity, then why did it matter?

Why was I not allowed to sew a dress that went down to my ankles? Since that would be more modest than the required, precise mid-calf length, it made no sense that even something so simple as that was forbidden. Would I go to hell if my dress touched the top of my shoes? Why was it that both too long, *and* too short of a dress was considered worldly?

What about if I wore a red or pink or lime colored dress; if that wouldn't guarantee me a spot in hell then why couldn't I make that choice? And earrings, if it wouldn't specifically send me there either then... why???

And why did woman have to wear two head coverings instead one to church? Was my head more sinful twice on Sundays and on Wednesday evenings, and needed to be double covered? The Bible said nothing about having to wear two coverings, so why was it a requirement?

If I could wear lose sweatpants under my dress when there was snow on the ground and wouldn't go to hell for that, then why couldn't I wear them throughout the rest of winter when it could still be just as cold as it was when it snowed? Why couldn't I wear pants under my dress when I rode my ponies, since sometimes it was a fight to keep my skirt tucked under me. It seemed like it would be far more modest to wear pants while riding, instead of my skirt flying up.

Why did Church have to be three times per week? There was nothing in the Bible about any of those things being requirements to get into heaven. *Not a single one of them.*

So, if those things weren't actually sinful, then why couldn't I have the freedom of choice to do them? And why was everyone so against the military, police, etc. Why couldn't I be a Christian protecting the very few people I loved in the line of duty? Protecting the innocent from those who wanted to do them harm seemed like a completely amazing, selfless thing to do.

I asked why they only focused on Jesus having died for them, and did not celebrate and morn the immense number of deaths that occurred to grant them their right to religious freedom? I pointed out that at minimum, Veteran's Day and Independence Day should, indeed, be a respected part of the Mennonite holiday routine.

The Mennonites enjoyed the freedom of religion; something which a countless amount of people *died for* their freedom of. Yet the Holdeman's themselves had never fought in war; they took their freedom for granted *without* a personal cost.

Poor grandpa couldn't answer all these deep questions of mine. He would try to scramble to find the words to explain at first, but as my questions persisted and knocked down his reasoning, he'd eventually just kind of smile a bit in his special way, shake his head slightly, give up with a chuckle and tell me that it was just the way things were.

Dear 'grandpa' was a patient, very special man, and he meant a lot to me. Even though he was a minister promoting and upholding all the rules, he was very smart, kind and understanding of my thoughts and questions. He was my family; and no matter how many times Ahaz continued to beat me for calling him grandpa, I never ever stopped.

Ahaz purchased a bit of land from an excommunicated Holdeman Mennonite within the Muddy Pond community and had part of it plowed for two large gardens. A large green house was built onto that land, and a pond dug out as well during that spring. He built a fence out there, too, and planned to move the ponies over because he expected at least for my Butter to till the ground with a plow he purchased. Ahaz then had a harness made for her at the leather shop.

He talked a lot about how everyone would have to pitch in, but I knew he really meant Travis and me. The youngest two boys were too small, mom would never do such a thing, and Sarah was exempt. Travis was only expected to do men's work, yet I was forced to do housework, had to sew my own clothes and work hard physical labor at the same time.

I was the only one multi-tasked with so very much, and every time I pointed this out and demanded to know why, Ahaz said that housework was women's work, and long days and hard work on the farm would teach me how to be normal. He said my sister was too delicate for such work; even though she was the picture of health.

It made me so angry. I didn't want to be forced to go to the farm, but of course he made me. Right after school, I'd have to go there and work the ground, spread chicken poop without gloves, plant various seeds and plants, pick out stones and endless weeding. He'd also put up a smaller greenhouse by the house and existing garden, and the amount of work to be done between it all was immense.

I utterly hated tending to the tomato plants most of all, because they were his favorite. I didn't want to touch them, but of course I had to.

I hated it; not for a hate of gardening, but for a hate of doing something, anything for him that would ultimately please him. For having to be near him. For having to stay out in the heat or chill until supper, for having my hands covered in blisters and then washing the dishes after eating with those same raw, burning hands. Oh, how I hated him.

There were some days I'd simply refuse to work, couldn't bear the choking, skin crawling feelings of being forced to be in his presence, of doing something that made only him happy. He'd beat the near daylights out of me and force me to work anyway.

I'd be shaking from the pain and bruises, yet still forced to work and accomplish gardening while adding more blisters to my hands. It made me feel so angry, so helpless that he could beat me until I eventually gave in just to make it stop. I even hated *myself*, for being so weak and giving up.

I got the most dreadful of cramps; they absolutely put me down. The sharp cramping pains were in my stomach and back and would shoot straight down both of my legs all the way to my ankles. Mom would laugh and say that if I thought I was in pain then, I had no idea what was coming, because when the day came that I'd have a baby it would be ten times worse. She thought I was over exaggerating; only I wasn't. It was incredibly intense at about a nine/ ten on pain scale, and I suspected this had something to do with what Ahaz was doing to me; like he was ruining my insides.

Ahaz would still force me to work the gardens and greenhouses during this, even when I could barely walk. He'd beat me for faking, for not acting normal, when I was already in so much pain.

Another thing that began to happen was strange spells where I couldn't hear well, and it sounded like I was under water. Mom kept saying I had wax in my ears and gave me peroxide to put in them frequently a few times a week at least. It would happen at the worst of times, such as when I was supposed to read out loud in class, which I'd have to do it anyway and the teacher and other students would give me strange looks and tell me I sounded odd.

During the forced group singing in the mornings at school, I knew I couldn't follow a tune with my ears like that, so I'd whisper-sing or mouth the words. But those nearest to me knew I wasn't really singing, and I'd get in trouble for it. No one believed my hearing was going from regular, to under water without warning. Sometimes it would only last a couple minutes, sometimes several hours, and it happened multiple times per day. Perhaps it was an ear issue, or perhaps a result of anxiety or from being beat; I did not know for sure.

It was happening at the house, too, so on top of being treated oddly at school for it, Ahaz would beat me terribly over it; for not talking normally on purpose for attention, he'd say. He told me he'd give me the attention I was looking for. Not normal... not normal.

Chapter Fifteen

Prior to my 'big' graduation from the whopping eighth grade, I was allowed to go hang out with Joyce at her house. She showed me a beautiful, small hope chest her dad had made for her, and I wanted one just like it. I asked her dad to please make one for me and much to my delight he did just that.

I treasured that little chest. It was perhaps only about 18 inches long, 18 tall, and about a foot wide, give or take a wee bit. It meant the world to me that he'd taken the time to make it for me. No, it didn't have any fancy carvings on it, but it didn't need them in order to be very special.

Somehow, I managed to get my math grade up to barely passing, although I wasn't entirely sure how because I still did not have a grasp on it by any means.

The closer the supposedly all- important graduation approached, the more horrified and anxious I felt. I knew that for one thing I'd be forced to be in the same house with Ahaz even more, plus be made to work the farm six days a week. He said that he wanted to grow crops to sell to locals and run it as a second business, alongside being a doctor and seeing patients in the back of the house.

Ahaz so enjoyed talking about how wonderful that was going to be, having me work so much. He also said he was pleased because this would give him an extensive amount of time to increase the amount of time he was able to spend dedicated to beating me into becoming normal. Only he used words like 'discipline' and 'correct', and I didn't know that I could call what he was doing to me beating. I was still calling it being horribly whipped.

I not only desperately wanted to continue my education inside of a school, but I also wanted to keep as far away from Ahaz as possible at all moments in time. Knowing I'd be trapped with him even more was terrifying, but I knew that no one could save me from him. I had panic attacks just waiting to graduate, knowing that far worse was to come.

Ahaz forced a table seating arrangement change. We'd always had assigned seating at the kitchen table; his was at one of the short ends / heads since he believed that he was to be honored and revered as a dominate male. My chair was all the way down the long side, at the end, in the furthest possible seat away from him without being directly across. But he made me switch to being beside him. Mom sat on his left; I was now on his right. And oh, how I *hated it.*

He had to spend many, many hours dedicated to beating me in order to enforce that change, since I kept deliberately either refusing to go to meals at all in order to avoid it or would still go to my 'old' spot. Being near him made me nauseous and made it even more difficult to attempt to eat, on top of the anorexia.

Ever since he had first raped me, I had utterly refused to look him in the eyes since then. And when it was unavoidable to be near him or having to walk within his vicinity, I'd turn my head deliberately to the side, even if it was at a wall as I went by. It damn near made him lose his mind with outrage over the clear 'disrespect', especially if anyone was around to see, or at church or within another Mennonite home where anyone could see. He couldn't do anything immediately about it in public because he had to hide the monster within him, but as soon as he'd get me back to the house it was all over with, and I'd know it was coming.

He would spend hours beating me for this intensely, while insisting he was *going to break me just like a horse, if that was what it took to make me act normal.*

Ahaz tried to force me to look at him while he raped me, too. But I would not give in, no matter what. I could control that much; I would *never* be his robot; I was my very own person. I was not his object to do with as he wished, even though he treated me as such.

The Muddy Pond community had their very own volunteer fire department. It was made up of just a few men since woman were not allowed such a lofty position. They did not get called out often, and they didn't work shifts hanging out at the department.

Every year in May, there would be a community auction on the property of that tiny fire department. All sorts of things were bought and sold, from tools to vacuums to cars and livestock. I had always gone every year before, but this year I couldn't bear to be forced to be around Ahaz, so I stayed at the house, hiding out and reading my precious books. Suddenly there was a phone call; Ahaz had bought a horse that had been otherwise destined for dog food.

I nearly lost my mind with excitement. I loved my dear Butter and Spice, too, but having a full-sized horse was my ultimate dream. Mom drove me out there to the auction, and there I met my new American Saddle Mare. She was scared and lashed out at anyone who attempted to get near her.

I was told that she had been owned by a local, well known trainer, who clearly beat his horses cruelly into submission by breaking their souls. This one he could not break by beating, so he declared her to be crazy and dangerous. One look at that wild eyed, fearful, angry, beautiful mare and I knew we were twin souls; beat and never quitting. Never truly submitting, never becoming robots. We were our own individuals, her and I.

On some level, even then, I somewhat understood that it was a manipulative chess move, similar to the one he had made in purchasing Butter. This was a strategic purchase to get me into the van and to the farm to work more easily, since that was where he intended to keep her. Ahaz also knew my love of horses ran so deeply through my veins that it would reduce the risk of me telling, and thus risk leaving such a priceless beauty. And he wasn't entirely wrong.

Grandpa was in a tizzy over the mare having been purchased for little ole Hannah. Maximus, Grandpa and others told Ahaz to not let me near the horse and to get rid of her fast. They said that since she had come from a great trainer who had deemed her unrideable, she must be truly crazy. And she honestly was dangerous by all appearances. People were worried and some even in somewhat of a panic for my safety. Grandpa even told me he was scared for me.

However, I had been preparing for this moment for years by reading all about Monty Roberts and his amazing training techniques. Nonviolent and gentle, he was the 'The Horse Whisperer'. I was not afraid, although I probably should have been. She was taken back to the farm in a trailer, and I noticed immediately her obvious hate for males. I didn't blame her; I didn't like them either. We were going to get along famously.

She wouldn't allow me to touch her at first, but I climbed up on the gate and just talked to her for the rest of the day. The next day was a Sunday, and it was awful to have to go to church before I could see my sweet darling. I spent that afternoon just hanging out in the pen with her, allowing her to come to me in her own sweet time. When I reached out very slowly as if to touch her, she'd jump back and run off, scared. But as I continued to quietly stand, she'd come back a bit later, getting just a little closer while I waited patiently and non-threateningly. We did that over and over, until finally she stood quietly while I carefully rubbed her, of course all the while watching out for signs of things going wrong.

By that evening, I was riding her, bonding, running free on that 'unrideable' mare. Now, she was still actually quite dangerous, but it was only out of reactive fear. She simply needed kind, loving, gentle hands. She needed me just as much as I needed her.

If anyone else went near her she'd go into instant fight mode, and I was perfectly fine with that fact because I didn't want anyone else to lay a hand on her, most especially Ahaz. I had zero desire to teach her otherwise and did not attempt to. I wound up naming that beautiful darling Wish, because she had been my long-cherished wish. Wish was a beacon of light to shine through the darkness that was my life.

Graduation came swiftly, and I didn't want to participate in the end of year program tradition. I was told that I wasn't allowed to refuse; I *had* to stand in front of them all and sing and act out a ridiculous short play right along with the other students. I did *not* want to be on display in front of everyone. I felt like I was going to throw up and got through it only because I had to. I felt dizzy and was afraid I was going to pass out.

There were three graduates in total, myself and a sibling pair of a brother and sister I had went through grades three to eight with. Group singing aside, the three of us alone also had to sing a song together with all eyes on us. My hearing went out, but I kept on singing, hoping I was on tune, knowing I couldn't get away with lip singing with only the three of our voices.

After the program was finally finished and we three were declared officially graduated, there was a flurry of buffet style snacks, with each household having brought a dish of some sort. And presents for us.

I didn't pay attention specifically to what the one graduating boy received that night, but when young boys graduated the eighth grade, they would be given things like a wallet, a pocketknife, or tools of their trade. The girls, and in this case myself and one other girl, were given items for our hope chests, which was a wooden floor chest you'd fill with things for your future household when you marry.

Some of the things I received were antique China serving bowls, carefully embroidered dishtowels, and delicately soft, silk woven doilies. Doilies are a beautiful, practical decoration of sorts, used for protecting a surface while placing, say, a candle within a glass on top of it.

From my adopted grandpa, I got a beautiful lamp with images of horses running across the glass shade. Now that most special of gifts was not just to put away; he knew I loved horses and oh how I adored that lovely lamp! It instantly became my most treasured possession, second only to my books, of course.

After graduating, the boys would generally go straight to work. In the case of that particular community, it was primarily carpentry there. The boys would start saving right away in order to have enough money to pay for a house nearly as soon as they reached maturity, so they could then propose to a woman and marry her.

The girls on the other hand stayed home to further learn how to become a proper housewife, to cook and clean while staying humble and submissive. They learned how to be wives, how to always submit to their husbands and to Gods will.

However, in my case that did not happen; I was not treated in such a kid glove manner. It was summer, and with a small greenhouse and garden at the house to tend, plus two large gardens and a large greenhouse at the farm, I wasn't allowed to have my teen years turn out so gently. In the summer, many days Ahaz demanded that I get up early, before the sun even rose in order to get out to the farm a few miles away by daybreak.

He'd force me to work until lunch when we'd go back to the house to eat, and then it was straight back to the farm to work until it was too dark to see anymore. This was about two- three days per week for full days like that, since the rest of the days he spent either seeing patients or trying to beat and rape me into submission 'to teach me how to be normal', as he said. Also, when full days were not spent out there, he'd still make me go out there to the farm to work at the very least in the afternoons and evenings once he was done seeing patients for the day.

There was no bathroom out there, so I'd have to go in the trees and hope that Ahaz didn't follow me out there. I felt desperately anxious about that. A good bit of the time, Travis went to the farm, too. But there were many times Ahaz forced me to go alone with him, while Travis stayed at the house to build things such as picnic tables.

Ahaz would take some of those opportunities to attack and rape me at the farm. He'd remind me not to scream, because I wouldn't want anyone to know how I was being so immature, not normal and screaming for no reason. Besides, no one would believe me anyway, he'd say. Because he was a doctor, a Mennonite and a respected member of the community, he'd claim.

He'd hold his hand over my mouth to muffle my screams when I couldn't hold them back myself. His hand would be dirty and smelled bad. I tried biting his nasty hand once, but that didn't go well; he slapped me hard across the face for it.

After, I had to go back to work in the garden while in pain, sobbing my eyes out and choking back vomit from the utter disgust, fury, and helplessness. It was difficult to see through the tears flooding my eyes to tell the difference between what actual plants or weeds was.

Of course, I also had Wish at the farm. She was my comfort, my love. She required a lot of patience, gentle kindness and training when I was allowed to be with her. Sometimes she would be wild when she was fresh out of the pen, and she'd take off with me on her back, bucking like a bronco. Which was perfectly fine with me because I had an excellent seat and stuck to her like glue.

My mom once came to the farm and watched me ride one, and only that one time. Wish decided to play bronco that day, and mom was terrified as she watched. After Wish had calmed down and was walking about nicely with me cheerfully still mounted on her back, mom said she'd never watch me ride again because she had thought she was about to see me die right in front of her. She did compliment my riding though, of which I felt very proud.

I would ride whenever I could get away from the gardens and greenhouse, even if I was in pain from being brutalized. Sometimes, I'd arrive back at the house at nighttime with blood on my dresses, but mom never said a thing. Nor did she fuss about how much new fabric I needed to frequently make replacement dresses. I was doing all my own laundry at this point, mostly out of embarrassment. And I also wanted to make sure my clothes were never mingled with Ahaz's... I couldn't bear to think of my dresses and such touching his clothes in the washer or dryer.

I begged mom to protect me so many times. From his brutality, from going to the farm and work entire days; to protect me for the horrendous things he did to my body. I begged her to tell Ahaz she needed me at the house, to keep me there with her and Sarah. But she never would. She had her precious Sarah and that was all she needed. I was nothing.... I was not normal.

It blew my mind how mom was capable of pretending I wasn't being hurt. She was very aware of it but chose to be a happy ostrich in the sand; see no evil, hear no evil, pretend evil did not exist. I even attempted to tell her on a couple occasions that Ahaz was raping me.

I did it in a roundabout type of way, trying to gear up to saying the horrible words. I felt as though she must surely know what I was working up to, as I stammered out that Ahaz was hurting me, touching me. She stopped me so quickly and told me to just quit it. Everything was deny, deny, deny. Nothing was wrong; everything was roses and lilies.

Travis talked Ahaz into buying him a weight set, and he began lifting faithfully, bulking up. He was tired of losing our wrestling matches, be they friendly or out of anger as they sometimes were. He also got some sort of muscle building powdered drink stuff to help. Soon, gone was the little scrawny kid, and he quickly turned into a muscled teen then; stronger, and faster than me.

I was having dizzy spells. Some of them were due to the anorexia and now- severe anxiety, at first. I was getting to the point of becoming truly fearful/ anxious being around people, and I thought this was triggering the original ones.

It started off slow, I'd be around people such as at someone's house for Sunday lunch, which made me feel uncomfortable and out of place. I'd get really hot all the sudden, then feel dizzy and lightheaded. My hearing would mess up, and everything sounded as though it was underwater and moving further away. Then I'd pass out, or nearly so cause generally with all the people around someone would notice something was wrong, grab and guide me to furniture before I hit the floor.

It was deeply embarrassing, and even more so when everyone around decided that I was faking it for attention. Even grandpa asked if I was faking it, which made me feel shameful because no one seemed to believe what was happening to me.

Then it progressed into something more. Every time the big spells happened; I had a rash pop up on my legs. It was very strange, with many tiny pinpoint size red dots, grouped tightly together to form into near perfect circles around ¼ to maybe ¾ inch across. They were also completely flat, and I did not feel any discomfort from them; if I had been blind, I would never have known the rash existed. My mom was very confused about it, but also could not deny it seemed to be connected.

There came a day when I had those dots in so many places: arms, legs, belly, etc. I couldn't walk. I could only crawl to and from the bathroom and was barely able to pull myself up onto the toilet even. Everything around me spun in nonstop circles. Even when I closed my eyes, the darkness spiraled, spinning round and round and round. When I opened my eyes and tried to look at the calendar on my wall, the calendar moved around in a big, nonstop circle.

This wound up going on for days on end, 24/7. I attempted to eat and did a little but was so nauseous from the constant merry go round it was incredibly difficult.

Mom realized something really was terribly wrong and took me to a dermatologist even though Ahaz said she wasn't allowed to take me, and they had a huge, yelling fight over it. But mom wouldn't back down this time and helped me out the door and into the van to head to the appointment anyway.

The doctor didn't know what the marks were and took a biopsy of one to send it off to have it looked at a big hospital. There was very basic bloodwork done in the meantime, which mom talked Ahaz himself into ordering at a local lab. Mom took me there, and I could barely walk so she had to help hold me up to get inside the lab. Everything came back fine supposedly, according to Ahaz.

There was another appointment at the dermatologist once the results came back from the biopsy, and the doctor said it was still unknown what it was; the great minds that had examined it were clueless. He recommended that I be taken to a neurologist since something clearly was wrong; he *knew* something was wrong.

But Ahaz absolutely refused and said that I was faking the whole thing. Mom gave up fighting and didn't take me in the end. Ahaz prescribed some sort of medication to me; I never saw the bottle and I do not know what it was. Whatever it was didn't do anything to stop it.

The longest dizzy spell I had lasted a couple of weeks in length. The world simply would not cease spinning. I couldn't read or do anything really other than debate whether or not the spinning was worse, or better with my eyes closed or open. Both were terrible and there was no good solution. One day, it just finally stopped all by itself.

It would continue to come back time and again throughout the next few years, but never again for that long of a time. It could happen for hours at a time, sometimes several times a week, sometimes less. And it was always accompanied with the odd rash. I kept wondering what the pills were that Ahaz were giving me, but I had no way to find out.

Chapter Sixteen

Over supper one night, Ahaz announced he had some sad news for all of us and wanted to prepare everyone. He said that he didn't want to upset anyone, but he did not expect to live much longer. Since his own dad had started having heart attacks at an unusually young age, Ahaz felt his own luck would soon change. He admittedly considered himself already fortunate to have made it to his current age without any. However, he anticipated this good luck would not continue, and his own heart would soon fail. He said that he feared we'd be lost without him, but he wanted us to be ready if it happened.

Now this announcement tickled me so much! In fact, I was so incredibly thrilled and hopeful over it that I could hardly contain my excitement. Beaming from ear to ear, I cheerfully blurted out something down the lines of asking just how soon, exactly, did he think he was going to die from a heart attack?

I swear he saw red. Or black; whatever color the devil sees. He was absolutely, utterly infuriated and his face turned red. If he had been a cartoon, there most definitely would have been steam coming out from his ears in that moment.

Ahaz jumped up, nearly knocking his chair over in his rush, completely enraged and probably embarrassed, too, that I had taken his solemn moment in the spotlight and dared to be so obviously, ecstatically happy.

I knew that I was in deep trouble but having the hope of his imminent death made me so happy, that I simply didn't actually care. It made me genuinely happy that monster was hopefully dying, which would ensure my freedom to live life to the fullest without all the pain he caused. I couldn't wipe the joy from my face.

Ahaz grabbed my upper arm and dragged me along to my bedroom, shoved me inside and told me to stay put; he was coming back for me. I heard his heavy, angry footsteps run to his room for the leather strap, switch and paddle, but I couldn't stop smiling in pure, hopeful joy.

He returned quickly, in a rushed fury and started in with the switch, hitting anywhere he wanted. In his anger, he forgot to only hit me where it would be hidden and instead striking wherever, anywhere, and everywhere. He was screaming that he would not tolerate my blatant disrespect and not normal reaction.

With the chance of freedom seemingly near, I felt stronger and bolder. I yelled right back that I truly hoped, with everything in me that he would simply die soon because he was a horrible person.

The bedroom door was still open, and my siblings Sarah and Travis came to stand just outside of it in the tiny hallway. They were laughing uproariously, and Ahaz was encouraging it. "Watch and see what happens for disrespect!" he roared. "It will not be tolerated!"

The smile still on my face that could not be contained only added to his rage, and he dropped the switch in exchange for the strap. Tackling me, he wrestled me down onto the floor and sat on my back. It was so difficult to breath under his weight; I felt as though I was being crushed, and each inward drawn breath was a struggle. He went to town striking my bottom and legs repeatedly with the strap while my siblings still watched and laughed... so much loud laughing.

Eventually he let me up, and he went to the kitchen for a drink break; he was sweating and stinking. Only Sarah now remained in the hall to laugh at how funny I looked. Returning, he demanded that I apologize for 'lying' and for being so disrespectful to him. He claimed that he was an upstanding citizen, doctor, Mennonite and a head of household and would not tolerate me not acting normal and telling lies... yet he was beating me to force me to lie. To force me to be *saddened by* his perceived impending death?

I utterly refused to lie this time; I simply would *not*. So, I clung to the hope, the truth, the happy thoughts of his coming death. I tried to block out the sounds of my sister's laughter and I refused to scream, refused to drop the smile no matter how hard he beat, bruised, welted and bloodied my body. I would not allow for him to take my genuine joy away from me; he could do whatever he wished, but I knew that he could not take that from me at least.

He continued to beat me for about a couple of hours, until he realized he wasn't going to win that one. He was finally worn out, exasperated and had other things to do. He was absolutely soaked in sweat himself, his light blue shirt now mostly dark and wet. He stank from it.

Since he was too tired to continue, he made me sit at the kitchen table and write. But not to write just anything; he got one of his parenting books out and made me hand copy entire chapters from it on proper discipline until the wee hours of the morning, until long after all my cackling in laughter siblings had went to bed.

It made my hand cramp and hurt but relishing the thought of Ahaz soon dying made everything a bit more bearable, including my sore and beaten body. I tried not to read the words as sentences, as only a single word at a time instead but it was difficult to focus on doing that.

Things like having to copy those books like that played a huge part in why I couldn't properly explain to grandpa and others what was being done to me for what I was; being beat. And him constantly referring to my beatings as discipline and correction; the laughter of my siblings; my mom always turning a blind eye and denying the terrible marks on my body existed, and even grandpa not believing from my description of these 'whippings' that lasted for hours. It all combined into what led to my painful silence.

It made me feel as though, even though I *knew* it was terrible, even though I *knew* it was horribly wrong; the beatings, the rape, the mental abuse, the way he forced me to lie to suit his own personal beliefs; everything added up to me knowing I could never prove it. In fact, I had no clue how to prove it, much less understood I could use the word beat instead of whipped.

You see, Ahaz would also point out over and over again, while he was beating me, that this was his *right* and in fact, *required* of a parent to do; to discipline the kids. He had always talked that way, as far back as I could remember. Obsessively. Top off listening to that, with how the Mennonites spoke of discipline and obedience; how I was even considered a bad influence and unruly for speaking out and not properly and submissively conforming to their ways; and the confusing lines between what truly was allowed, and what truly wasn't, was incredibly blurred in my eyes. Was I being 'disciplined?' Was he truly allowed to 'whip' me until I lay bruised and broken on the floor? Rape me when I could barely even move enough to weakly fight back? The library books said he couldn't do that, at least, yet he was.

Ahaz had always been big on the books about disciplining kids. He'd always collected and read them, but by this time, it had turned into a literal obsession of his. He bought an incredible number of books like that, and when he wasn't seeing patients, making me work the gardens alongside him, or busy raping and/or beating me; he was reading about how to dominate 'unruly kids.'

Because that's what it truly was all about, dominating me. He wanted my complete and utter submission with immaculate, unfaltering control over my thoughts, words, actions, and body; and he was trying so incredibly hard to figure out how to accomplish that. He also clearly, sadistically enjoyed it.

However, I was just as determined to not ever be broken by him. I knew I was born my own person with rights, and I would never let him win. I would never allow myself to be broken; I'd stand up for what was right no matter what pain it brought to my body. I could take it, I thought. I could bear it until I was free. Until he died... or I turned eighteen. And I would never stop fighting for more education, for the right to be creative; for the right to be free. I would never stop happily dreaming of his death.

I occasionally talked to that wonderful correction officer, Lisa, whom I'd met after taking the liberty of spending a night alone in the woods. My mom knew I did this, and so did Ahaz. I wanted to tell Lisa about the abuse so bad, but I didn't know how.

During one of our casual conversations, I did once ask her a few things specifically about sex. I was still figuring out how a consensual, wanted sex experience was different from the form of torture that was being done to me. She seemed a bit uncomfortable over the phone but did answer all my questions fairly well.

A couple of times she even came to see me and brought a gentleman friend of hers who was a police officer. I was enthralled with him since I wanted to be a cop, too. I also talked to him on the phone several times, asking questions about what it was like to be a cop, and what the police academy was like.

There were days when I had just been brutalized and snuck the phone to call one or the other of them, crying; depressed, in pain, suicidal. I wanted to say the words, but I felt they couldn't help me, so I didn't. How could I prove anything at all, when I *knew* my laughing siblings and ostrich mom would back Ahaz? Their words would leave me with zero evidence. My word against every single one of theirs.

Besides, was I even *being* brutalized, if Ahaz had the 'right' to beat me, and withhold education under the cover of freedom of religion in the Mennonites, and overall being a complete ass as the 'head of household'? Being 'whipped' for blinking in a way he didn't like, for protective or cold arm crossing, for saying the word kids, for calling the minister grandpa, for asking questions, for being curious, for a thirst to learn; nothing that was happening could be proved as abuse and I knew it. Not with lying siblings, and an ostrich mom.

I did know at least that Mennonites were supposed to save themselves for marriage, which was spoken of from time to time in church but of course no real specifics; they didn't actually talk about the ever-mysterious sex. Yet I was aware that Ahaz was not supposed to do that awful thing to me. But I knew he'd never admit to it, and who would have believed me anyway? Mom sure didn't when I was trying to explain and tell her he was touching me in a bad way; but I was pretty sure from the quick way she cut me off that she *already knew*. And it was such a deeply embarrassing, shameful thing that trying to tell others was... well, I really didn't want anyone to know.

Without evidence or truthful witnesses, that meant nothing actually happened, right? And I believed if I did say something, that no one, including Lisa nor that officer, would actually be able to succeed at getting me out; that Ahaz would make my life so much worse if I dared to tell them. He would talk his way out of it, point out how unruly and undisciplined I was for bucking against his and the Holdeman Mennonites orders. He'd just have talked in circles about discipline and how he was trying to get me on the right path to acting like a normal person.

Ironically, I felt as though it was better to have *hope* to hold onto that I would one day be free, than to have all hope of freedom from pain squashed down and completely eliminated. The more people that did not believe me or were helpless to get me out of there, the more I believed no one could.

It's so difficult to explain in a way that makes sense, but he held such an incredible, fear and controlling power over me it was all encompassing and had spent years dedicated to making it seem as though these were all things that he was *entitled* to be able to do to me, which rendered me helpless.

It felt as though I was suffocating, drowning. It was at such a high level that I did not even fully understand that it was happening. I thought I was strong because I tried to fight back, because I fought to not give into having to tell the lies that he tried to make me tell. But I was wrong. And even I couldn't fully grasp the hold he actually had over me nor the many years of being mentally programed to think it was allowed in some form or another.

I suspect that Ahaz was so confident in believing that no one could stop him, that he fancied himself truly untouchable. Perhaps he felt since he didn't hit me with his fists, that he wasn't beating me. Perhaps he thought raping me was his right as the honored 'head of household' and knew I'd never be able to prove anything. Perhaps he truly was so messed up in the head and saw himself as so powerful while I was so tiny, that no one would ever believe me.

I think these reasons and so many more is why I *wasn't* completely forbidden from talking to the officer and Lisa, although he definitely didn't *like* me talking to them. He didn't fear repercussions from the words of a mere girl; with the god complex he had; he never would have imagined anyone would have ever believed a kid over him.

He had also spent all my life dedicating to making sure my word was meaningless and useless. I was 'not normal'. I was dubbed a liar, bipolar, and both mom and Sarah had also contributed greatly to this happening. It seemed as though everyone wanted only lies from me.

Lies were beat from my lips; lies were expected of me. To lie and act as though women are not powerful, even though I could feel the strong woman power rushing through me. To even lie in silence by pretending that both Ahaz's and the Mennonites rules were acceptable to any degree.

I was *angry* from the abuse. I was broken, even though I always remained defiant and stood proud, refusing to be turned into a robot. He damaged me so much, both inside and out. I was far more broken than I could even admit to myself, because to face the brokenness fully would mean there was no hope left.

Seeing Joyce at this point outside of church was now rare. I desperately wanted to spend time with her, and her kind family. Finally, I was allowed to go for an overnight sleepover, and it was glorious!

Joyce had gotten her hands on a cassette player, and her parents actually knew about it. In her room, she had a handful of few cassettes with music on them, and we listened and reviled in the forbidden nature of it.

She also showed me a guitar that had been found on a trash run. It was missing some strings, but we played with it and pretended it was in perfect condition and worth a million bucks. Just hearing any sort of musical instrument was amazing to me. I determined that I was going to learn how to play the guitar as soon as I could get out of that place to freedom.

I did try to figure out a way to tell Joyce what was being done to me. Of course, I had always complained about how terrible Ahaz was, but I needed for her to know just how bad. When we snuggled up together on her bed at night and she was half asleep, I was tried to make the words come out of my mouth that Ahaz had touched me in terrible ways, but I couldn't speak out in a blunt enough way for her to understand. Joyce mumbled back asking what I was saying and said that she was tired.

She soon fell sound asleep, and I remember crying as I whispered to her sleeping form beside me, about how he got on top of me. I thought perhaps since I had been able to whisper some of the words out loud, that this was kind of like practice. I had to be able to tell someone, yet it was so deeply shaming for anyone to actually know. But I could do it one day. I thought I'd try again in the morning maybe. Only I didn't.

Sarah and I did the dishes every evening after supper, unless it was a night I was forced to eat and then go right back to work at the farm. We took turns on who washed and who dried them.

We were also the primary ones taking care of little Alex, my sister and me. When I wasn't otherwise being worked or tormented, running free in the woods, on horseback, embroidering or reading. So really it was probably my sister as his primary and me as his secondary caretaker.

Mom was laid up with back pain and depression, and on serious pain killers. She slept an awful lot and wasn't able to do much other than force herself to cook supper and be made to go to church, pickup and drop off kids from school, and her multiple trips to town each week just to escape.

She actually did up and leave several times, too. One time I remember crying as I watched her take a suitcase with her out the front door. I remember begging her not to leave me, to take me too; she *had* to take me, couldn't leave me behind, with *him*. But she didn't even say anything, her eyes were glazed over, and she looked like she was in a fog, completely out of it. She left, but came back the next day, pale and acting as though she had never left, as though perhaps she'd just been to the store and back.

I had never been more relieved to see her, yet all I hoped for was that she'd leave again; this time with the rest of us kids in tow. I needed for her to free us; but when I begged for exactly that, she told me to stop asking. She said that wasn't going to happen. By that point, I believed her. My only hope of freedom left was reaching my eighteenth birthday, and somehow finding a way to hold on until then.

I always managed to find time for reading and romping alone in the woods as well. I'd frequently stay up quite late until midnight or later reading my precious books and learning every little snippet of information I could about the great big world outside of my own. I read about true history stories because I felt it was important and vastly interesting. I read about ghost stories, fiction, crime and romance because they thrilled me. Horse training books and anything to do with horses, really, was also a continued favorite go-to. Monty Roberts techniques especially were the most fascinating to me, as I used his ways on my horse Wish to relax her.

I still made sure to ride Butter and Spice some, and even taught Butter how to plow the gardens. She wasn't incredibly impressed with the whole harness and plowing gig idea at first, and I was forced to watch Ahaz beat her horribly for it. I screamed at him for hurting my pony but was powerless to make him stop. He beat me dreadfully with the whip for acting not normal, stepping in his way and even for daring to try to stop his actions.

One day Ahaz decided that he wanted to take Travis and I blackberry picking in a fellow Mennonites field. It wasn't like the good picking by the house; this area was overgrown and scary. I didn't want to go and be forced to be near him, so naturally he beat me until I was weak and shaky. Then he dragged me to the van, forced me inside, and off we went. I felt sick; I hated being forced to be around that disgusting person.

While picking the blackberries, I was moving from one bush to another when I heard a sudden buzzing. Instantly I froze, thinking it was coming from the bush a few feet in front of me that I'd been walking toward. Then I felt tickles on my legs and looked down to realize in horror I had *stepped on top* of a ground bee nest, and the angry bees were coming out, crawling up my legs.

As soon as I noticed them, I panicked, and as soon as I did, they all started to sting at once. I started running and screaming while being stung by many bees at the same time. Ahaz and Travis saw and heard my plight, and they laughed while I cried out from the painful stings.

The bees were trapped under my skirt and stung my legs so many times. They were not just limited to there, though; they got my arms, hands, chest, back, face and neck, etc. Not sure how long the bees chased and stung me, but at some point, it was over, and they were gone.

Ahaz grumbled about how enough blackberries hadn't been picked yet in-between his laughter, but he did wind up taking me back to the house when I would only stand still, crying, and I refused to pick more. He said he'd let me put something on them at least and then he'd make me go back to make me continue the berry picking.

I was in misery already, and thinking of having to go back, to continue to be around him, only served to add to it.

Thankfully I wasn't allergic to bees, but of course all the sting sites swelled swiftly and were obvious. When Sarah saw one of my eyes were swollen halfway shut, she found it absolutely hilarious, and started laughing hysterically at how funny and not normal I looked.

Mom was a bit more sympathetic and gave me ibuprofen, and a baking soda and water paste to put on the many stings. She told Ahaz that he surely couldn't make me go back to that field; that was one of the few times she actually convinced him of something, and although he made a fuss about it, he gave up on berry picking for the day.

That evening, I was forced to sit at the table for supper and endure my sibling's snickers and outright laughter and comments over how funny I looked. It was not amusing to me whatsoever.

Ahaz got it into his head that the word 'father' was the highest term of respect, far more so than anything else. The deacon told him that being called this was the highest honorable respect for a man of his position, and Ahaz announced this while on the way back to the house one day after church.

He demanded that us kids call him that, and while we were at it; we should refer to mom, as 'mother'. I knew right away I would never, ever call him that; in fact, I had already stopped referring to him as anything. He was not a man to be respected; he was a monster. The monster that I was forced to live with.

He insisted we practice saying those words; I alone utterly refused that horrid monster. If father stood for a position of honor and respect, then saying it would be just like ought right lying. Plus, I could never and would *never* willingly stoop so low as to honor such a loathsome, disgusting creature.

Ahaz was utterly furious I refused to oblige him and do as he had ordered. And he set about correcting that situation as soon as we arrived back at the house. He collected the strap, a switch and wooden paddle and proceeded to beat the daylights out of me.

I held my chin high and refused to break; refused to give him the pleasure of screaming. I gritted my teeth together and took it for as long as I could, acting like it didn't hurt. This made him even angrier, and he hit even harder, putting his all behind it and doing everything he could to hurt me as much as possible until I couldn't stop the screams from tearing out from my throat any longer.

Now that... delighted him. I could see his satisfaction, feel his excitement from it. But that did not slow him down; naturally he persisted, still swinging with all his strength. I lost my inward fight and tried to run from him; he grabbed my upper arm and yanked me back hard enough to bruise from his fingers. While struggling to hold me in place, he reached for and changed out his choice of beating tool before continuing.

On and on and on it went, until he was nearly worn out. Stopping, sweating, and breathing hard, he demanded that I call him father, insisted that I respect him. He ordered me to say, "I love you, father," to which I refused. I would not lie... so after he stood there panting for a bit, on it went until he stopped again to see if I was ready to give in.

He also kept telling me to look him in the eyes when he spoke to me, but I would not give him the satisfaction; the mere thought of it made my stomach roll.

"Normal people don't refuse to look in their fathers' eyes," he said. "Normal people follow the directions of their father without question. Normal people respect their father. Normal people are grateful to their father for correcting them... say 'Thank you, father,' to me right now... You aren't acting the way a normal person acts." Not normal... not normal... not normal... I had heard that nearly every single painful day of my life.

I told him disdainfully that he could *never* force me to call him that. That I hated him, and I reminded him that anywhere I had to be with him would *never* ever be my home. That one day in just a few years, I would be far away, free and he would *never* be able to hurt me ever again.

This increased his rage instantly, his face was beet red, and he continued to strike me with a serious amount of force, changing out his weapon of choice again. He yelled that this place was my home and would always my home, that he was my father and would be treated as such. He was a doctor, a Mennonite... a head of household and demanded only the upmost respect... he was going to 'correct' and 'discipline' me until I broke, until I gave in. Until I *believed* it, he said. Until I did every little thing he wished without a word of question; and did it with an obedient smile on my face.

He kept stopping because he'd never handled physical exertion well, and he always had to have his breaks here and there. But per the typical, Ahaz wound up beating me until I could barely move. The door was closed this time, but I could hear my sibling's laughter off and on, clearly amused from my screams, along with the whacking sounds. There was no one and nothing to stop him...

Should I simply have done as he said? Heck to the no. I would happily show respect to honorable men and woman, toward respectable people such as my beloved grandpa, but *never* to Ahaz. He was not deserving of respect, and I had to stay true to myself, to my beliefs, and not allow myself to be forced into lying yet again. It was incredibly difficult., because staying strong meant intense added suffering.

But truly when it came down to it, if I had given in, he still would have come up with random reasons to beat and rape me for his sadistic pleasure no matter what. Which was something he often did, anyway. Not normal... not normal.

"If you have nothing nice to say, don't say anything at all."

This rule had been whipped, and later beat into me from the time I was a tiny girl. It sounded like a great rule that many kids are asked to follow, but it meant so much more to Ahaz. To him, it *didn't* mean to be polite as it was phrased, but the true meaning was to *lie*. To blend in. To not even have thoughts except for those of cheerfully blind, unquestioning obedience.

To him, it meant that I wasn't even allowed to have an opinion, even if I said it nicely. It meant that I couldn't say anything that sounded more intelligent than him. It meant I wasn't allowed to be creative, because any form of creativity must simply be a lie; I couldn't possibly be naturally creative, as a mere female. It meant if I was asked a question and I answered honestly, I'd be beat.

Ahaz never wanted anyone to catch even a hint of how miserable things were in that house. We were one big, happy family according to him; perhaps in some part of his mind, he truly believed that amid all his insanity. Mom would be punished by him if she didn't smile enough or talk just the way he wished for her to in public.

What happy family? My mom was miserable and obviously depressed. She was a worn-down woman at the hands of Ahaz and hated being Mennonite. Suicidal herself, for being trapped and quietly abused behind closed doors.

Ahaz clearly wasn't happy that he couldn't force me, his supposed-to-be-normal- robot, to work the way he wished it to be wired, as easily as he could force my mom. But then again, he got such an immense amount of pleasure out of beating me weak that I am sure he wasn't nearly as unhappy about it as he put on. I was his outlet. I was a little girl, sacrificed to that monster. I was just the girl called not normal.

I utterly hated being trapped there with that horrid man and not being permitted a single independent thought. I hated being hurt, being worked intensely, hated the Holdeman Mennonites rules that simply didn't make logical sense. I hated how Ahaz forced part of his body into mine. I hated how my siblings joined together to mock me, hated how I was an outcaste my whole life. I just wanted to be free. I wanted to fit in, somewhere, with other strong people, learning how the world ticks in every way.

When I tried to seek help from multiple trusted members in the community, I was told that people 'knew' I wasn't telling the truth because I would avoid eye contact during a tense situation; for example, talking about anything that made me uncomfortable, feel attacked or hopeless as to what to say because the truth was never believed, so what was the point of continuing to converse at all if others had already made their mind up? With truth supposedly most easily judged by fierce eye contact without looking away even for a mere instant, I was screwed.

Facing someone's eyes straight on meant possibly seeing the shameful truth of my own agony reflected within their own. Eyes are the windows to the soul, or so it is said.

The lack of eye contact was pointed out many times, the most memorable times coming from Maximus. Yet I actually looked up to him as a strong person; as someone I wanted to be like. He wasn't just a Holdeman Mennonite, he was smart, too. Even though he didn't understand what I was trying to tell him. Even though he'd act like I wasn't being completely truthful when I tried to explain how I was being 'whipped'. He just told me that all kids get spankings and pressed me to understand that I was overexaggerating which just made me give up in trying to find further words to explain the shameful things being done to me.

Maximus told me I was very intelligent, and he was one of those rare ones, like grandpa, that truly believed I *didn't* have to be a Mennonite to be a Christian and go to heaven. He said I was capable of doing anything I wished to in life. He said I could get my G.E.D. after I turned eighteen and I could even go to college. But I didn't *want* a G.E.D; I wanted to go to attend high school. I wanted to have a real chance at a real education, right then. I felt that eighteen was far too late when *I had to know everything about the world right then.*

That was the most frustrating part about talking to him, because I *needed* help to get out, to be free of the horrible 'whippings', sexual abuse and the pure insanity surrounding me. I *needed* an education. And the only way for all that to happen, was to get out. To find my own path to freedom.

Maximus also explained bipolar to me more, the same as my mom had. By now I believed it, too, with so many saying it. I could be happy and smiling one moment and then the next, refusing eye contact and crying, or outraged and fighting back the injustices being done to me.

I must be bipolar; that must be it. Something was wrong with me. From the dizzy spells to the severe stomach pain, to something being wrong with my ears at times, to the

221

whippings, to how Ahaz treated me; I must be overexaggerating. I must not be seeing things clearly because I was being told that being bipolar meant I didn't have all the proper chemicals in my brain to stabilize my emotions. That's why I was so depressed, anorexic and even wanted to die.

That's why no one else who witnessed me being hurt wouldn't help and merely laughed or ignored my pain; I wasn't being abused. He had the right to hurt me. Even though I knew he didn't; I knew that something was terribly, horribly wrong with it all. He *couldn't* do those things to me, surely. But no one could seem to understand how much pain I was in; how desperately I needed help. It made my head spin in confusion; that must be the bipolar effect, right? Was I insane? I must be insane, because only I could see what was being done.

At the same time, I *knew* my pain and torment came directly from Ahaz. From my mom, for refusing to leave and make my agony end. From the Mennonites, some of whom were encouraging my abuse. Most especially the deacon, whom Ahaz talked to frequently about how to get me under control and reported back to me all the dreadful suggestions for upping my pain level the deacon had. Like whipping me until I broke and submitted to his will and fell in line with the 'right path'.

I thought people must surely be able to *see* what was being done to me; and see how terrible I was; 'not normal', beat, raped and hurt so terribly. It made me feel as though I was a horrible, dirty piece of trash, in spite of also knowing that I wasn't. I knew I was worth more than that, but I was just a girl, born into the great big free United States of America; yet tossed about without any consideration of my rights to freedom from pain. Of choice. I was nothing and no one. The words I spoke held no power, no weight; my voice had no sound. Not normal... not normal.

Chapter Seventeen

2004, Age 15

At the tender age of fifteen, I was now old enough to, and *expected* to join the youth group. They'd get together about once a week to sing hymns, play volleyball, or eat supper together, and they were strictly overseen by two married couples.

No dating, courting or anything even remotely resembling it was permitted at all, no hand holding, and most definitely no two of the opposite sex wandering off to quietly speak alone as such things were forbidden.

I didn't enjoy going to the youth group; I felt out of place, with no sense of belonging there. I was self-conscious and would feel nauseous as I wondered if they could see how different I was, how bruised and broken in spite of the outwardly strong, sarcastic cover I put on to try to hide it. Disdainful, even. How could they laugh and giggle so innocently, when horrible things were happening?

I did go to those groups with my older sister for a bit, just to escape that house and win a few moments of false freedom. But eventually the pain of doing such simple things as singing hymens to a god who never stopped my monster became too much, and I stopped going. Everything felt so fake and pointless.

Ahaz said that as a youth now, I was allowed to go more places. It was common practice among the Mennonites for the youth to travel frequently amongst other congregations. For the males, it was to find their bride of choice. For the females, this was to increase their chance of being seen by a potential husband who might pick them. Especially since as a female, they would become an 'old maid' at the mere age of twenty, so being seen was important.

I got to go see a pen pal of mine named Trista at the Murray, KY congregation for a few glorious days. We used decorative rubber stamps and ink to make cute handmade cards, and I very much enjoyed getting to hang out with her. She was far more willing to discuss exploring worldly things with me, unlike most of the other Mennonites.

While I was there, I spent a lot of time talking to Trista's mom, Jessica. I told her some about what I was going through, but since I described things with using words like 'whipped' and complaining about a lack of education, it didn't get me very far with a Mennonite.

Jessica talked to me about something called Manic Depressive Disorder, and said she believed I just might have it. This was based off of my depression and she asked if I was disassociating and thinking things had happened that actually hadn't. And no, she was not a health care professional by any means; Jessica was a housewife who had been diagnosed with that exact same disorder. She quite nearly convinced me that perhaps I had it, on top of being bipolar. Was I crazy?

After that conversation, which she also talked about to my mom, it only made it easier for Ahaz to spread the word around that I was 'mentally ill', and those in the Muddy Pond community seemed to eat it up without question.

My sister and I were permitted to ride with my elder minister grandpa and his sweet wife to a neighboring congregation in Fountain Run, Kentucky, to a wedding. It was quite near to Tompkinsville where I had grown up, only about a twenty-minute drive away.

The distance between the two towns was actually the only reason I wished to go in the first place. I contemplated on running away to my grandparents while I was so near to them; but I had never forgotten how they didn't want me, back when they had gotten custody of Thomas. I knew they wouldn't be able to help me.

I had to great other female members of those congregations, and others that I went to, with The Holy Kiss. Lips to lips with complete and utter strangers, from young girls to teens and women of all ages. It made me feel quite anxious, but I *had to* kiss them; couldn't shy away from it. It was all a part of the facade of a life I was forced into living. Yes, I had willingly joined even knowing I'd be required to participate in such an act, in the hopes being a Mennonite would stop Ahaz from hurting me. But it hadn't. And I hated the kissing.

One day, my mom took me, Sarah and little Alex to eat at the Cracker Barrel in Cookeville. Only there was a big surprise waiting for us; Nana and my mom's sister, Aunt Mandy were there to meet us! Sarah and I were sworn to absolute secrecy, and we all had a long, delightful lunch.

I was so relieved to see them, and this gave me a glimmer of hope that perhaps mom was getting back on track to getting us out of there. Maybe there was still a chance that we could be free.

Nana always had to be a joker, and she told me in front of everyone that I needed an underwire bra to 'lift and separate' my boobs. She made graphic movements in front of her chest as an example. Everyone laughed and I did too a bit, but I was also very embarrassed. She gave me a pull over sweater, and I put it on right away, excited to have it.

I asked for them to please take me with them and said how much I hated being trapped as a Mennonite, especially with that horrid Ahaz. Nana of course was helpless to do anything to help, but she did pull out her camera and snapped a few quick photos of each of us. She said that she'd keep them, and when I was able to get out, she'd give mine to me. Nana of course knew we weren't allowed to have our pictures taken.

On another incredible day, a top-secret meeting was arranged, only this time it was between Thomas, Sarah and I at the Burger King in Monterey. He was now eighteen years old, and he'd requested that my Grams set the whole thing up quietly. Part of the deal was that mom had to drop my sis and I off; mom couldn't go inside of the restaurant or Thomas would leave immediately.

The conversation was kept pretty simple and was a bit awkward. So much had happened in the six years since we'd seen each other, and our lives were so vastly different, it was difficult to know quite what to say. Not to mention remembering the last day I had seen my brother. He seemed quite nice now, and all grown up. I wished that he'd take me back with him, but he couldn't. Thomas told me to hang on, because I would soon be old enough to leave.

Joyce, Sarah, me and just a couple others met in the church basement once to work on a quilt. Joyce's older sister who was excommunicated, worldly and under the avoidance met us there, and she kindly snapped a picture. She said I'd want it one day, and she was right.

The two pictures taken that year were the only ones taken since I was nine years old. Aside from random tourist strangers whom I was certain had pics of me, especially from when I'd been on the playground while in school.

All those secret meetings made me long for my freedom even more. I was staying up even later at night, pouring over my priceless books full of knowledge. I learned about everything from ballet dancers to Lipizzan horses, about wars and the Holocaust, worldly birthday parties, alcohol, drugs, other countries, and most importantly about love. Of both loving relationships, and loving families. Families where there was no beating, no terrible abuse, and where dancing & singing along to the radio was a supposedly frequent event.

I learned about the kids who could go to big schools & had bright futures with real education, and even college. I read about murder, mysteries, & dating. When I came across words in books I did not understand, I used the dictionary to find out what they were. I even read the old encyclopedia's that were on the living room bookshelf when I ran low on library books. I simply *had* to learn and soak up everything I could since no one else was going to teach me.

Outside of the books and trips to the worldly grocery store, I really had very little idea of how the real world worked. How people interacted with each other when there were so many things to discuss other than what dress, or quilt they planned to sew next, or what new recipe they'd found. I wondered how they even had relationships, and how the interworking of dating really happened in real life. I wondered what worldly friendships looked like, and if it was just the way it happened in books.

I wondered if worldly people took all their freedoms for granted or if they relished every single moment of every single day, reveling in their freedom of speech, of thought, of movement, of choices. I imagined that it must be absolutely amazing to live a life outside of the one I had been raised trapped within. I was an adventurer at heart, forced to live a painful existence.

I carefully calculated the exact number of days left until my eighteenth birthday, and it was a depressing length of time away. I started to mark every single day on my wall calendar with a countdown number, so when I felt the worst, I'd easily be able to check how many days were left and repeat that number to myself as a comfort. Only it didn't turn out to be comforting; the number of days were far too many and I wasn't sure if I could hang on that long.

Shortly after I'd done that, while Ahaz was beating me and claiming that I was his to do with as he pleased, I pointed at the calendar and screamed out that I hated him and told him exactly how many days were left until I was free from both him and the Mennonites *forever*. I told him I was going to leave at midnight on my freedom birthday and there wouldn't be a single thing he could do to stop me.

It infuriated him as I knew it would, and he beat my body harder and yelled at me that I was not normal, disrespectful, and had no right to say such things. I'd known saying that would make it harder on my body, but in my mind, it was worth it. Because I was proving that he would soon be powerless over me, and I felt as though I was fighting back by speaking *the truth*.

But with every beating, every rape, every time someone didn't believe what was being done to me, a little more of what made me into being me was being shaved away bit by bit. As much as I wanted to live to the ripe age of eighteen; I also wanted to die. I wanted for the pain to end.

It felt like I was suffocating, and I couldn't escape it no matter how hard I tried to. My birthday was so incredibly far away, I didn't know if I could suffer through and live for that long or not. The pain was too raw, too deep, too horrifying, too real.

Sometimes in the quiet of the night, the intense pain would be stronger than I felt I could bear. I had to get out of there, that house, that room, and I did just that. I'd slide open one of my windows and sneak outside. I'd lay on the trampoline and stargaze at the vast sky above me and dream of what it would be like to go into outer space. Or I'd take a walk down my favorite, well-worn trail in the woods and think about what it would be like to never have to go back. Eventually within an hour or so, I'd head back and slip back inside through my window.

At some point, it was realized that I was leaving some nights, and Ahaz accused me of running away. How was it possible for someone to be running away, when I was coming back each time and was only gone for brief periods of time? The truth was irrelevant to him though, and he wouldn't listen to reason.

Soon after that, my mom took me to Cookeville for groceries and when we got back, I headed straight my bedroom to curl up with a book. As soon as I touched my doorknob, I realized right away that it was a different shape in my hand. Looking down, I saw that this one had a key turn lock on the *outside,* facing into the hallway.

I went into a panicked, hopeless, angry rage out of pure fear and helplessness; I had to get the feelings out of me somehow. I entered my room and grabbed some of the beautiful things that had been gifted to me at my graduation from my hope chest and smashed them against the wall viciously.

I had no idea how to otherwise express my feelings of trapped, powerless rage and hopelessness. What I was doing was merely a futile, outward example of my inward turmoil. Mom was shocked at my outraged screams and the sounds of forceful breaking of things, and she yelled out for me to stop, but I couldn't. Instead, I ran to the kitchen and grabbed a knife.

In that moment, most of all I wanted to kill Ahaz. He'd came running when the screaming started and was edging near to me with arms held out, acting as though he was going to try to restrain me. I also I wanted to kill myself because I felt like a caged animal. Instead of doing either of those things, I scared the top of the kitchen counter with the knife while mom and my siblings screamed out in horror.

Ahaz yelled at me to not do that, and he said normal people do not act that way. He said he'd changed the lock on my door and also put alarms on my windows so I couldn't run away, because my rightful place was there with my 'loving family'. Ahaz claimed that he had to make sure I stayed where I was supposed to; he said he was doing it for my own good.

Even more strongly then, did I wish to kill him. My windows having alarms on them would make me truly trapped. Only I didn't actually have it within me to attempt to harm him, mostly due to fear of what he'd do to make my life even more painful; but I *could* take his own power away by breaking things.

I ran past them all and into my room with the knife still in hand and smashed some more pretty, delicate things against my walls while my shocked siblings snickered, and my mom cried loudly. Ahaz called the police to tell them I was completely out of control.

An officer came and tried to talk to me, but I *couldn't* talk back; I just sobbed instead, hot tears of panic streaming down my cheeks. Couldn't he see the lock on the door was on the wrong side? Couldn't he see that I was damaged and not simply an unruly girl? Couldn't he free me?

Instead, the officer took the knife from me and talked to me about Juvenile Detention, where destructive, disruptive delinquent teenaged girls go. He told me that it wasn't a place a nice little girl like myself wanted to be, that I needed to do as I was told, and not destroy property.

After the policeman left, Ahaz beat me dreadfully for having dared to harm his property, including my own. He told me, as he commonly did, that even my own things were all his; he owned everything inside of that house, including me.

Before he finally left me beaten and broken on the floor, he first checked that each of the window alarms were working, then he locked the door on his way out. That was the first night I was locked in; the first night I felt panicked, trapped and fearful of the sound of a key slipping in a lock.

Ahaz used this situation to spread around that I was 'running away' at night, and when he had kindly tried to protect me by changing a simple lock on the door to keep me safe, I shockingly destroyed his property. The accusations of being bipolar, unruly, and manic depressive were looking even more true to those in the Mennonite community. And even among my siblings who also believed that I was mentally ill, a troubled teen from a 'loving family' with no reason to act in such a way. Not normal... not normal...

Every night from then on, I was kept locked up inside my bedroom. As well as off and on at times during the days when Ahaz wanted to make a point that I had no personal freedom; that he controlled me in full. Sometimes I had to pee when I was locked in, and since no one would answer my fists pounding on the door and yells I needed out, I started keeping a couple of cups in my room to use for those times.

Each moment, day, week, month and year seemed to drag on forever. Trapped between being incredibly restricted, forced to play mind games, raped and beaten with an increasing frequency and now frequently caged within my own bedroom on top of it all. It was a relentless nightmare from which I could never wake. During the night, he haunted my dreams. During the light of day, being forced to be even remotely near Ahaz was far too intolerable to stand.

Maximus came by to see me one day when I was incredibly depressed. When he pulled up in the driveway, I made a beeline straight for his car and hoped right into the passenger seat. I was crying and desperate for help. It seemed no one could help me, but I thought perhaps if anyone would, it would be him.

He did most of the talking at first, asking what was going on and how he could help me. I managed to choke out that Ahaz was 'whipping' me horribly, and that he'd do it for hours on end, even for an entire day, at times.

Maximus asked if I was actually sure that was what happening, but he asked it in more of a way that suggested there was no way it could be true. I said yes and started to explain that Ahaz took breaks. He cut me off at that point, preventing me from explaining this more. He stated that it was literally, physically impossible for anyone to whip someone for hours; I must be overexaggerating and making something seem worse than what it was.

When I told him that I was being locked into my bedroom at night and sometimes during the day, he said that was for my own safety. He made it out to seem acceptable, allowable, just the same as Ahaz, mom and everyone else I told did.

My tears continued to fall, and my nose began to run from it, too. He wouldn't believe me nor allow me to fully explain, and I gave up. There was no help to be had; not from him, at least. I had no voice; no power; I was just left to live with the pain swirling round within my mind, the evidence of which was clearly marked across my body.

I was so confused by this point, even I continually questioned if I was just a horrible kid who was simply being 'properly disciplined'. Did I even, indeed, deserve to be locked up for taking short walks after dark? I only desired fresh air and to soothe my mind during them, why did Ahaz continue to call me a runaway for such a simple thing he refused to listen to?

With so many around me telling me repeatedly that I wasn't being abused... wasn't I? My head spun with the craziness of it all; I knew it was all reality. I wasn't crazy, and I wasn't hallucinating. But why didn't anyone else see it? Why did they hide it, seemingly from both themselves and from everyone else? From me, even, odd though it was. It was incredibly confusing.

I hated myself for not being able to stop him. For not being stronger. No matter how many exercises I did, I was never strong enough nor fast enough. I wanted to kill him; to put my fingers through his eye sockets straight to his brain, beat his head with a rock until it was bloody & completely pulverized. Or shoot his body 100 times over with a gun or bow & arrows; I wasn't picky. I fantasized about all the ways he could die, but I couldn't do it myself. Fear paralyzed me and made me weak.

Ahaz made it clear so many times that I was only born to serve first him, and later on, a husband of his own choice. As a mere female, I had no freedom. My thoughts and words held no real meaning; only an adult male's words did.

Not normal... I couldn't escape the words from resounding in my head amid the immense loneliness I felt, the severe depression, and the suicidal thoughts. Not normal; for refusing to thank my abuser for abusing me. Not normal; for happily clinging to the hope that he would soon die. Not normal; for being depressed, for refusing to eat much more than was barely necessary to survive. Not normal; for asking, begging, pleading, reasoning & demanding to continue my education. Not normal; for wanting to have a radio, wear my hair down, wear pants, jewelry, makeup, nor for wishing to go to my first movie theater. Not normal; for not releveling in the joy of having been granted such a happy family.

Ahaz was convinced he was going to heaven and that he was a devoted Christian. He seemed to truly believe that, and that he was beating and raping the devil out of me somehow. He fooled so many into believing that he was so godly.

He didn't touch the other kids, not like he did me. He didn't beat them ever, not to my knowledge at least. He did whip the boys at times. But it was minor, and to all my knowledge, it never lasted long.

The dizzy spells I was having continued, most commonly lasting for hours at a time. The world spun round and round until I wasn't sure if I was the one spinning, or if everything surrounding me was spinning. Everything moved in circles; I couldn't focus on anything. It was incredibly overwhelming, sickening. Ahaz said I was a liar; he said there was nothing wrong with me and ordered me to stop acting like I wasn't 'normal'.

He'd beat & rape me even during the episodes. I wasn't able to fight back- the strength simply wasn't within my body. I could hardly walk, much less struggle to make him stop. So weak... spinning... the pain didn't feel quite so bad during it all, at least, seemed more surreal, nearly like a dream somehow. Only it wasn't a dream, it was reality. My reality that I was forced to live through and endure.

I was hiding as much as possible in the woods and started wearing sweaters even when it was too warm for anyone else to wear one. It made me feel safer, to have that extra bit of fabric wrapped around me. Comforted. But that was, per usual, 'not normal' and I'd be beat for that, too.

Strange how something so simple could result in such beatings. He had to keep the cruelty going, though. Maximum pain for up to hours at a time, without actually breaking my bones.

The mere thought of me possessing natural problem-solving skills was completely intolerable, unacceptable, and 'not normal'. Ahaz would beat me on and on while demanding to know the truth of *where* I had learned whatever intelligent, creative thing I'd said.

I attempted reasoning with him, explaining that whatever it was had just popped into my head. I'd ask if he *wanted* me to lie to him and willingly offered to go ahead and lie if he so wished it, just as long as he knew it was a falsehood, I figured that would not technically make it into a lie. But this, as well was unacceptable and increased his own fury to the point he was absolutely livid.

Eventually, after refusing to lie for as long as I could bear, I gave in to the pain and exhaustion and would come up with a plausible lie. For example, I'd claim I heard it from my best friend Joyce or read it in a library book. He would beat me even longer then, for having held out so long. Even telling the lies he demanded from me could not actually stop him.

Ahaz still had me copying good behavior and proper discipline books for hours at a time, mostly when he had to see patients and wanted to make sure I didn't have time to relax, or late in the evenings. He also started forcing me to stand with my nose to the refrigerator for hours. But since I was a strong-minded girl, not a mindless minion, I always fought every step of the way in everything until he'd beat me near senseless. When I'd finally give in and do as he demanded, he'd smile a disgusting smile as though he had won.

I repeated to myself frequently that giving in for self-preservation reasons was *not* betraying myself nor my basic human rights I was fighting for. He never won my mind, never quite conquered my soul, never 'broke' me in full in spite of his incredible efforts to do so. Or so I thought. I had no idea how truly broken I even was.

When mom would let me go out to the grocery store with her, it was becoming harder to go with her. I now cowered because of the shame I felt ran so deep. I tried to keep my chin up high and not show it, but I was dying inside. Every trip out into the 'real world' brought stares; the stares which I had endured all my life.

Curious, disdainful stares, even out the corner of their eye stares, happy stares, even uncaring glances. And then there were those who ignored me out of disgust for how I was dressed. I wanted to scream at those worldly people that I was truly one with the world, I was merely forced into being a Mennonite. I inwardly begged them not to stare, but to instead see me for who I truly was.

I also hoped that somehow, someone would see the horrors in my eyes and come to my rescue. Yet I knew it didn't work as easily as that, and I knew better than to run up to strangers and try to quickly tell them what was being done to me, when others who *did* know me, didn't even attempt to protect me when I'd told. But I thought about it.

Mom *finally* stepped up and went to the ministers several times about what was being done to me. She did this without me knowing until after. She told them things like he was whipping me too hard, for too long, being overly cruel and locking me in.

When Ahaz was questioned about my treatment by my grandpa and other Holdeman Mennonites, he'd talked in long circles about how important discipline was, and how unruly I was for refusing to fall into my rightful place. He pointed out again that I was 'troubled, a runaway and mentally ill'. He said that both my mom and I were over exaggerating, and eventually out of fear for herself, even mom would give up and agree that yes, she must have misunderstood the situation.

Instead of reporting the abuse to true authorities, the ministers decided to believe Ahaz each time. In spite of what I'd been saying, and in spite of even my mom going to them. Could they not see we were obviously under distress?

I was drowning, suffocating, wrapped up in everything that was happening, and no one could stand against him. Not normal... not normal.

Chapter Eighteen

2005, Age 16

The feelings of hopelessness were becoming more overwhelming. I felt trapped, caged and terrified, especially at night when I was locked in. Suicide was looking better and better, but I clung to thoughts of my eighteen birthday and of beating Ahaz at his own game by making it until then and going on to be strong, free and worldly. His treatment of me was turning me into someone I had not been born to be; powerless, pain filled, anxious, fearful and I lashed out due to it.

In summer, my sister stayed home to do housework as usual. I'd be in the garden/ greenhouse weeding away many days, skin sliding off my hands from blisters and eventually toughening into thick callouses. Year round, it was the greenhouses. Winter I hated most of all. I was so terribly cold, and it was only slightly warmer within those plastic walls than outside of them.

My bare legs felt frozen, my skin red and chapped. But I wasn't allowed to put pants on as a barrier from the cold ground, and a thin dress did little to protect me. My fingers would go numb from trying to dig in the cold dirt, and I broke fingernails to the quick, like it was going out of style. I was his personal slave.

It got to the point that I didn't even want to go out to the farm to ride Wish, nor see Butter who had been moved out there as well. I even started completely refusing to go at all, for which Ahaz beat me for dreadfully. Painfully. He tried to lure me there with promises of being able to ride my beauties. Some days I let him beat me until I couldn't hardly walk just so he wouldn't force me there. Other days he'd stop short of that, drag me to the van and push me in then take me there.

On the days when he'd eventually give up on making me go, once I had gained enough strength to move, I'd slide down the top of one of my windows since my door would commonly be locked after such an incident. No one else knew the tops of my windows slid down, and there were only alarms on the bottom part of them. I'd stumble around the back of the house, go into the woods and find my favorite spot to cry. I reminded myself of how many days there were left over and over, and told myself it wasn't so far away now, even though it felt like a lifetime.

I'd sneak back the same way I'd gotten out before Ahaz got back from the farm or anyone bothered to realize I was gone. Getting back in was harder, but the stump I had placed under one window long ago for the cats to use to get in and out of my bedroom was still there, and of great help.

I cut my skin with my own fingernails from the anguish within, some of the cuts were actually deep enough to leave permanent scars. Arms, legs, stomach, wherever. Ahaz hated when I did that, because that didn't fit in with his perfect idea of a flawless, obedient, normal robot. Also, because some of them would be visible to anyone especially on my arms if I didn't cover up, which ruined the illusion of what he wanted.

I was accused of attention seeking due to the self-harming. As for Ahaz and the Holdeman Mennonites that said it, they were not entirely incorrect. Although I was cutting myself due to the inward pain, I *did* want people to know and *see* that I was in agony. I *wanted* for someone to hear, to understand my cries for help. I was also told I was attention seeking with the anorexia, too, but in all truthfulness, it was a very real eating disorder that I had. I couldn't make it stop; didn't even know how, much less had the strength left to fight it. I was broken... so much more broken than I was even aware of.

Not normal... not normal. I needed to get out. Needed to escape; needed my freedom. How could no one see? How could they all think me merely unruly and ill; I *needed* for everyone to *see*. I needed *help*. How could the Mennonites even think that I was ok, when even my body language was growing more fearful, especially around Ahaz.

There came a brief, wonderful interlude to it all. My pen pal, Trista and her family were going to Miami, Florida for two weeks. They were seeking medical treatment for their daughter Trista there, for a long-term condition and wanted me to go with them to support her through it.

Somehow, someway, with a combo of both of Trista's parents, and my dear elder minister grandpa, they talked Ahaz into allowing me to go with. I was so excited and felt so free, and I felt as though I could finally be me while I was there. It was a wonderful experience, and when we weren't at the treatment facility, we were exploring the mall, going to the beach and swimming in the hotel pool. I was so free, at least for a little while.

The mom, Jessica, actually asked me at one point if I was being abused by Ahaz. She specifically asked if I was being raped and used that exact word. I guess my body language was throwing off enough clues by that point, along with the little ways I tried to let people know, that somehow, she or grandpa had finally picked up on it and conspired together.

Jessica promised she could try to get me out if that was the case, said that her and grandpa could talk to Ahaz and convince him to let me go live with a different Holdeman Mennonite family in another congregation, at least for a little while. But that didn't sound like a lot of help to me.

I hesitated and nearly told, but I knew there was no way I'd be safe from him simply in another Mennonite house. I knew that Ahaz would never allow it, anyway, to have his plaything taken away permanently. He'd beat me terribly if I told the truth, then he'd convince them otherwise and I'd still be trapped, this time with even less hope. So, I said no.

Grandpa wound up asking me as well and promised me the same thing Jessica had; that he'd try to convince Ahaz into letting me live elsewhere. But when he did, I told him no, too.

I couldn't say it; I couldn't tell; they couldn't help me. I knew they would never report it to the police or The Department of Children Services because that would mean I'd be taken and put into a worldly home, which would have been an unacceptable thought to them. I was on my own, and just had to make it a little over another year until freedom.

Shortly after they had asked me, came a day on which I had been both beaten and raped; their offer was my first thought. I was shaking, barely able to dial the right numbers once I had got ahold of the phone. I called first grandpa, then Jessica. I tried to tell them each, 'You know that thing you asked before? It's true, Ahaz has been raping me, I'm sorry I couldn't tell you before. Can you help get me out'?

I thought they'd help me now, since they had, indeed asked me first, strangely enough. Even if it was at the risk of Ahaz not letting me go, at least they could try. But that isn't what happened, in fact, they no longer wanted to hear it. My mouth made the words, but they did not care. Since I'd said no the first time, they believed I was now lying. They both told me if it had been true, I would have jumped at the chance to say so the first time. A liar... not normal, not normal.

I began trying to desperately make it all make sense in my head. The truth mattered to no one, I was nothing, I was trapped, all rights stripped from me. I began to pretend I had a secret boyfriend, and even left tidbit 'clues' in my journal because I knew Ahaz would see it and it would infuriate him that he was not the only person that could touch me. I wanted to take his power away, and I also thought that if he thought someone had touched me, it might disgust him enough to never rape me again.

In the journal, I wrote that I had snuck out and went to a worldly party. While there, I got dizzy, fell asleep and woke up with blood between my legs. I wrote that to make Ahaz angry on purpose, to 'prove' I was my own person. But I was actually talking about him, and how Ahaz raped me frequently. On some level even then, I suspected I was being drugged, just did not fully comprehend it.

Of course, Ahaz and mom read it because they read everything I wrote in my journals, in addition to opening and reading any mail I sent out to my pen pal or received.

Ahaz was furious and he beat me for hours on end, then raped me savagely. Yet in my mind, I still thought that I was the one winning somehow, because I thought that I had proved that I was more powerful, unstoppable and stronger than him because I was making *him* feel powerless to not be the only one able to touch me.

I even told him that I could and would have sex with anyone I wanted. In fact, I *did* want to. I *wanted* to know what it was like to not be raped. I *wanted* to have the right, the choice, the option to have a boyfriend. I didn't even have worldly teen girlfriends much less anyone to date, but I sure continued to pretend I did once I saw how furious it made him.

I know it may not make a lot of sense as to why I did that, but you see... I was so deeply messed up by that point, I was grasping at straws. Yes, I provoked him on purpose, because I thought that was what not giving up without a fight was. I thought that was the only way my helpless self could have any power. I was not an animal; I was an independent woman, and I would be free no matter what it took. I was born in the land of the free, with the right to education and to not be abused. The land where woman had fought and won the right to vote, to wear pants, to not be mere objects for male satisfaction. I *had* to be a part of that world. I was *not nothing.*

Mom pregnancy tested me after that journal entry, made me pee in a cup. But I wasn't pregnant. Ahaz pretty much always put a condom on his appendage before attacking me, and I had read in books that this was a form of pregnancy prevention. This also would have also reduced the amount of evidence.

That evening mom insisted on taking both Sarah and I into town to the DQ in Monterey for blizzards. I hardly ever got such a treat, and should have been excited, but something was wrong; something bad was going on. Mom didn't seem quite right, and her words seemed forced. Her face was drawn, and she looked as though she had been crying.

I looked over at Sarah who was giggling and smirking by the front door, where she was standing beside mom, and I felt a wave of horror come over me. I didn't want to leave the house, but mom insisted that I had to, so I followed them out the front door and off we went. Once there, we went inside the restaurant and I ordered my favorite, a Reese's blizzard, and we stayed to eat it at a table at mom's insistence. I could barely eat the ice-cream. My sister kept that ridiculous grin on her face, that 'I know something you don't' look, and wouldn't tell me anything, nor would mom. I felt sick and anxious.

When we arrived back at the house, as soon as I walked in it was obvious something had happened. Travis was laughing in the living room, and Sarah was now openly, wildly laughing as well. Mom looked even more pale, and Ahaz was standing in the short hallway holding a drill grinning from ear to ear. He moved out into the living room as I panicked, not knowing what was happening and I made a dash for my bedroom; only to find that there was now a deadbolt on the door. This was no twist turn lock, it had a keyhole on each side, in and out. The horror within me rose.

I felt incredibly trapped and sick but for some reason I still went through that bedroom doorway, feeling hopeless and not knowing quite what to do. As soon as I was within the room, Ahaz locked it. I broke the few trinkets I had left, slamming them against the wall with a resounding smashing sound as the delicate bits cut into the wallpaper and left marks. I screamed, and screamed, and screamed... I felt like I was suffocating.

I soon realized that Ahaz had also nailed the bottom of both my windows shut, because he thought I had got out through the lower part in spite of the alarms. But I still knew something he didn't; that the top half of my windows slid down.

A few nights later after he'd beat me dreadfully, I climbed out the top of one of the windows. I wandered down the road, walking slowing and breathing in the clear night air, dreaming of freedom. The road was little traveled that late, so I didn't expect anyone to see me. I didn't want to go back but eventually I turned around, knowing if I got caught out, I'd be in deeper trouble than it was worth.

As soon as I was back within sight of the house but not quite there, a police car pulled up alongside me and stopped me. He asked how old I was, where I lived, and what I was doing out so late. I pointed to the house but was too scared to talk and went into full blown panic inside myself. I knew that now I was completely screwed for sure; Ahaz was about to find out that the top of my windows slid down, and I'd be 100% trapped if that happened.

The officer got out of the car when I wouldn't talk to him, and that's when he noticed the terrible bruise on my face, that covered nearly all of one side. I could hear the alarm in his voice as he asked what happened to cause that, but I couldn't tell him. I knew he'd never be able to save me, never be able to make it stop or get me free from the clutches of Ahaz, it would all just be covered up yet again.

"I fell." Was all I told the cop and I didn't even bother to make up where it had happened.

He looked down the way at the clearly one- level house, back at me and asked if I was sure that was what had happened, because he didn't believe me.

Again, "I fell," was the only thing I would say. I didn't even attempt to make it sound believable, because I felt as though it didn't matter anyway. Everything was pointless. I felt as though I was hopelessly trapped and left to endure alone until I was eighteen, after so many had failed me. The truth didn't matter anymore; no one could help me.

Then the officer told me to get into the back of his car, which I did. After he'd shut me in, he got into the front driver's seat and told me he could help me, but he couldn't do anything if I didn't tell him the truth.

But all the beatings from Ahaz, and blind eyes from others proved to me that the truth didn't even matter; none of it mattered. If I dared to tell, it wouldn't get better, it would get far worse for having dared to try; of that I was convinced. I couldn't escape my fate by telling this nice man, a complete stranger.

He sighed, put the car in gear and pulled into the driveway of that horrid house. The officer stayed there in the car with me for just a few minutes, asking again who had put the bruises on me, but still, I would only respond that I had fell.

I *knew* that the cop knew something was wrong; just as much as I knew he couldn't protect me. Couldn't save me from the force that was Ahaz.

The officer finally offered me a last chance warning to explain the awful bruising, and then gave up and got out of the car. I fought back tears as I watched him walk to the front door. I knew that I was in such deep, deep trouble. I wanted to scream for the cop to wait, to please come back; I wanted to tell him; I couldn't tell him.

After just a couple of minutes, the officer came back and opened the back door for me to get out. I resigned myself to my fate, headed inside and hurried past my mom and Ahaz. I stood just out of sight in the hallway by my bedroom door, because I couldn't even get into my room with it deadbolted shut.

As I had dashed through the light of the living room, the officer had noticed the giant bruising on my arms; most specifically, the entire blue and purple handprint left behind by Ahaz's cruelty. He commented on it and said he hadn't seen my arms until I had come inside into the light; he sounded upset about that.

I heard Ahaz tell the officer I had a boyfriend and he'd been abusing me. He said that I was a completely out of control unruly teen and said they didn't know what to do about it. Then Ahaz asked the officer if it was possible for someone to do something like that to *themself*.

Now, of course the officer did not know that Ahaz was a doctor. And I feel like mentioning that is important as well, because a doctor probably wouldn't ask a question like that. It seemed as though Ahaz was merely trying to cue the cop into believing I could potentially be that unstable.

The officer answered that yes, of course it was *possible*, but also said that he did not believe that was what had happened to me. He told them that I was either protecting the person that did it to me, or I was *afraid* of the person. I could hear the suspicion in his voice, and I felt like he might actually know that Ahaz was the one who'd hurt me. I hoped that he did. Maybe he could help me after all?

I wanted to run out from my spot by my door, point at Ahaz and scream to the cop that it was him; that I had been locked in and only snuck out for a breath of fresh air and for a few moments of secret, stolen freedom. I wanted to scream that he had been raping me, beating me, refusing to allow me a proper, worldly education, and tell him all the reason for which Ahaz beat me for.

I wanted to tell him *everything*. But I couldn't. My voice, my words had been proven over and over again to be worthless. Silenced. All those in the Mennonite community would back Ahaz up, same as my siblings and mom. My own words were nothing and meaningless.

Ahaz could even 'prove' how terrible I was by me having ran away before at 13, which he sometimes liked to point out. That was just one of the ways to prove I was an unruly delinquent no one should believe. There was also that stupid journal entry, plus me saying I had a forbidden, worldly boyfriend, and the day cops had been called for me scratching the dadgum counter tops with the knife and breaking things. My lying siblings and parents who'd say I was just angry and unruly; not abused. The self-inflicted cuts on my body gave Ahaz an easy out, and now he was saying the rest of the damage was from the supposed boyfriend. Even my tiny anorexic body would work against me; mom and Ahaz would say it was from me faking an eating disorder for attention.

Also 'proven' unruly by the Mennonite standards. Wanting to wear pants and *not* wanting to be a Mennonite were pretty serious offenses. Demanding an education and wanting to hold a job in a place of power as a female was also awful in their eyes. Even the pure fury they saw was within me, counted against me. The Mennonites didn't care about my pain; they only cared that I fell into line as a submissive female. For these and so, so many more reasons, I stayed silent and just cried quietly.

As soon as the officer left, Ahaz came at me demanding to know how I'd gotten out; but I didn't say a word. At first, he thought I had picked the deadbolt, but as soon as he realized it was still locked, he used the key to unlock it and entered my room. The top of an open window still obviously slid down was all the answer he needed.

He closed the window, deadbolted me back inside that room, got the tools from the garage and then nailed tops of my windows shut from the *outside,* same as the bottom ones were. And that was that. He didn't even beat me more that night, just left me to panic and cry out my pain; 100% locked in then.

Both mom and Ahaz told other Mennonites I had run away that night to see my boyfriend, and when asked I didn't even fight it; I agreed. What did it matter anymore, anyway? I was breaking apart, losing myself. Losing my very mind.

Maybe that cop could have helped me that night. Maybe he could have made it stop; maybe he could have got me free, but I would never know for sure. Maybe I was right that he couldn't have helped me. I wish I could have told him; this would become my greatest regret in the upcoming months. I relived that night over and over again within my mind and swore I would never pass up another chance. I had to be free.

Ahaz found a security company and scheduled a day right away to have a security system installed on the house, which was very non- Mennonite like. He said it was to protect me; to make sure I stayed where I was supposed to stay, 'with my happy family' where he could continue to 'discipline' me to ensure I became normal.

I was kept locked into my bedroom until it was time for my windows to be wired, then mom let me out and took me into the living room. I watched the installers as some walked by and tried to beg them for help with my eyes, to somehow let them know I needed help; but they turned their heads and seemed to deliberately avoid my gaze.

I couldn't hear everything that was said, but I did overhear a small bit of what Ahaz told one of those men while they were standing in the kitchen. Ahaz said that I was an unruly delinquent runaway and he had got the security system to help protect me from myself.

Didn't they see the deadbolt on my door? Couldn't they see it? They had to; I just knew. Deadbolts are not usually on bedroom doors, and couldn't they see the nails in the windows? Did they think them being nailed shut from the outside was a typical thing? Couldn't they help me? Couldn't they *see*? Didn't they have the power to call the police and free me?

While it was being installed, I felt hopeless, near dead inside, and deeply suicidal. Had I done this to myself? Did I deserve this? Was all this truly legal, as he claimed? It must be, since no one was willing to help me.

Had I entrapped my own self by climbing out the window and 'running away', although I hadn't run away? By pretending as though I had a boyfriend, and even by pretending that I'd had sex with someone else, just to take his power away and to prove he wasn't the only one that could touch me. Was it legal to lock up girls who were like that? Was I bad? Did I deserve this for fighting against Ahaz in the only ways I knew how to?

The alarm was tested, and the volume cranked up incredibly high to a terrifyingly loud level. It was finished; the installers were now gone. I could hardly believe that I had missed what I knew might have been my very last chance. I was now deadbolted into my bedroom, security system always on, except for when Ahaz dragged me out to work, or if I was let out to use the bathroom.

Ahaz was very happy with the higher security, and he made sure to tell me that this was going to help me act like a normal person now. He was going to make sure I was never able to leave my happy family again. But I still knew I'd be able to get out on my eighteen birthday, I could at least have that much, right? It was most definitely illegal to be denied freedom once midnight would strike on my birthday just a little over a year away.

Sometimes mom would let me out to wash dishes or to clean the living room, but it was only under the guard of either Ahaz, or Travis. Travis would watch me, partially crouched, hands held out at the ready to snatch me, swaying from side to side preparing to run after me if I attempted to run outside through one of the exit doors. He looked excited and thrilled with the task. I could not even use the bathroom without being guarded from the other side of the bathroom door.

Travis being so eager to play guard I also felt was my fault, that it must be payback for all the years of fighting with him even though most of those fights had been mutually friendly fun. Some hadn't been though, especially the more trapped and angrier I felt, and I felt I deserved him now treating me in such a way. Travis was now bigger, stronger and faster than I was.

I began refusing to work in order to prove I had the right to refuse my abuser. I stopped lifting my arms to do the dishes when I was let out, or to work at the farm. No matter how hard or long I was beat for it, I would not do any of it. This made Ahaz furious; he wanted not only an obedient robot, but also a working one; one that would work from dawn to dusk and tell him, 'Thank you for letting me work, I love you, f***** (Ahaz)'. Topped off with happy smiling eye contact, not fighting when raped or beat. Complete and utter, flawless, mindless obedience.

Ahaz was incredibly angry that no matter what he did to my body, no matter what he ordered, or even if he forcibly dragged me to the farm to work that I would not work at all; would just stand, arms hung limply by my sides, no matter how much he hurt me for it.

He grew more frustrated with having lost even more control, and no longer being able to force me to work. He told me that except for going to the bathroom, I'd be let out only for the duration of time I was willing to work under guard or politely go to church like a normal girl.

Ahaz seemed to think that beating those options into me would force me to obey his commands, but he was wrong. I had no intention of doing hard labor for him, nor for going to church to play pretend.

As the days progressed, I was let out less and less. I wasn't able to hold it when I needed to use to bathroom for so long and the small cup I had wasn't enough. When I tried banging on the door or walls, no one came unless it was my siblings to laugh from the other side of the deadbolted door, or Ahaz to beat me for not acting normal, while making so much noise. I stopped trying.

There were times when I balled up clothes from my closet to use the bathroom on, which was humiliating. Sarah took my laundry while laughing and gagging one day, because my room and dirty clothes smelled of urine; she declared that I was hilariously disgusting and asked when I would grow up and be normal.

One day when I was let out by mom to use the bathroom under guard of Travis, I saw a small, blue sand bucket with a yellow handle, laying just across the hall inside the door to the room my three brothers shared. When I came out of the bathroom, it was still just sitting there; so I moved fast to grab it and hurried into my room as quickly as I could. Travis didn't stop me from grabbing it since I wasn't going toward an exit, although I assumed he had no idea what it was for.

I had to use the bathroom in that small bucket, and I'd empty it when I was let out once in the morning and once again in the evening for just a few minutes. I was so embarrassed of that bucket and would hide it between the hall wall and my skirt to try to conceal it from mom, Travis, or Ahaz as I walked the few steps to the bathroom with it to empty it and freshen up myself. No one ever asked if I needed to use the bathroom more than twice in twenty-four hours. No one gave it a single thought, not even my mom. No one cared.

I was in a near constant state of anxiety, mixed in with a heavy dose of panic attacks. I'd feel like I could barely breath; I simply had to have fresh air. I begged to be let out; I screamed, I beat on the door, punched the walls. Lost my mind... trapped. I tried to pick the deadbolt keyhole with a bobby pin and even attempted with the pointy ends of hangers. Nothing worked; I simply couldn't do it.

There wasn't a lot left to do in my room. I had a box spring and mattress sitting on the floor, a chest for clothes, a mirror in the closet, my small hope chest with barely anything left in it that I hadn't smashed. I also had a journal and pen. The bookshelf hanging on my wall was the most important, as it was filled with books. In fact, I had far too many books to all fit on it, and even had a few stacks here and there about the room.

I tried to remember to count down the days until my freedom birthday. I tried to immerse myself in my books, most especially reading Dee Henderson's over and over, focusing on the strong women portrayed within those pages.

Mom would bring me food and sometimes new books from the library, and I lost myself in the beautiful tales of the outside in the real world, of freedom. Somehow, I didn't fully see my mom as being a part of my torment, even though sometimes she was the one to turn the key. Even though she didn't stop it and was aware of what was being done to her baby girl. Even though she denied everything; denied that I was even abused much less so terribly.

I'd managed to play right in his hands through my power struggle to be stronger than him. Through me deliberately trying to prove he could never truly dominate me; I had indeed lost. People now truly believed I was a wild delinquent or had been born mentally ill. A misfit... not normal... not normal.

The ministers came to try to talk to me several times. Mom came to my door and so sweetly, within their hearing, begged me to please come out because they wanted me to talk to them. I did go out a couple of times, once the door was unlocked, but then just sat and cried mostly, perhaps spit out a few angry words before being taken back into my essential jail cell.

The other times, I refused to comply. I heard them talking through the door, from where they'd be in the kitchen, or living room. Hearing both Ahaz and mom expressing such deep concern to the ministers for their troubled teen and doomed to hell soul. I felt so incredibly, deeply betrayed by my mom.

I was told that I was going to be excommunicated. Ahaz tried to force me to go to church and I did go a couple of times that winter. I hid in the women's bathroom, crying in one of the stalls, hardly able to stop crying long enough to even go to the service. I especially didn't want to have to sit with the youth girls at the front of the church; I wasn't one of them. And I didn't want cry during the service and so many people behind be able to tell. But that was where I was supposed to be.

God had forsaken me; he hadn't saved me, nor struck Ahaz down. If he was real, he was a cruel God that looked down and didn't care about my pain. Did he enjoy it? How could I serve a God so awful as that?

I felt like an empty shell, and I could feel my mind slipping away from the years of abuse but tried to hang on and cling to thoughts of my eighteenth birthday. Had to find a way to survive the onslaught surrounding me.

I wanted to scream and tell them all inside that church; scream out everything, until someone understood. But I felt no one would hear, much less believe. I had set myself up so perfectly, without understanding the consequences of what was to come from it. I was dubbed unruly, mentally ill... from a supposedly wonderful family, with no reason to be so *upset* all the time. Why was dear little Hannah so *upset?*

How could the Mennonites only be worried about my *soul,* instead of someone standing up for my *body*? My *mind*? I wondered and I couldn't understand it. How could my beloved grandpa have stood down? And Jessica, too, even though she was in another congregation. I had told them both about the horrible 'whippings.' Even about the rape, *because they already somehow knew, and recognized what was being done to tear me apart.* Maxwell, whom I had told I had been being beat for hours on end? They all knew I was being deadbolted into that room; so many within the community were very aware. The extra strict, stoic deacon; how could he stand behind encouraging Ahaz over the years to hurt me?

The Mennonites excommunicated me for reasons such as refusing to bend submissively, for having a 'boyfriend', and my years of outspoken insistence of wanting to have rights and be one of the worldly. For demanding rights such as immediate public-school education and more for so long. They believed I clearly was not a part of them any longer; and for in that, they were, in part, correct. I had never been a Mennonite at heart.

This made me feel more alone than ever; I was now one of the excommunicated and was to have 'The Avoidance' upheld against me.

The sound of his footsteps coming through the living room and down the short hallway haunted me even when he wasn't there. Even in my dreams I could hear it. I knew the sound of every wooden floorboard under the fall of his steps and knew how he'd pause for a moment outside the door; perhaps enjoying eyeballing the deadbolt, knowing I was trapped on the other side of it. His breathing would deepen audibly and grow faster.

I could hear the key slip into the lock, and the smooth grating sound of the key against the inward mechanisms of the lock as he turned it within, and the slip of a noise as the bolt slid open. The sound of him gripping and turning the doorknob; the sound of the door creaking open... him standing there. Coming in. Him talking. Hurting me. Helpless...

The beatings and rape continued. He hit me, even kicked me here and there in-between the paddle, switch and leather strap. Now when he'd come to hurt me, he'd deadbolt us both within. I wanted to kill him, to get the key and escape, but I did neither of those things. He promised to break me like a horse many times. He'd chase me round in that small room when I tried to run in circles from him while he continued to strike me. Nearly as though he were fiercely and abusively lunging a horse.

I'd spit at him; tell him he was disgusting and say that he'd never be able to break me nor truly trap me. I said that he could hurt and contain my body but that didn't mean he could ever take away my mind. I told him I was going to leave at the stroke of midnight on my eighteenth birthday.

Ahaz laughed and asked who was going to let me out; and just how, exactly, did I plan to leave? He said that he was going to keep me until I was twenty-five years old, because I was clearly behind in mental development since I was unable to ever act normal and submit to what he knew was best for me. He said I was clearly not yet a woman and wouldn't be until I was twenty-five years old. Ahaz told me that he would be able to retain custody of me until I was mentally normal and old enough to take care of myself.

The strongest fear I had ever felt hit me like a train, as the shocking power of what he was saying slid over me. That was the first time he had told me he was going to keep me, even after I was legally an adult. It occurred to me that him claiming I wasn't a woman contradicted him having told me I was a woman at the age of thirteen, when he first raped me.

I was in shock, denial. I didn't know how to respond, and for possibly the first time I did not have a snappy come back pop to mind. I was terrified, petrified and most definitely not ok. I wasn't a strong teen on the verge of adulthood fighting for my very rights in that moment; I was just a tiny, helpless, scared little girl all over again. I was nothing. Not normal... not normal.

No one would be coming for me. *No one was coming*. I realized in horror that he could, indeed do exactly what he was saying. He could keep me as long as he wished, and no one would ever know. The Mennonites even had abandoned me, my mom, my siblings; and I was under The Avoidance. All the missed opportunities to tell flashed through my mind as though it was on a video; I had done this to myself. And now I was trapped, forever.

When he left me there in that room, more broken than ever before, after the final sound of the deadbolt sliding closed and his footsteps walking away; I felt as though that was it. I was never going to be free, not in life, at least. I knew if I could not find a way out of that room, I could at least find freedom in death. Finally pain free.

I didn't care about hell; if hell existed, I already knew that I was most definitely headed there. I would rather burn forever in flames than to endure what was being done to me. He had turned me into everything I had never wanted to be; a liar, a helpless female and more. I had to get out, so I didn't have to die. Had to.

Crying, I crawled into my closet, curled up and wrapped my arms around my knees tight. Part of me just broke; a part that had thus far still been strong. Curled up in that closet, I shattered. Over and over his words repeated in my head; every single hope I'd had, was taken away that day. I felt like I couldn't breathe, as though I was going to die from just how badly I hurt.

Chapter Nineteen

2006, Age 17

My siblings thought it was so hilarious that I was deadbolted into that room and continued to laugh at my plight. They thought I was a horrible person, bound and determined to go to hell. And perhaps they were right.

Maybe I really *was* bad. Maybe it really *was* me. Maybe I should bow down and give in, instead of allowing myself to be beaten into something terrible; some horrible shadow of a person whom I could barely recognize the reflection of within the mirror.

I was no longer keeping my hair bound up in a head covering. In theory I was free from the Mennonites, except for those within the very house I was trapped. Ahaz demanded I go back to wearing my hair twisted into braids because to leave it unbound was sinful. But I refused and said I could leave it down if I wanted to. He beat me for that repeatedly, and every single time I dared to point out he could not force me to be what he wanted; I wasn't even a Mennonite.

In the face of either suicide or survival, I decided to trick him into thinking for a time, that he had won. That he had finally done it; beat me into submission. Perhaps then he'd leave me alone. Maybe he'd stop. Maybe I could even gain his trust and be able to find a chance to get free. And by this point, I *was* actually so broken, it wasn't that difficult to do.

At first, Ahaz seemed confused and untrusting of this new me. He grabbed my chin and turned my head this way and that to no reaction. My arms remained limp at my sides, I offered no resistance. Then he became visibly pleased; and a conquering smile slid across his face.

For the next couple of weeks, I acted like a robot. I did as he wished. I did not talk at all. Did not fight when he raped me. Did not flinch when he beat me. Did not scream. Did not respond when he yelled at me, nor when he told me how not normal I was acting.

I took my mind far, far away from there and tried to dull out the agony both within, and without my body. Tried to numb the physical, mental, emotional and sexual pain to the point it didn't actually hurt quite so horribly. I put myself into a fog of nothingness. It was honestly nearly a relief, to the point I started to numb out even when Ahaz wasn't in that room with me.

It really didn't take too long before Ahaz seemed to become afraid and unsatisfied with my limp, lack of fighting body, from which he could not even force a single scream. The lines in his forehead wrinkled in worry. I truly think he was genuinely worried that he'd broken his favorite plaything, even though breaking me was what he had fiercely tried to do for years.

He grew increasingly irritated from it, and I could see that through the haze. He tried to hurt me more and more; to touch me in different ways. I dulled my mind out, went to a place far away inside my mind where there was no pain, where I was not trapped as a prisoner, and where no one intended to hold me captive until I was twenty-five. Where I didn't have to use the bathroom in a tiny bucket.

Ahaz decided to beat me with everything he had in him; he seemed determined to make me 'snap out of it', to fight back, to scream, to respond to his torture. He was angry and worried, telling me that he was going to force me to stop acting that way, and act normal instead.

I fought to stay in that foggy place far away. I did everything I could to not react. To stay still in one spot and to let him strike me repeatedly with a stick, paddle and strap. With his fists. I let my arms hang, and I tried to dig deeper, further away mentally. I refused to make a sound, nor to flinch. Just had to keep my body relaxed. Had to keep it up so he'd trust I was so broken he'd let me out of that room...

Ahaz kicked my legs out from under me and continued to kick my body while I was down on the floor, taking my breath away, and brought the leather strap down on me furiously over and over, changing to the switch, the paddle, and back. On and on.

I couldn't fight it anymore mentally; emotionally. Suddenly everything came rushing in and I could no longer block to dull my senses; the full hopelessness of the situation I was in rushed through me, mind, body and soul. I was powerless to stop the shrieking screams from rushing out from my throat, to stop my body from reacting, flinching, nor from trying to crawl away. I couldn't stop the rest that followed, either. Tears streamed down my face, and I was just a broken little girl. I was nothing. Not normal... not normal.

Ahaz was once again seemed very happy that he now had his plaything in working order.

I wanted to die. He kept reminding me that he was going to keep me until I was twenty-five, that I wasn't normal. Not normal... he was going to make me normal though, he said... no matter what it took. No matter what he had to do to me.

I cut my skin with my own fingernails, digging down into the same lines in my skin over and over to make them deeper and deeper. I knew I didn't need a knife to die; I could open my wrists with my own teeth or nails. I could end it all, bleed out on the floor, and never have to feel again. A part of me truly wasn't ready to die yet though. I needed to fight, I needed to find the strength to. I had to find the way to get out. Had to cling to it, but it was so far away, and I was fading...

The fear I'd feel when I heard him coming toward my room... each step resounded loudly within my ears. I felt panic, and the urge to run, but there was no escape. Nowhere to go, no place to hide. The sound of the key being pressed into the lock, the grating sound as the key turned in the keyhole, the slip of a noise of the deadbolt sliding open... It was a moment of true horror, with nothing more to do than to wait and see what he had in mind for tormenting me that day.

About a couple of months after I turned seventeen, I was let out to use the bathroom. When I came out, Travis was in his bedroom right beside the bathroom instead of strictly guarding me. I realized and *ran* just as fast as I could through the living room and threw open the front door and ran outside.

The alarm blared loud and terrifying. Travis was already nearly right on my heels, with Ahaz just behind him. I knew I couldn't outrun Travis, and he was about to grab and drag me back inside. I avoided his grasp, and he ran faster, around and in front of me, stopping and spinning around with the woods at his back to face me again, cutting off my easy way out.

Ahaz was behind me, and both of them were edging closer. I was in a fearful panic; I knew I couldn't be caught; knew I might not be able to get out again. I realized the pile of rocks picked from the garden were right beside me, and on impulse I scooped up a couple of good-sized rocks as quick as I could to defend myself with and spun around to throw them at Travis. I don't think I hit him, but he backed up and half crouched, a smile on his face while excitedly swaying from side to side. He was ready to run in any direction I might try to go; ready to outrun and tackle me.

I turned right around, grabbed more from the pile and pelted rocks at Ahaz, who was trying to inch in on me closer. I was trapped and lashing out. I truly wanted for Ahaz to die for what he had done to me, how he had destroyed me. How he kept me locked up, beat and raped me a countless number of times. Broken me.

He seemed incredibly shocked that I would dare to do such a thing as I threw the rocks hitting his head, his shoulder. Ahaz looked surprised, hurt and confused, and he yelled at me to stop that; but I didn't. He threw his hands up, trying to protect himself from the rocks.

In a panicked, trapped rage I advanced on him with a handful of rocks in one hand, throwing one right after the other. He turned and ran the few steps to the van in the driveway, opening the driver side door and climbing in. He closed the door, locked it, and I could see the look of relief on his face; he felt that he was safe. He assumed that I'd never dare to throw a rock through the glass...

Travis was advancing behind me, creeping closer to try to grab me. I ran the few steps forward and threw my last rock straight through the glass window of the van, directly at Ahaz's head.

Mom came outside on the cement walkway in front of the house, yelling and crying. Ahaz pulled the cell from his pocket to call 911; I think he told them I was trying to kill him.

I was scared when he called 911, because it hit me just how 'bad' it would look to police. Even though I was the girl who was locked in, this would just 'prove' more that I deserved to be treated that way, in other people's eyes. With police on the way, and mom demanding to know why I dared to behave so badly, I gave up.

Ahaz talked to the officers as soon as they got there, and mom was still very upset. I was sitting on the cement walkway, having to listen to Ahaz run through his list of reasons I was an unruly delinquent with mental illness, when I had no reason to be that way. He asked about pressing charges and wanted to know if it would be possible to have me put on house arrest.

One officer talked to me, and I nodded to agree I was out of control for no reason. Even though the goal had been to escape, I felt as though I now somehow looked bad to the point that the officers wouldn't believe me; speaking would have been a waste of breath.

When the officers left, I was escorted back inside to my bedroom and locked within.

A court date was scheduled for a short time later, around March 2006. Ahaz kept saying he was going to have me put on house arrest for it, and he'd make sure I could never leave again, never escape. I was his; until I reached *his* age of maturity at twenty-five years old.

Ahaz said he could have the house arrest easily extended for years, especially if I ever tried to run away again, because breaking house arrest was a crime. He said that the police would always bring me back for him if I tried, and my time there would be extended for it. Because I belonged to him, because I was not normal and even the police knew it... because normal people do not stone their loving f***** (Ahaz), he said. Normal people do not run away... not normal... not normal...

Leading up to this court date, my mom took me from that room and drove me out to the Cookeville mall to find a store bought, worldly outfit for court. She told me that it was because I was a young lady now, and since I was excommunicated that her and Ahaz wanted to respect my wishes. She wouldn't let me get pants, but I was allowed to choose something in a skirt that was dressy. I picked out what I thought was a beautiful blue & black skirt, with blue top & matching jacket to go with it.

I thought about telling someone there at the mall. I thought about screaming out what was happening; I thought about running. But Ahaz had said the police would bring me back... he said they were on his side. That what he was doing was right. It was allowed.

By then, I felt just as insane as they tried to make me out to be, just as bad. I had broken things, stoned Ahaz, wished for him to die... wanted to kill *myself.* Cut myself, could never be submissive, couldn't accept a lack of education or the ways of the Mennonites, nor of the ways of Ahaz, lying down. But I'd *had to* fight back somehow. I'd *had* to find a way to be free...

had to prove I *wasn't* broken by showing my strength, the power within me... the power that was fading away into the depths of pure despair.

Ahaz was coming to my room less often as the court day drew near. I thought he was scared of me now since I had shown him what I was capable of... thought maybe I really could get out of there at eighteen, maybe he'd be so scared that he'd let me go. Maybe there was hope after all?

As soon as the court day came, both mom and Ahaz took me. I was fighting tears, depressed, knowing if I tried to tell anyone, they wouldn't believe me. I was a true delinquent now in other people's eyes.

When I walked into that juvenal courtroom, I realized how out of place I was. The other teens there were in torn jeans, mostly. Yet there I was all dressed up in an outfit I now realized made me look grandma-ish, not worldly. I thought I heard a couple of snickers, but I dared not look around too much; I didn't want anyone to see the shameful shadow I'd become.

I realized at some point that it was not kindness that had led to this new clothing purchase; it was to make me appear as though I had more rights and choices than I actually did, being dressed in modern clothing instead of as a Mennonite.

Ahaz and mom were both right beside me the entire time. Someone came to ask me questions, someone who maybe could have helped, someone kind. They sat beside me, on the bench where I was right beside Ahaz and mom. Ahaz reminded me to 'make sure I told the truth'. AKA lie.

The questions I was asked were something down the lines of if I was safe. I wanted to grab that person and hide behind them; I wanted to ask to talk alone; I wanted to blurt out everything.

Instead, I hung my head low and whispered out the answers that were expected of me. Even there, I did not feel safe. I did not feel I could say what was happening, because how would I prove it? It was my word against theirs. I was nothing, no one. Powerless.

There was an officer there, one that had responded to the 911 call. He called me a delinquent, and other things, too, when he talked to the judge. I felt deeply embarrassed and ashamed. Although he wasn't wrong, he still had everything wrong. Why couldn't he see something was terribly wrong?

Ahaz asked the judge to put on house arrest, and to order me to do community service in his greenhouses and gardens. It was 'their only hope of getting me under control', as he said. The judge set another court date in April 2006 for my fate to be determined.

I hoped the judge would put me in juvie- I *wanted* to go to jail at that point, in order to be *free* from Ahaz. To exchange one jail cell for another, if that was what it took. On the other hand, I feared it would mess up my wanting to go into law enforcement. How could such a troubled mess be allowed to be an officer, anyway? How could someone so broken, ever help a single person?

Back to that horrid house, and back to that awful room. Ahaz assured me I was definitely going to be on house arrest, forced to work and be his for years more. For my protection. He said again that he could have it extended for years past my birthday, especially if I tried to run or refused to work.

The fear, humiliation, the pain of everything felt like it was choking me, swallowing me whole. Even in counting down the days until my eighteenth birthday didn't help now, because it was too far away, and it was crystal clear I would never be allowed to escape even then.

The deadbolt, nailed shut windows, fancy security system, and a guard when let out twice per day... the laughter, and impending house arrest... I couldn't breathe through the pain. I had to get out... but I didn't know how. The more I fought, the more I was being swallowed up. It felt like I was trapped in quicksand; and I was about to die.

I had to die. I cried over it, agonized over it, could barely breathe from it. There was no other option. I cried for the strong young girl I had been born as; I cried for what I was now. I cried for the future I would never have. I cried because I knew I was going to hell; because even I thought I must deserve it. I cried because I couldn't tell if I had done this to myself or not; I couldn't tell if it actually was his to legal right to do those things to me. The books from the library said it was all wrong; the people, on the other hand, said it was just fine.

On April 3rd of 2006, mom let me out in the evening to shower. I took my bucket with me and emptied it, rinsed it out and showered. I took as long as I thought I could get away with, finished up and came out.

Surprisingly, I didn't see anyone, which was strange. I put the bucket back in my room and quietly tip toed back out into the hallway, peering into the living room, eyeballing the front door at first. But even though I didn't know where Ahaz and Travis were, I figured they'd probably appear and catch me just as soon as the alarm went off, blaring.

Then I spied the black business cell phone laying on the side table by my mom's recliner and walked as toward it as quietly as possible. I heard her, my mom, in the kitchen just as I laid my hand on the phone and quickly slipped it down the front of my dress, hoping the elastic at my waistline of my hand made dress was tight enough to not allow it to continue sliding on down passed it.

Mom came around the corner from the kitchen right then, seemingly carefree and not upset I wasn't where I was supposed to be. I took a deep breath in, trying to puff out my stomach and make my waistline thicker so the phone wouldn't slip past the elastic and drop onto the floor. I quickly hurried back to my room without a word. She locked me in and walked away unworriedly.

I took the phone out and hid it in my closet. I was so terrified of being caught that I felt sick. I didn't even know if I would be strong enough to make a call or not.

From that moment on, I waited in fear. I thought someone might notice that the phone was missing and come after me. I dared not to make a call until everyone was long asleep; they'd hear me talk, perhaps even if I whispered and rush in to stop me.

I tried to figure out who I could even tell as I waited. Grandpa had turned his back on me, and the rest of the Holdeman Mennonites that knew had proven they had no desire to help me. I thought about calling 911, but I didn't think they could help me, didn't think a delinquent being locked in a bedroom counted as an emergency, right? I didn't want to risk being yelled at or getting in trouble for wasting the time of a 911 operator.

I remembered that I'd seen hotline numbers in the back of a Chicken Soup for The Soul book on my bookshelf. I was shaking. I wanted to die; I couldn't be there any longer. I cut myself with my nails in anguish as I waited, thinking how it would be so easy to dig just a tiny bit deeper and cut open the arteries in my wrists, or bite them open with my teeth. I knew one did not need a knife to die. I was crying, overwhelmed, and terrified. How could I tell someone; could I even do it? I couldn't let this chance go by. I had to do it... I could do it... Not normal... not normal... would anyone help me? Save me?

I felt like this was my last chance. I had to either tell someone or kill myself to find my freedom. I couldn't keep breathing in that room another day; I couldn't endure one more beating, nor one more time of being raped. I had to have either fresh air and blue skies, or the fiery flames of hell.

The house grew quiet as the night grew later. I was so anxious, and I kept having to pee in my little blue bucket. I worried about what if someone did come; what if someone saw I had a bathroom bucket? The thought was humiliating; I couldn't let anyone know that. But I had to risk it. I had to tell.

Pain rushed through me as I tried to make a choice between attempting to tell one more time, or to give up; give into the darkness, bite my wrist open and fade away into oblivion. The tears streamed down my face, I felt like I was choking, suffocating. Dying. I was nothing. I was not normal.

Around 1 a.m. on the morning of April 4 of 2006, I chose one of the hotline help numbers in the back of that book, and I shakily dialed the numbers. I had no idea what I was going to say; I just had to make the pain end. I had to be free. I had to have help. I felt as though no one wanted to hear the truth though.

Someone answered. I was sobbing and could barely speak, but managed to say that I wanted to die, that I couldn't take it anymore. I said I was cutting myself, that I had a knife and that if no one could help me I had to die. I thought if I said I had a knife someone might actually come for me, since a teen being locked into a room was apparently ok, I didn't mention it, nor any of the other horrible things that had been done to me through the years.

The person on the other end contacted 911 and kept talking to me. I wasn't listening much, but I still had the phone in my hand. I just knew I was either about to be freed, or about to be dead if no one came. I couldn't survive even a single day past April 4th, 2006. Not even another hour.

Police cars and an ambulance showed up, lights on, turning onto the gravel driveway. I could hear them and see them from out of my bedroom window, and I panicked; felt like I was going to throw up. I hung up the phone quick in my fear. I knew I was in deep trouble now that my call had brought those people, I knew Ahaz would never allow me to be taken anywhere.

I didn't know what to do; the time was here. I thought for a moment that I needed to hurry and bite my wrists open because I surely had to try to die before they could reach me, before I saw the disbelief and accusations in their eyes. I knew that those people were going to come in there, see I didn't have a knife, and they'd walk away from me. They wouldn't see any more than anyone else had. Ahaz and mom would tell them I was mentally ill, a delinquent. That I didn't act normal, and they'd leave me there.

But there was no time left; there was pounding and yelling at the front door. Deep, terrifyingly loud voices yelled out that they were the police and to open the door. I was shaking, trying not to vomit in fear of what Ahaz was going to do to me for this.

I was so incredibly afraid and in a full-blown panic. They would see that I was locked in; they would see I needed help. But could they save me?

I grabbed my bucket of pee and hid it in my closet out of panic. I couldn't let them see it, because they'd be even more disgusted by me. The police and paramedics were still at the front door, banging on it furiously while yelling and shouting. No time at all had passed yet it felt like it was drawn out on and on...

Ahaz yelled out too, then I heard him open the front door. I could hear my mom, too, and their combined confusion. More yelling, and from the sound of it the men kind of pushed their way in, shouting to know where the girl was because they got a call about a girl cutting herself.

Mom shouted back that my room was down the short hall on the left. I heard heavy footsteps cover the short distance incredibly fast and I knew exactly when they realize the door was deadbolted shut.

There was more yelling, this time for the key to the deadbolt on my bedroom door to be brought immediately. Ahaz found the key and brought it to them; my door was unlocked and... there I was. Tearful, scared, my body bruised and cut, but not to the point of needing ambulance care.

I felt ashamed that they were there, ashamed that I had called. Ashamed and hopeless, because they were going to declare me an unruly delinquent and leave me to Ahaz's abuses when they saw I didn't have a knife like I'd said. Leave me in that room, to my fate. I knew I would never get another chance; yet I couldn't speak.

They tried to talk to me, but I couldn't seem to talk back from the immense fear of not knowing what horrible thing was about to come next. I remember one officer seemed like he was disgusted, so I felt like they all must be. So much shame... so much pain. I was wrapped up in it.

Ahaz was trying to push through the guys and tried to demand that they leave. He kept repeating that he was a doctor, and they could leave me in his care. He said I was a delinquent that had been running away, and going to parties, I had a boyfriend and they had to protect me from myself. He tried to make it sound like I was crazy.

I was handcuffed and put in the back of a patrol car, while Ahaz continued to yell and tried to stop them from taking me. They took me to the hospital, and I was put into a small room.

I could hear when Ahaz arrived. He was shouting for people to let him into that room. He was a doctor... an almighty doctor... plus as a 'parent' he knew what was best for me. He was going to take me back 'home' and seek his own proper mental health care for me. He insisted loudly I was a liar... that no matter what I was saying, it was all lies.

They didn't let him in the room; I had guardians watching over me, but I didn't know whom exactly. All I knew was I was told he had been forcibly removed from the premises by security, but not arrested. I felt safer; I felt like just maybe someone could protect me this time. Now if only they could see that I wasn't horrible and merely a nearly grown, broken girl.

Someone let my mom into that small room. I wouldn't look at her because the pain and agony of her betrayal burned through me, crushing me, breaking my heart. She dared to ask in her fake, cover up tone of voice what could possibly be upsetting her little Hannie Annie? Whatever could be wrong?

I wanted to punch her in the face, to scream at her to stop pretending; to *help me*. But she had already dedicated so many years to turning her back on my cries that it no longer mattered. I had no words for her.

People wanted to touch and examine me, but I didn't want to allow anyone to touch me. I just cried, knowing if they sent me back, I would be forced to die. Forced to kill myself. I knew Ahaz would make sure I never left that room ever again; never had another chance. This was it.

There was a man there that asked me many questions, and he was very nice and kind. He asked me if I had ever seen a movie called Fried Green Tomatoes, and I told him I wasn't allowed to watch movies. So, he told me a bit about it instead and said I needed to watch it when I could.

He asked me questions about if I was being hurt, and I couldn't answer properly. I couldn't tell him the truth out loud because I still felt as though no one would ever believe me. My voice had been silenced by all those who should have protected me. Who *should* have been more worried about my pain; my fate; than my soul.

That man spent a good bit of time with me, but I don't know exactly how long. He asked a few times if I was being sexually abused and only received silence as his answer. Then he'd change the subject and I was happy to discuss worldly things with him such as about that movie. Eventually I was finally able to very slightly nod yes, when he asked if I was being sexually abused. He promised I'd be protected, but said I was going to have to talk. Only I couldn't talk; not about that.

All I could think about was not the freedom ahead, but about how much Ahaz was going to hurt me for this. I couldn't tell the man the name of who was hurting me. I was scared. Sure, Ahaz had been kicked out of the hospital; but what if I still had to go back there? How could anything even be proved?

I was offered food, but I was too scared to try to eat, too sick from the fear. At one point I was told that I was going to be taken to a teen's mental hospital. There was a woman officer who took me from the E.R. to there. I was afraid, but very happy I didn't have to go back to that house just yet.

Now I had momentary freedom, a tiny shimmer of the littlest bit of hope. But all that would end the second I'd be forced to return; I knew I still wasn't safe. I had to find the strength to talk, but could anyone save me from him? Not normal... not normal... maybe I really wasn't normal. Maybe I deserved all this. Maybe he really was allowed to do it.

Chapter Twenty

At the Peninsula Hospital in Blount County, Tennessee, I barely spoke, mostly just took in my surroundings at first. Staff tried to ask me a lot of questions, which I either ignored, or answered sarcastically. I was petrified of what was to come, and sarcasm especially was a go-to self-protection mode of mine. To 'prove' I wasn't broken, somehow. That I was still alive. That I wasn't a robot. That I had not be beaten into nothing.

The staff noted down that anorexia was suspected, and that I had about 20 cuts on my body. Most of these were from my own cutting of myself. Since Ahaz had cut back on the severity and frequency of the beatings due to the upcoming court date to have me put on house arrest, there were not nearly as many injuries as usual.

I was given a set of scrubs to wear, with pants included! Wearing them made me feel incredibly strange and even sinful due to the years of them being utterly taboo. Would I go to hell for it? Maybe, but I was still thrilled to have them on.

I was surrounded by other teen girls and female staff wearing pants as well, who thought nothing of it. I found myself actually a bit excited to be able to be so near to, and to talk to these mysterious worldly girls. I wondered what their lives were like, and if they were escaping from something as terrible as I.

The staff kept trying to get me to talk more than a few words to tell them what had happened. Staff seemed to be, for the most part, very gentle souls. I had a favorite, of course, and she reminded me of my sweet third grade teacher. She was petite, kind, and soft spoken; yet I also got that strong woman vibe off of her. She was perfect, in my mind, and exactly the type of person I wanted to be.

We had group classes and therapy stuff. I still didn't speak much, was to wound up within the trapped torment of my own mind. I didn't want anyone to know where I came from nor what I'd went through; I merely wanted to be a teen on the verge of adulthood, nothing more, nothing less. I had to escape from the years of torment in every way... Not normal... not normal...

The psychiatrist seemed aloof, and I didn't like him at all. I most definitely didn't feel comfortable talking to him about what I'd been through. He didn't wind up putting me on any medications, which made me happy. I thought he must know I wasn't so bad after all.

Ahaz was extremely angry that his control had been forcibly taken away from him, and he wanted me back in that house, inside of that deadbolted bedroom *immediately*. He tried to pull me out of there multiple times, but wasn't allowed to do so, thankfully.

He lied to the hospital, not that I expected any less than that. Ahaz said that I had been very sick as a baby, and ever since then had always needed 'special treatment'. Yet he also contradicted himself by saying all my milestones were on time, and of course then there was the fact that I wasn't actually allowed any form of medical treatment, including not even getting simple immunizations.

No one asked for proof to back up what he claimed. *What special treatment? Other than being deadbolted into a room, raped, beat, mentally and emotionally abused?*

Ahaz described me to staff as 'being intelligent but lacking a lot of academic skills.' Lack of allowed education, much? I'd *begged* for a proper education. He also claimed that they'd signed me up for G.E.D. classes since being in the hospital.

I knew that this was a scrambled attempt to make it look better for getting me out of there and I hoped the hospital didn't fall for it. He had no good intentions toward me.

He insisted that all my mental problems stemmed from when he lost custody of my older brother Thomas when it was decided 'as a family' to become Mennonite. He said that Thomas did not want to do this and *chose* to stay with Ahaz's parents and that I was resentful because I hadn't *also* been given a *choice*.

Yet he then claimed *his* dad had been angry we left his own Baptist church in Tompkinsville, and that's why he 'falsely' accused Ahaz of abandoned his son, Thomas. But I was a *witness* that day. By law, what happened met the lawful definition of abandonment, or so I assumed. Not to mention he'd abused that poor boy for years, until he'd turned Thomas into a monster of sorts as well.

Ahaz told them I had undergone a trauma and was acting out due to it and showed the hospital that journal I'd written in about going to a party, which I had written purely to upset *him*. He said he had no idea who raped me... umm... how about *yourself???* Over and over again, for years.

He told them about the event I 'stoned' him in, but left out all the important parts, naturally. He said the past couple of years had been very hard, that I was out of control and their only hope was to have me put under house arrest at the upcoming court date for the stoning.

I was asked later, about the things he'd said, and I actually agreed with that journal entry and said yes, I'd been raped by my boyfriend, and yes, I'd stoned Ahaz but wouldn't tell them why.

I wasn't protecting Ahaz; I was sick with fear and trying to protect *myself* from more shame somehow. On top of the years of no one believing, I also felt an overwhelming need for no one to know the horrors actually inflicted on my body; it was humiliating to tell what had been done to me for so long. Nor did I want anyone to realize that I wasn't nearly as strong as I put on the facade of pretending to be. Not normal... not normal.

Finally, after a few days I started talking, leaving breadcrumbs that I needed someone to follow. I told the psychiatrist small clues, like how I felt in jail at that house, felt locked in, and was literally locked into my bedroom at night. Couldn't go outside even during the day nor take walks, couldn't go to school, and didn't feel safe; wasn't safe. I *needed* for someone to follow these to *help set me free*.

I also said I'd kill myself that if I was forced back there, and this was not an idol threat or plea for attention; it was simply a fact.

In spite of feeling far safer inside the hospital away from Ahaz's painful reach, I still felt the need to try to escape from there. I didn't think anyone would ever believe me over that horrid man even if I did tell, and I knew I had to get out before it was too late. I wanted to be able to *live*. I felt as though a homeless life of hiding and eating from dumpsters was a far sight better than being trapped. The only issue with that was that there were always staff watching, and I didn't know if I could escape in time.

A meeting was set up with Ahaz, mom, me and someone to supervise it on April 16, 2006. I didn't want to go; I cried and absolutely refused. A woman pretended to make a 'deal' with me and claimed I would be allowed to leave whenever I wished. So, I pointed out that meant I could walk straight in and right back out; but she said that wasn't how it worked. Sounded like an utterly useless, lie of a fake deal in that case if I truly couldn't leave right away. She made me go and sit in a chair in the same room as both mom and Ahaz.

I refused to look at them, nor to say a single word. But out of my peripheral vision I could see mom's hands clutched together in her lap, twiddling her thumbs around each other slowly. She did that only when she was nervous and lying to cover up Ahaz's crimes.

Mom asked why I didn't want to come home; did something happen? This question made my heart feel like it was shattering with the betrayal. *Did something happen???* Well just moment, let me see if I can think of anything... hmmm... oh wait I got it! *You allowed your husband to torment and abuse me with your knowledge for years, yet you dare to ask; did something happen? Bitch.*

Tears slid down my face throughout all her proclamations of love for me. She said she just wanted for me to come home, and asked a few more questions while pretending ignorance, such as, "How can I help my sweet Hannie Annie?" Even her questions were lies, only asked for show; and I felt even more betrayed by her than ever.

Ahaz didn't say much, and I knew he was trying to pretend he wasn't the dominate lord over every single thing being said, that mom wasn't speaking rehearsed lines, even though she was. Eventually, I was finally allowed to leave the room.

Immediately following that forced visit, I had a complete, helpless breakdown. I went into the bathroom and just... shattered. I was crying; I think I was even screaming. It felt like I was losing my mind; feeling as though no one could protect me; no one could stop him; no one could save me. Not normal... not normal.

Staff was near, and one woman came to the bathroom door to talk to me. She asked over and over what had happened, what I was thinking and saying that she couldn't help me if I didn't tell. But if it told, I would be kept safe and I wouldn't have to go back; I'd be protected, she promised.

My heart was pounding so hard and fast, I felt like it was going to explode right out of my chest. I couldn't see through the tears clouding my eyes and streaming down my face fierce and free. My lungs burned and tightened; air was hard to get in and out of them.

I knew that in telling, it would still only be my word against theirs. I thought I'd be sent back anyway, as the unruly delinquent that Ahaz and the Mennonites made me out to be. Or that I'd be told by even the hospital staff that I really did deserve every bit of it; that he was allowed to 'discipline' me in that way and deadbolt me in because I was a delinquent, a runaway. And there was no way to prove he'd raped me, either... not normal... not normal.

Eventually I was able to gather the courage to at least nod yes to the woman, that I would tell. She got me out of the bathroom and took me across the hall to an empty room and motioned for me to sit on one of the beds. I was so incredibly afraid, with tears still pouring down my cheeks.

Somehow, I managed to just barely choke out the words that it was Ahaz who had been raping me since the age of 13. That he'd beat me with his fists, and even kicked me.

The woman comforted and reassured me again that I would be protected, and then left me alone briefly while she went to report what I'd said.

After telling, I felt a combination of relief and fear. Could I truly be free? I doubted it, but still a glimmer of hope shinned.

The Department of Children Services (DCS) was called in, and along with came an officer who had been at the first court date for the unruly charge. I felt very afraid when I saw him; I thought he had come to tell DCS what a horrid girl I was, and that everything would come tumbling down and I'd be forced back into that prison of a house. I thought that for sure suicide loomed in my future.

But I had it all wrong, and what he said replaced my fears with hope. He told me that he'd known something was very wrong that day, by the way Ahaz, mom and I acted. I felt so much relief, as though I was not actually as alone as I felt.

DCS and the officer reassured me many times I was safe and that I had nothing to fear from them nor from the process of gathering information, and most importantly; nothing more to fear from Ahaz. They were going to protect me; I was safe.

I had to go through details, telling them about the rape and even the condoms while they asked questions to urge me on. However, I should have talked far more; I kept what I said at a minimum from the incredible amount of fear and utter shame.

I also talked about Thomas, said that Ahaz had abused him prior to me, and my grandparents now had custody. I *didn't* tell them how horrible the day was when I last saw him. I *didn't* tell them I had watched my brother Travis die, nor how scared I was when we were driven out of town with nothing but the clothes on our backs, leaving Thomas behind in Kentucky. Leaving every single, tiny thing I had ever known in my short life.

I *didn't* say that I'd been 'whipped' for hours or for an entire day at times; because I thought since the Mennonites said it was impossible, no one out here would believe it either. And I had been told over and over that what he was doing was allowed and didn't even meet the definition of beating. By Mennonites, mom, Ahaz, even some of my siblings.

I *didn't* tell them about being called 'not normal' all my life because I didn't understand that the mental/emotional abuse was also actually a crime. To Ahaz and to the Mennonites, it was his right.

I *didn't* talk about so many things... how he manipulated my mom, how he sent her cowering into a fearful lying mess. I *didn't* say he had forced me to drink vinegar, and even forced soap down my throat. I *didn't* say I'd already tried to tell for years, but no one believed me; not even the literal witnesses of the abuse.

I *didn't* say that I was being deadbolted in except for being let out twice a day; nor that I had been forced use a bathroom bucket, because the *shame* from having to use a bucket ran so incredibly deep. And the fact that I looked 'bad' and unruly were still not far from my thoughts; hadn't I set myself up to deserve that, according to everyone?

I *didn't* report that Ahaz said he was going to keep me until I was twenty-five years old, because I knew he'd have just denied it.

I *didn't* talk about the ways of the Holdeman Mennonites; nor that I had quite literally kissed approximately a couple hundred of adults and girls of various ages, strangers included as a *minor* for the sake of their Holy Hiss. Because all those around me had acted like it was all completely ok, even though it had made me very anxious and uncomfortable. It was supposed to be a part of practicing their freedom of religion and therefore legal, right?

I *didn't* tell them I'd been forced to work hard labor in the garden and greenhouse; because according to Ahaz and the Mennonites, there was nothing wrong with being forced to work them, even though I'd had to work many times up to 12 hours in a day and was viciously beat to be forced into it.

I *didn't* tell them I'd had to file patient paperwork starting at a young age, which probably went against HIPPA for the private things I saw and kid labor laws.

DCS were able to get a judge to sign an order to remove the boys from that house, and to put all four of us in foster care. At this point, my brothers were 14, 10 & 4 years old, and my sister was nearly 19 so this of course did not apply to her.

Mom told DCS she did not believe the sexual abuse had even happened, and Ahaz never actually confirmed nor denied that he'd done it. He did say that he thought I'd would say something like that and wanted us kids to be put in a Mennonite home at least. When he was told that wasn't going to happen, he stated Travis would learn about condoms in no time in a foster home.

Funny that Travis learning about condoms was Ahaz's worry; condoms were what Ahaz used when he raped me.

When Travis was questioned, he said he did not believe any of it, and that I was always trying to start trouble. This I could understand; all he saw, to him, was a very angry older sister who refused to conform to being a Mennonite, never fit in, and challenged every outlandish rule every step of the way. Who needed to be severely 'disciplined' to 'correct that not normal behavior.'

Dennis told DCS that I did not like being around his dad, and he didn't know why. From the mouth of babes... he may have been just a boy, but he should have been further questioned. At 10, he could have told them the things he had witnessed; how his sister was 'whipped' terribly for hours, for starters, because he was also a witness at times.

Alex was never questioned; he was just 4yrs old. Could he, in all his innocence, have revealed anything if the right questions had been asked? At four, he still could have told them his sissy was kept locked up and hurt. Any of them could have.

Travis, Dennis and Alex were then taken to a worldly foster home, where I would soon join them.

But due to the focus being primarily about the rape; the boys were not asked the right questions. Why were more not asked? Why was the questioning so incredibly brief? Why did no one dig more?

Perhaps not surprisingly, DCS never looked at my bedroom. Not at the deadbolt, the nailed shut windows, the bucket containing pee that may or may not have already been removed. Nor the intensely loud, brand new alarm system. Everything was right there for them to find, they only had to *look*.

Those pieces to the puzzle, of being deadbolted in, was completely lost at this point since DCS never looked for a police report of that night, nor even seemed to realize a police report *had never been filled by any of the responding officers.* No pictures were taken of the room, either.

Although DCS did receive the hospital reports, either no one actually looked at them, or they skipped over the documented parts where I had briefly spoke on being locked up at night and not being able to go outside even during the day. I had *no idea* the trail had ended on that. I *assumed* that DCS knew what little I had told the hospital, and what my bedroom was like.

Since no one said anything about it to me I *thought* that those things were approved things to do in their eyes, too, just like the Mennonites had said when I'd spoke out about being locked in.

My sister Sarah was *never* questioned. If only DCS had talked to her, had done a real investigation, I truly believe she would have told them. *Because she didn't know that what was being done to me was wrong; she wouldn't have felt the need to protect or cover up anything. None of my siblings knew they could or should automatically tell; because of Ahaz and the Mennonites portrayal of everything. They set us all up to believe what was being done was legal and **his right.***

Also, I feel that considering it was a tight knit, Holdeman Mennonite religious community, *someone else* within the community *should have been questioned*; ministers, anyone. My voice was gone... *I needed someone else to be my voice.*

Chapter Twenty-One

On 4/20/2006 I was transported from the hospital to the same foster home my brothers were at. Dennis and Alex were both excited to see me; Travis, on the other hand, was not. He would barely even acknowledge me, in fact, he completely ignored me except for a few snide comments muttered under his breath. He blamed me for this, his always troublesome sister, always acting 'not normal' and refusing to fit into the neat little Ahaz and Mennonite molds.

Wee little Alex clung to me those next few days and would scarcely leave my side, which made me feel better just to have him to love on. Dennis was pretty laid back and enjoyed watching TV and learning how to play a video game system called The Cube.

Being in a house with a TV was so incredibly strange. I was introduced to the Discovery Channel and so much more. There were so many buttons on the TV remote to memorize what they did.

I actually felt guilty for watching those moving figures on the screen, but at the same time so, so good. Was I going to hell for it? Maybe, even probably. But since I was already a horrible, dirty person bound straight for hell anyway; what did it matter? I was free to make that choice for myself.

I felt such a strange mix of emotions from fearful, relieved, happy, and excited, to terrified that the worst was yet to come. Travis kept looking at me like I was disgusting, useless; like I was nothing. Not normal... not normal.

After just a few short days, there was a court date to determine whether or not we'd be allowed to remain in custody. A crowd of Mennonites showed up to it but weren't allowed inside the courtroom. I felt incredibly afraid; this was it and I just knew I'd be forced back. I was in full blown panic and overwhelmed with fear.

Since the boys did not disclose any abuse to themselves or to me and there was no proof that they were being harmed, they were to be sent back. However, I was able to remain in foster care, thankfully.

Ahaz was supposed to have a psychosexual evaluation and complete a sexual perpetrator treatment. Mom was supposed to go into counseling to learn how to accept what had been done to me, but they wound up never doing those things.

The boys and I were then taken to the DCS office, where Ahaz and mom came to pick them up from the parking lot. I didn't want to be outside, but that's where I was made to stay for some reason. I suspected this may have been a reaction test to see how they would react around me, but neither even attempted to speak to me.

Travis went straight to them, but both Dennis and Alex ran from Ahaz when they saw him. DCS was going to take a picture of each of the boys before they left, but Ahaz stopped them citing religious beliefs and he also made it plain that this was not The Churches rule; it was his belief alone. Now *that* was a provable lie! It was literally one of their religious rules.

After the boys went back, my foster mom received about $250 to take me shopping, so she took me to the local Walmart. I picked out pants, a dress, shoes, t-shirts and of course personal items. It was incredibly exciting and felt so right and so wrong at the same time. Then she took me to get my ears pierced, and my hair done after that.

I got a nice haircut and some blond highlights put in my plain brown hair. I nearly didn't recognize myself in the mirror, just kept staring at the reflection of the girl looking right back at me. With worldly clothes on, hair down and colored, ears pierced... it was an absolutely incredible moment. Huge. I felt very guilty, wicked and worldly, yet happy right alongside it.

Lisa was no longer a correction officer and now she worked at the DCS office. I was delighted to see her again, and she said she'd always known something was wrong all those years. Knowing that she had been able to tell, made me feel slightly better and more validated.

If only my voice hadn't been so silenced, perhaps I could have told her everything, the one familiar face amongst all the others. But by that point, I only wanted to hide from and run from my past instead of dive deeper into the torment, I couldn't handle telling more than the little I already had.

My DCS case manager (CM) tried to get me into counseling right away. Only there was one tiny issue stood in the way of that; I couldn't talk because the fear and mental abuse ran so incredibly deep. It didn't help that even DCS didn't seem to have an issue with my having been deadbolted into that room because they sure weren't mentioning it, so I figured no one else would be upset by the other things, either.

I was soon taken to an older female counselor who seemed confrontational, impatient, and demanding. She *ordered* me to tell her what happened and why I was there, to which I silently refused. In fact, the only type of questions I would answer were simple and basic ones, like my name.

By the end of that session, the counselor was so incredibly frustrated that she marched me back out to my waiting foster mom, threw up her hands and said I had a defensive disorder and that she refused to work with me.

Neither my foster mom nor the CM were happy that I'd managed to fluster the woman and they put me under a lot of pressure to cooperate with a different counselor. Eventually it was thankfully decided that they'd back off and allow me more time to adapt before they found someone more qualified to work with me.

I thought that all I had to do was forget, to throw myself into this new worldly culture, embrace my freedom and all the pain would go away. I thought I could squash it down and hide from it, but I had no actual idea the severe impact the PTSD would actually have on me. Even though I had already been experiencing the awful symptoms of it for years.

I was very excited to be enrolled in G.E.D. classes, which was accomplished only after much difficulty. My CM eventually managed to get my tiny school file from one of the school board members back in Muddy Pond, and then was able to get the Adult Learning Center to co-operate with the unusual situation after some difficulty.

On May 2nd of 2006, I took the G.E.D. pretest and scored a 2720, passing every single topic and excelling in language arts. It was high enough to be able to have the real test scheduled for just a few weeks later. My CM said that no matter what happened at the next court date coming up in July, at least I would have my diploma beforehand.

In the meantime, I was taken to my very first movie theater by my foster mom on the evening of May 12th. I felt anxious, wicked and excited as I walked in, and didn't know what to expect exactly. My foster mom told me to keep my movie ticket because I might want it one day, so I put it into my pants pocket for safekeeping.

We got popcorn and drinks before going in to watch a movie called RV, starring Robin Williams. Once inside of the actual theater, I didn't like how dark it was; hadn't even known it was going to be dark. Nor did I like how incredibly loud it was, but I did find the movie itself quite amusing. Later that night, I glued the movie ticket into my brand-new scrap book so that I'd always remember.

On May 23rd & 24th came the big G.E.D. test days. I was incredibly anxious and fighting the panic attacks all along the way while trying to hide them.

Somehow, I managed to pass with a score of 2890, thanks to all those years of sneaking with my mom to the library. In fact, I was told that I scored in the top three in the state of Tennessee and was even given a cake because of that at the graduation ceremony the following month.

In June, it was officially decided to indicate Ahaz only for sexual abuse against me, and to unfound that I had been beat by being hit and kicked previously.

I wasn't fully aware of how everything was working out at the time. However, I did know that when the court topic was brought up, people *only* talked to me about the rape. Not the beatings, nor the deadbolted room; and I still wasn't sure why exactly other than it must have been allowed because I was bad. I truly had no idea that nearly every single tiny bit of what I'd been able to say had basically been lost along the way.

There was so much more to it than just than just the rape, and all the information could have been gathered if anyone had done a proper investigation. This was a failure on multiple people's parts. From the police to the hospital, to the DCS. Everyone was trying to help me; and yes, they did get me out, but I needed more than that. I needed for a trial to happen; for some kind of justice to be served. For the words I could not say in depth to be found and heard.

In mid-July, the big court date came. I was shaking and didn't know how I was going to walk into the courtroom; how I was going to keep breathing through my lungs being squeezed tight, much less somehow talk on the stand.

There were many people there for me, all a part of DCS but some were not actually on my case. They were simply there to support me, which was at least somewhat reassuring.

I didn't know how I'd even be able to say the words on the stand. I didn't know how I could face the furious Ahaz; whom I knew was so angry that I had told even that little bit. Mom, who would pretend hurt, pretending to be so worried for her daughter. I hoped that somehow, she would tell the truth, speak out and tell the judge not just a little but *everything*. Even after all this time, all the years of betrayal and fake ignorance; I still hoped my momma would be able to save me.

Mom, Ahaz and their attorney all lied, and even though I knew it was coming, I still felt hurt by my mom. It crushed me so deeply, and I felt betrayed by her as she denied and outright lied to authorities.

My body was shaking when I was called up to the stand, and I felt as though I might not be able to force my legs to walk but somehow managed to and I was put under oath.

I thought for sure that I was going to vomit and was afraid of what the judge would do if I lost my stomach right there. I wondered if I would I be in trouble for that? I looked around to see if there was a trash can nearby but didn't see one. I wondered if I was allowed to get down from the stand and go to the bathroom to throw up but was afraid to ask and I didn't think I'd be allowed to speak out of turn to ask. I also didn't know if I could, or should, ask the judge, or make the request to my lawyer who seemed so far away. So, I just kept trying to keep it swallowed down my tight throat.

I never looked at neither Ahaz nor mom, but I could feel Ahaz staring at me, and felt my skin crawl with increasing panic. I was asked a lot of questions, and then Ahaz's attorney handed me my own journal and asked that I read a very small, selected bit out loud. I read the requested part, and then continued to read beyond it.

All the while, that attorney kept telling me to stop. Because the 2nd part I was reading ruined the attorney's ability to manipulate and twist the 1st part. The judge did not stop me, nor pay any attention to the protesting, upset attorney who was trying to stop me from reading.

Instead, that judge listened intently as I read, until I stopped shortly after at a spot of my own choosing. I felt a moment of power, of being strong; of being heard. I was not too broken to still fight back just a little.

With his plan now ruined, Ahaz's attorney sputtered for a bit, gave up and took his seat.

My own lawyer pointed out what Ahaz had said the day the boys were picked up by DCS, because in his very own words, Travis would learn about condoms (in worldly foster care); and it was also pointed out that Ahaz had raped me using condoms.

After everyone had had their turns talking, the only thing left was for the judge to make a decision. Fearful tears slipped down my cheeks while I waited for what seemed like forever.

In the end, it was my word against his, moms, and those of my siblings denying any abuse. There was no actual proof, beyond a shadow of a doubt, that I had been raped by him.

If the judge made the wrong decision, I had already made a plan to take matters into my own hands to find the only other freedom that I knew of. I knew that I'd never, ever go back to that house and be trapped for years in tortured agony; I couldn't live with enduring any more pain. I figured there was no point in telling anyone of Ahaz's plan to keep me there for years, because he'd only deny it, and my words would mean nothing.

As I waited, I braced myself to run and thought about what I was going to have to do if the judge attempted to sign me back over to Ahaz. I'd jump up from where I was seated around so many people and run across the courtroom all while biting the arteries in my wrists open fast enough that none of the shocked people would be able to react in time to stop me from it. I hoped that by the time I was grabbed, it would already be too late, and no one would be able to stop the bleeding nor repair my shredded veins before it was all over. Finding peace from torment comes in many forms...

But the judge surprised me and based off of the previous unruly delinquent charge that had been filed, the judge used that to declare that I was indeed unruly, and in need of rehabilitation and treatment under the charge of DCS for an undetermined amount of time.

Through my blur of panic, I didn't fully understand what was actually happening. I knew that meant I wouldn't have to go back, but did it mean that I'd have to go to Juvie instead since I was a delinquent? I was also upset because I thought that meant the judge believed Ahaz and thought that I was really was bad; not normal... not normal.

My CM met with the judge in his chambers after it had all ended, and then she better explained to me what had happened. She said that the judge made it very clear that this didn't mean he didn't believe me, but that his hands were tied with the evidence he'd been presented with. So, he did the only thing that was within his power as a judge to protect me and ensured I didn't have to go back!

I was assured that there wasn't actually going to be any sort of delinquent rehab thing, but instead we were going to focus on making sure I was as prepared and adjusted as possible for turning 18 and being on my own out here in the real world.

Ahaz was incredibly angry of course; absolutely infuriated that it hadn't went the way he'd planned. He had pulled the stoning incident card, assuming that would prove I unreliable, unruly, a liar, not abused, and that I would be 'rightfully returned to the care of my loving family'. Instead, the very smart judge had used that very thing to protect me.

I'm sure that he was deeply insulted anyone would dare to not do exactly as he demanded. Ahaz and his attorney filed an appeal right away to contest the judges' decision, now saying that I was *not* an unruly delinquent in spite of having said repeatedly that I *was* unruly.

This appeal court date was set for a day in August, but thankfully Ahaz's attorney was not able to be present for it, and Ahaz refused to show up without being lawyered up. Due to this, the date was reset for November, and I hoped someone deliberately had a hand in making that date as far away as they could get away with.

With the appeal looming over my head, I still felt as though I was living on borrowed time. That at any moment, it would all be snatched away and I'd never breath fresh air again.

Every day, I waited for him to come after me, and everywhere that I went, I felt as though had to stay hypervigilant to ensure I'd see him coming before it was too late. I also feared that if I actually spotted Ahaz, I wouldn't be able to move, fight, or even scream out as he grabbed and took me.

At night, I dreamed of him in horrible nightmares. To heck with the boogieman, I had my own, very real monster. Due to those night terrors, I primarily slept on the loveseat in the living room instead of in my own room, mostly so I could be closer to the front door.

My fosters were pretty understanding about it, and there were some nights that my foster mom sat up with me when I couldn't sleep. Everyone there learned very quickly not to touch me while slept, or they might get automatically decked if they weren't fast enough to get out of the way of my fist. This was also something that happened during the day, as well, the automatic punching out if someone near surprised or startled me.

I couldn't stop the panic attacks, nor the flashbacks even in daylight. All around, I was surrounded by triggers, and although I was eager to make new, worldly friends, I learned that people felt an incredible need to ask a series of small talk, get-to-know-you questions, such as, 'Where are you from and where did you go to high school?'

Those simple questions would send me spinning into a world of panic within my mind. To me, these were loaded trigger questions because no matter how I tried to answer them it only seemed to bring about more curiosity. And to me, that brought more pain.

I started trying to ward them off by pretending to suddenly remember I needed to quickly do something I'd forgotten about, in order to avoid the questions. Other times I even lied just to nip it in the bud. Both ways made me feel terrible and panicked.

People were far too curious about my accent. Due to my age at the time of switching to Mennonite, I had easily slipped into matching the distinct way they'd spoke in Muddy Pond, and no remnants of my original accent remained. I thought that perhaps if I could change it again, fewer people would ask where I came from. So, I paid close attention to how those around me sounded and began to copy them. I practiced so hard, to *not* sound like a Mennonite. This was not something that could be accomplished overnight though.

I also had to change the way I phrased things in general. For example, if I commented that it was 'a terribly beautiful day outside'; I was looked at like I'd grown seven heads. But in Holdeman Mennonite terms, 'terribly' was actually a pleasant exclamation used for expressing joy or excitement over something.

Interacting with people was complex, even with the questions not counted in. I had thought that by putting on worldly clothes, having my hair down and appearing to be modern would actually make me worldly. I thought I'd blend right in and make the past disappear, the pain, the fear, the mental and physical agony. But it didn't work like that. My pain from the past felt as though it would never leave me, it was an overcasting shadow by my side.

I now stood out in a way I could never have anticipated. I had always thought I was quite plain looking, but as it turned out, according to all the compliments, whistles, catcalls and up and down looks I got by the college boys and others while shopping with my foster mom in Cookeville, I'd apparently been wrong. It was overwhelming, especially at first. Although a part of me definitely liked it an incredible amount, the attention also made me feel strangely uncomfortable and anxious at the same time.

I had thought learning everything I could from books would have been enough to prepare me a bit more; but *nothing* could have prepared me for teen worldly girls. The other girls in the foster home I was at enjoyed teaching me things at first, because I was a novelty.

They couldn't believe I didn't know the names of all the famous 'stars' of Hollywood, nor that I I thought 'makeup' was an all- encompassing term; I didn't know that eye liner, mascara, foundation, concealer, etc. all had their own individual names. The teen girls laughed when they realized I really didn't know; they found it funny.

My foster sisters asked what my favorite music genre was, and I had no idea what they were talking about. They literally had to explain it to me, and this seemed to be funny as well. I didn't think they meant bad by it; it was more of surprised, amused laughter.

The first trip to the little local movie rental store was overwhelming, to say the least. There was such an incredible number of movies to pick from and I had no idea where to start, much less what to pick. Of course, I had seen movies in passing in Walmart and such, but I had no idea what was a good one to watch and what wasn't, nor what made the difference. The shows I'd seen at a young age had been very few, and I didn't exactly want to watch Barnie the purple dinosaur anymore.

I felt like I was doing something exciting and sinfully wrong by being in that movie shop due to the many years of it having been forbidden. The other girls walked about together, excitedly chattering about all the grand choices and the many movies they had already seen. Eventually I'd finally just randomly pick one.

On one of those visits to the movie store, I found Fried Green Tomatoes and watched it, just like that man in the ER had told me to, and I quite liked it.

My foster parents gave me the freedom to walk the very short distance to the small-town library, in Gainesboro, Tennessee. I loved having the freedom to wounder amongst those aisles to choose a new book to learn more from without restriction. I read romances, mysteries, forensics, science, freedom, love, hatred, and history. I took as many books as I could carry back each time, to engross myself deeply within the world held inside of each one.

I wanted to go to college; and in fact, I had dreamed for years about going to Yale and Harvard, because I had read about them and knew one of those was the best place for me to learn the very most from. But with only a G.E.D. plus lack of real education, those places were definitely overshooting, and my CM and others discouraged me from even applying. They said I should go to a small community college instead, considering where I had come from.

I took my A.C.T. thanks to my CM setting it up, and even completed a couple of community college applications with a bit of help and was accepted.

It didn't take long to go from being cautiously happy over being free from Ahaz, to realizing that something was still horribly wrong. To suddenly understanding that whatever this was, the stupid PTSD and the horrible anxiety I felt might, might not go actually away. I began to realize I wasn't sure I could fight through it to even be able to go to college.

When I now thought about being in a giant classroom, inside a huge college on a giant campus, it was terrifying. I also knew that there would be even more people would ask questions that I couldn't face, such as the most horrible one of being asked where I was from.

I did express this to my CM, and to my foster mom as well. They were very displeased and did not understand. How could they, when I did not fully understand myself? It only served to get me education lectures. I just needed for one of them to understand, and to be able to comprehend just how severe what I was going through was.

Sadly, this seemed to be more attributed to simply being nervousness, or teen wildness or something instead of it being truly understood that the PTSD symptoms I was experiencing were affecting even my ability to do what I had always dreamed of for so many years of furthering my education. I didn't need lectures; I needed help to learn how to cope with it.

I was being made to see a counselor weekly at this point, but I pretty much just went because I had to. And plus, I got to play with the therapy poodle the counselor brought to the office with her. She tried having me do silly things like attempting to get me put together puzzles, which I humored one time and refused beyond that.

I couldn't talk to her about the past, but I did tell her about the anxiety because that was something current. I don't believe she fully grasp what I was experiencing, even though she did diagnose me with long term PTSD. Not without knowing the extent to what all I had endured. If I could have told her, that probably would have made a difference.

In November, mere weeks before my birthday, I had to go to court once more for the appeal. I was petrified and didn't know if the judge would be able to save me this time or not.

At court, Ahaz and his attorney ranted on about how the judge was incorrect, I was not an unruly delinquent and never should have been ruled as such. He said he needed me 'home' with my 'family' before I turned eighteen, because that was what was 'best for me'.

His lawyer had subpoenaed my counselor to testify in court that day, but she was unable to make it and sent an affidavit in her place, stating within it something down the lines of I had diagnosed PTSD and in her professional opinion it was in my best interest to remain in state custody.

Now, the judge could have easily accepted this affidavit and proceeded, but instead *the judge declared that he wanted to hear from my counselor in person and rescheduled the appeal for the beginning of January 2007; weeks after I would turn eighteen!*

Ahaz had a complete and utter tantrum in the middle of that courtroom over this, saying he wanted to take back even having asked for the counselor; he didn't want to hear from her anymore. He yelled that I must be home before I turned eighteen, and he didn't want any more court session after my birthday. Ahaz even loudly fired his attorney on the spot and the scene he made was simply outlandish. I had no idea why the judge did not find him in contempt and put him in jail for the way he was acting at least; but he didn't.

Ahaz had to leave the courtroom but didn't go far. I was told that he was lingering in wait for me in the lobby, so I had to stay in the courtroom for a while longer until he was escorted out of the building and security made certain he was long gone.

Celebrating, happy and relieved it was finally truly over, I was taken back to the Department of Children Services office and given lunch. I had to stay there to ensure Ahaz wasn't coming after me, then I was taken back to my foster parents via the scenic route with extra turns en-route to ensure my safety.

Those days spent in foster care were simply amazing. No longer was I called 'not normal' and gone were the beatings and worse. Even the long, strange dizzy spells, times of my hearing going out, and severe stomach pains were no more. Gone was the strict, ridiculous dress code and religious rules that didn't even line up with the Bible. I had freedom from pain and freedom of choices.

On my birthday in mid- December, my foster mom bought me an ice-cream cake which I was very excited about. Until my actual mom called to say that Ahaz had a gun and had said he was coming to kill me with it. She said that I needed to stop whatever I was doing and get out as quick as I could. Mom also told me that Ahaz didn't know she was calling.

I took one of my foster sisters with me and we walked the short distance to the tiny police station nearby. The restraining order that had been on Ahaz through this all had no expiration date listed, and I wanted to ask them if it expired on my birthday, or if it was still good.

A nice policeman assured me that it would still be good since there was no end date listed. I nervously hung out there for a bit longer, and then called one of my new friends I'd met when I got my G.E.D. to come pick me up and get me out of town.

Off I went on the run to start a brand-new chapter in my life; I was finally eighteen years of age, free and independent. I had survived my monster this far, but could I do it again?

Epilogue

If you or someone you know is experiencing abuse in any form, you *must tell*. Use the correct words and describe it to the best of your ability.

Will your abuser make you feel as though the abuse is your fault, or that you are *bad, crazy*, or even *deserve it?* Yes, absolutely. They may have even bribed and manipulated you for your silence, and now perhaps you even feel ashamed for not having told yet.

Do not allow them or anyone else to stand in your way of freedom from abuse, for those reasons or any others. Will it be painful and feel utterly shameful to tell? *Yes.* But it will all be worth it in the end.

It is possible that whom you chose to tell may not believe you, or even if they do believe, they may not choose to seek help for you. This only means you must *tell someone else,* as many times as it takes! Tell every single neighbor, teacher, etc. and do *not stop until someone helps you.* If possible, go to or contact your local police station. Call 911 if need be, The Department of Children Services in your area or even a help line; find someone safe who can help get you out!

If you are given only temporary freedom and the horrible scenario does happen that you are forced right back into abuse, *do not stop talking about it.* Tell people repeatedly until there is simply no way they can refuse their assistance. Scream it, whisper it, do *whatever it takes* to be free and *do not give up.*

Remember this:

THE TRUTH WILL STILL BE THE TRUTH NO MATTER WHAT OTHERS MAY CLAIM; SPEAK YOUR TRUTH LOUDLY!

YOU DESERVE THE RIGHT TO FREEDOM FROM ABUSE.

YOU DESERVE THE RIGHT TO AN EDUCATION.

YOU DESERVE SO INCREDIBLY MUCH!

YOU ARE AMAZING!

YOU DESERVE TO BE FREE!

NOW IS THE TIME TO FIGHT FOR YOUR FREEDOM

Made in United States
Troutdale, OR
08/24/2023

12333002R00176